ON THE EDGE OF SCARCITY

Syracuse Studies on Peace and Conflict Resolution
Louis Kriesberg, *Series Editor*

ON THE EDGE OF
SCARCITY

Environment, Resources, Population, Sustainability, and Conflict

Edited by MICHAEL N. DOBKOWSKI
and ISIDOR WALLIMANN

With a Foreword by John K. Roth

Syracuse University Press

Copyright © 2002 by Syracuse University Press
Syracuse, New York 13244–5160

All Rights Reserved

First Edition 2002

02   03   04   05   06   07   6   5   4   3   2   1

The paper used in this publication meets the minimum requirements of American National
Standard for Information Sciences—Permanence of Paper for Printed Library Materials,
ANSI Z39.48–1984.∞™

Library of Congress Cataloging-in-Publication Data
is available upon request from the publisher.

ISBN 0-8156-2918-4 (cl.)
     0-8156-2943-5 (pbk.)

Manufactured in the United States of America

Contents

Foreword

Bottlenecks and the Ways Out

John K. Roth

Despair is no solution. The solution lies in analysis, in hard thinking and questioning, and in purposeful and informed action. To that goal this book is dedicated.

> —Michael Dobkowski and Isidor Wallimann,
> *The Coming Age of Scarcity*

WHEN HUMAN BEINGS LACK what they need or want, terrifying sights often follow. Scarcity is grim. Of course, scarcity and *scarcity* are not the same. The former refers to a condition in which something may be in short supply, but in principle nothing prevents that obstacle from being overcome. Such scarcity can encourage hard work for what is wanted. It may spark progress that provides what is lacking. It may even be wealth's partner, because fortunes have been made in finding ways out of need. Scarcity of this kind is not too much for optimistic hopes to bear, but what if scarcity runs deeper? What if scarcity means not a temporary shortfall or a relative lack of what people need or want? Could there be *scarcity*, not a condition in which things we need or want have just run low or run out temporarily, but one in which those things are gone beyond replenishing? If the answer is yes, then scarcity might as well be a four-letter word, because it keeps company with the most obscene characteristics of its closest kin: poverty, disease, greed, exploitation, war, ethnic cleansing, and genocide.

Although this book explores scarcity's multiple dimensions, its most profound concern is not about temporarily short supplies. Concentrating on scarcity of the more basic and unforgiving kind, it focuses on consumption-driven and wealth-obsessed human policies that are taking us not just to "the edge of scarcity," as the book's title puts it, but over the edge and into circumstances that we are extremely reluctant to acknowledge, let alone correct. Thus, as I consider the articles that Michael Dobkowski and Isidor Wallimann have published in this timely revision of their book, I remember two fascinating figures in Western civilization. As important as they are different, one is named Cassandra, the other Wittgenstein.

Greek mythology identifies Cassandra as the daughter of King Priam and Queen Hecuba of Troy. Loving Cassandra, the god Apollo, whose domains included light and truth, bestowed the gift of prophecy upon her, but when she did not return his love, Apollo took cunning revenge. Although Cassandra got to keep her gift of prophecy, which frequently produced warnings about tragic consequences if her words went unheeded, Apollo ensured that no one would believe her truthful forecasts. Nevertheless, the Trojans and their Greek conquerors disbelieved Cassandra at their peril.

The social scientists and humanities scholars who have written the essays that follow are latter-day Cassandras. We should hope, however, that such a description fits them only in part. My reading suggests that, like the Cassandra of old, gifts of light, truth, and prophecy have been bestowed upon them—not by a god but through their hard thinking and questioning. The issue is whether their insights and warnings about scarcity will be disbelieved and dismissed as Cassandra's forecasts were—not because some divinity has taken cunning revenge but because the self-assurance of those people who control the lion's share of the world's wealth and power will prevent them from apprehending the dire straits that lie ahead.

Only when it was too late did people realize that Cassandra knew what was going on. That fate does not have to be ours where scarcity is concerned, and here is where Ludwig Wittgenstein comes in. Arguably the twentieth century's preeminent philosopher, Wittgenstein is famous for saying that the aim of philosophy should be to show "the fly the way out of the fly-bottle." He envisioned a scene where a fly had unwittingly flown through the neck of a bottle and could not find the way out. There was a way out, but buzzing around to the point of exhaustion and death, the fly could not find it. With help, however, the outcome might have been different.

Dobkowski and Wallimann write about impending bottlenecks that put us in potentially catastrophic circumstances. They see four factors—population growth and constraints on land resources, energy, and environmental carrying capacity—converging in new ways to produce "absolute deficiencies" and "impenetrable limits" that cannot be overcome by the capitalist market system, increased productivity, or scientific progress. So it was that my reading of this book made me think of Wittgenstein and his fly-bottle, which provides an apt metaphor for the human condition as the twenty-first century unfolds. Without realizing or intending it, indeed thinking we are doing exactly the opposite, we may have flown into scarcity's fly-bottle. Without help, we may not find good ways out. Fortunately, the contributors to this book share Wittgenstein's motivation. Their essays often have special sections that map ways out of the dilemmas they foresee. The ways out, of course, will not be recognized, let alone followed, unless the problem analyses that contextualize them are taken seriously. Wittgenstein cannot help if Cassandra is not believed. The contributors to this book play both of those parts admirably. The book's outcome now depends on what its readers do.

The Coming Age of Scarcity was the title for this book's first edition, which appeared in 1998. With the twenty-first century under way, editors Dobkowski and Wallimann revised that title while the essayists reworked their articles. Neither the new title, *On the Edge of Scarcity,* nor the updated essays are causes for optimism. For the edge of scarcity, especially if people do not think that is where we are, is more immediately ominous and threatening than an age of scarcity vaguely described as coming but not yet here. My foreword in the first edition of this book said that *The Coming Age of Scarcity* scared me. It did so because I believed what Dobkowski and Wallimann wrote in their introductory essay. Those words, which are only slightly modified in the new edition, packed the following punch: "The genocides of the twentieth century have unveiled the true heart of humanity. At our center lies an ability to commit evil of an almost unimagined degree. . . . The unthinkable has already happened; the idea of future catastrophes is therefore not unthinkable."

Much of what I said about *The Coming Age of Scarcity* holds true for *On the Edge of Scarcity* as well. Like the first edition, the second deals with evil. It documents ethnic cleansing and excavates the world's killing fields. Sadly, it anticipates mass death and genocide in the twenty-first century even while trying to prevent them.

The contributors to these pages know evil when they see it. They intend for their readers to see it, too. They succeed—so much so that this book does more than scare me. It leaves me depressed, almost to the point of despair. Perhaps it will do the same for you. The world's expanding megacities and refugee hordes, as well as pressures for and protests against immigration, are only one sign of an unrelenting global population crunch, which increasingly leaves the world with more people than anyone needs. A world with more people than anyone needs is a deadly place. It is a stage set perpetually for mass death and genocide. Surplus people are only one of the preconditions for mass death and genocide. Roger Smith's essay rightly argues that scarcity is another. As this entire book suggests, moreover, the specter of scarcity—most of it human made—is likely to be even worse in the twenty-first century than it was in the twentieth. That judgment is credible in spite of the hosannas sung to globalization, unfettered markets, and economic prosperity that are touted as "really different this time," as if contemporary monetary and business policies have abolished severe economic downturns, and as if the solution for the growing disparity between rich and poor is a high-tech tide that deceptively promises to raise all boats. Especially in an increasingly materialistic United States and among privileged young people who are short on memory, prone to take unprecedented economic prosperity for granted, and bombarded by promises that there are no limits to future standards of living, it will not be easy for *On the Edge of Scarcity* to get the hearing it deserves. Reminiscent of Cassandra's world, that result will come at humanity's peril. As far as human-made deaths are concerned, no century has been more devastating than the twentieth. The political scientist R. J. Rummel, who tallies the statistics of mass death unleashed by human power, helped to document that fact in his 1994 book, *Death by Government.* Written before genocide in Rwanda and ethnic cleansing in Kosovo added to the devastation in the 1990s, Rummel estimated that "the human cost of war and democide together"—the latter distinguished from war-battle dead and defined as "the murder of any person or people by a government," including genocide and other atrocities—reached more than 203 million in the twentieth century. Although "Never again!" still resounds after Auschwitz, post-Holocaust history has nearly turned that cry into an all-too-hollow cliché. The fact is that genocidal killing has taken more lives since the Holocaust ended than it did in the first half of the twentieth century. The arrival of a new century, moreover, will probably not bring relief. The twenty-first century threatens to produce even more human-made death than the twentieth.

At least thus far, attempts to prosecute those people who have been accused of genocidal crimes against humanity in Rwanda and the former Yugoslavia do not inspire confidence that the threat of arrest and punishment will do much to deter genocide's fury. Nor can one take heart from the observation that projections about the future are uncertain because history is always full of surprises. As historical analysis helps to make depressingly clear, more often than not history's surprises are lethal to the point of catastrophe.

In every contribution to this book there are plenty of reasons for despair. John B. Cobb Jr. clearly analyzes developments in the United States that are producing an underclass of the permanently unemployed. This underclass, he rightly fears, is likely to be regarded not only as superfluous but also as cancerous. The prescribed treatment is unlikely to be kind-hearted. Kurt Finsterbusch shows how scarcity creates social inequality, which threatens democracy. Waltraud Morales underscores that violence thrives when economic deprivation prevails. The impact on women and children, in particular, is devastating. Ted Trainer regards present society as unsustainable, Virginia Abernethy sees incivility and disrespect for law stalking U.S. life in the twenty-first century, and Chris Lewis appraises what he sees as "the collapse of globalized modern industrial civilization." These examples illustrate the fact that each essay contains nasty surprises for those readers who think the future will be benignly open forever.

On the Edge of Scarcity drives home the sobering point that, in one way or another, we are approaching the end of the human world as we have known it. Do not misunderstand: An apocalyptic doomsday is not at hand. The world is not going to end anytime soon, but times on the edge of scarcity are changing decisively nonetheless.

Sometimes the ending of an era is a cause for celebration. Ironically, in an age of mass death and genocide, such a conclusion would be unrealistic. The conditions accounting for our deadly age will die hard. As if they realize how unpopular their views may be, the essayists are aware of the Cassandra-like reception they may get. Far from a diminished sense of purpose, however, they feel an urgency that intensifies their efforts. Whatever happens, including even the corrective and constructive changes that the authors recommend, the shifts are likely to be wrenching and violent. Things will get worse before they get better—if they do get better. One reason is that for too long too many of us, including even people who have the means to buy this book and the time to read it, have enjoyed the world that is too much with us. Much as we deplore mass death and genocide, we will still find it extremely difficult to bring about the global changes that are needed to check it. Even while trying to prevent mass death and genocide in the twenty-first century, we may also resist the changes—especially economic ones—that are really needed to eliminate them.

The many beneficiaries of existing circumstances will not set aside their privileges easily any more than the wretched of the earth will placidly accept their desperate conditions of scarcity. As the pressures mount, and they will, parties on all sides are going to defend their interests. In too many cases, moreover, the defense will be by any means—wrenching and violent—that are perceived as necessary. History may prove such judgments wrong, but that outcome would be so surprising that only the foolish bank on it.

This book calls forth dark moods within me. Nevertheless, it evokes other moods as well. Perhaps it will do the same for you. At least in my case, these "and yet" moods are neither removed from nor located beyond the darkness with which this book engulfs me. Their movement is a stirring within that darkness, but the movement is not easily named. What I feel is *not* captured by words such as *hope* or *conviction,* and even less do my feelings contain much that a glib word such as *optimism* implies. The stirring aroused within me by *On the Edge of Scarcity* is best expressed in the negative. It is reflected in the words from Michael Dobkowski and Isidor Wallimann that are quoted at the beginning of this foreword: *"Despair is no solution."*

As I explore my feelings and write the words that they have provoked here, I do so as a philosopher and teacher who has spent most of a thirty-five-year academic career studying the damage that the Holocaust and other forms of genocide have done. Reflecting on the essays in this book, I have been reminded once more that teachers—and sometimes their students, too—are constantly stalked by despair. How could we not be?

Most teachers are idealists. However jaded we may become, most of us became teachers because we wanted to mend the world. That hope, however, encounters discouragement aplenty. History, especially genocide's history, provides it. So does teaching, which is a less-than-reassuring activity when humankind's future is at stake.

We are all beginners every day. No matter how hard we teachers try, indifference persists, prejudice remains, ignorance endures, and no place on earth guarantees safety from the destruction that such forces can unleash. Education's gains take place against stiff odds; learning is not a matter of evolutionary progress. Every year, every class, means starting over because wisdom does not accumulate. Teachers often know how Cassandra must have felt.

Teaching about the Holocaust and genocide makes me more melancholy than I used to be. It makes me realize how much despair lurks around every classroom door. Even more, however, such teaching makes me understand that those recognitions are not the conclusion, but instead they must be the stirring in the midst of darkness, the insistence affirming that despair is not the solution. To let despair have its way would be to give every genocidal act a victory that it does not deserve and must not have.

Where scarcity, mass death, and genocide are concerned, however, what is the solution? Is there such a thing? Perhaps, but if so, what ingredients does it contain? Responses to those questions—good and thoughtful ones—are found in this book's pages, especially in the essay sections called "Ways Out." Those responses start with the editors' insistence that "the solution lies in analysis, in hard thinking and questioning, and in purposeful and informed action," which are the goals to which this book is dedicated. Beyond that, I will not further identify the ways out that the authors suggest. It is better for you to discover and test them on your own. As a prelude to those proposed ways out of the impending and deadly bottlenecks that are being produced by population growth and constraints on land resources, energy, and the environment, I will add only two more words of anticipation: a warning and then a fact.

The warning: "If we stop remembering," says Holocaust survivor Elie Wiesel, "we stop being." The memory and analysis of scarcity, mass death, and genocide found in this book warn against despair. If we do better than Cassandra's listeners, the effect of that warning can be to sensitize us against indifference, which is despair's best friend and evil's welcome accomplice. As for the fact, the essays in this book can sensitize us against despair and indifference because history shows that the threats of mass death and genocide are human made. Those threats are not inevitable, and no events related to them ever will be. Mass death and genocide—and usually scarcity, too—emerge from decisions and institutions that depend on or-dinary human beings, on people like us who are responsible for our actions and who could act differently and better than we often do.

If we heed the warning and do not deny the fact—especially in an age of scarcity, mass death, and genocide—then we will keep working to mend the world's broken heart, and perhaps we will find our way out of scarcity's fly-bottle after all. In spite of much of its content, then, this book awakens, haunts, and challenges me in ways that I ignore at everyone's peril. I bet it will do the same for you.

Acknowledgments

THE TWO OF US came to the study of scarcity and conflict from different disciplines and from different sides of the Atlantic Ocean. That we could produce this joint effort is a tribute to the centrality of the issue, to the respect we have for each other, both personally and professionally, and to our commitment to multidisciplinary work and interchange.

We have spent more than a decade studying genocide, fascism, and other forms of human cruelty. We who study mass death do so in the hope that it will preserve life. We don't want our subject to become commonplace and even familiar; we want to bring it to the forefront of public discourse.

We wish to thank colleagues in our respective institutions and other friends and students who have provided an intellectual environment that was conducive to productive work. We are particularly grateful to the contributors for the prompt submission of their essays and the high quality of their work. We benefited from the advice and counsel of Louis Kriesberg who, as always, offered honest and insightful critique and support. We are, of course, responsible for any errors that remain.

A special acknowledgment goes to Melody Joyce, who typed, retyped, formatted, merged, and otherwise helped prepare the final manuscript for submission. Thanks also to Robert Mandel, former director of Syracuse University Press, who encouraged this project from its conception, and to John Fruehwirth, then managing editor and now acting director.

Finally, there are our students and colleagues at our respective institutions, friends, and families who sustained, distracted, and encouraged us.

To Karen Dobkowski, who fills my life with joy and meaning; to my mother, Bronia, who continues to be a source of strength and guidance; to my children, Batsheva (and her husband, Dov, and their beautiful

Leora), Jonathan, and Tamar, who also did their part by reminding me why the issues in this book are important. And to the many friends and colleagues of Isidor Wallimann around the world, who sustain his efforts to understand the factors that contribute to scarcity, inequality, and mass violence.

Contributors

Virginia Deane Abernethy is Professor Emeritus of Psychiatry (Anthropology) at the School of Medicine of Vanderbilt University and edits the bimonthly journal *Population and Environment*. She is the author of several books, including *Population Pressure and Cultural Adjustment* and *Population Politicis: The Choices That Shape Our Future*.

John B. Cobb, Jr. is Professor Emeritus of Theology at the School of Theology at Claremont College and a Director of the Center for Process Studies. He is the author of *Sustainability and Sustaining the Common Good* and coauthor of *The Liberation of Life* (with Charles Birch) and *For the Common Good* (with Herman Daly).

Craig Dilworth is Reader in Theoretical Philosophy at Uppsala University, Sweden. His major works are *Scientific Progress, The Metaphysics of Science,* and *Sustainable Development and Decision Making*. He is also the editor of the volume *Intelligibility in Science*.

Michael N. Dobkowski is Professor of Religious Studies at Hobart and William Smith Colleges. He is the author of *The Tarnished Dream: The Basis of American Anti-Semitism, The Politics of Indifference: Documentary History of Holocaust Victims in America,* and *Jewish American Voluntary Organizations*. With Isidor Wallimann, he is the coeditor of several books, including *Genocide and the Modern Age: Etiology and Case Studies* and *Genocide in Our Time*.

Kurt Finsterbusch is Professor of Sociology at the University of Maryland, College Park. His major fields of interest are environment and society, social-impact assessment, and sociology of social change and development. He is the author of *Understanding Social Impacts* (1980), *Social Research for Policy Decisions* (with Annabelle Bender Motz, 1980), and *Organizational Change as a Development Strategy: Models and Tactics for Improving Third World Organizations* (with Jerald Hage, 1987). He has edited many volumes and editions in introductory sociology and social problems and in the area of social-impact assessment. He is currently working on a book on the impacts of society on the environment and the impacts of environmental conditions on society.

John M. Gowdy is Professor of Economics and Director of the Ph.D. Program in Ecological Economics at Rensselaer Polytechnic Institute in Troy, New York. His latest book (coauthored with Carl McDaniel) is *Paradise for Sale: A Parable of Nature*. He has authored and edited several books on sustainability, hunter-gatherer societies, and evolutionary theory in economics. His recent articles have appeared in *Ecological Economics, Land Economics,* the *Review of Income and Wealth,* and the *Review of Social Economy.* In 1995 he was Visiting Fulbright Scholar at the Economic University of Vienna. In 2000 he was Guest Professor at the University of Zurich and at Tokushima University in Japan.

Chris H. Lewis is Senior Instructor in the Sewall Academic Program at the University of Colorado at Boulder. An environmentalist, intellectual historian, and cancer survivor, he is currently working on a larger study of the collapse of global industrial civilization. He places his hope in the ability of local communities and regional economies to survive and prosper after this collapse.

Waltraud Queiser Morales is Professor of Comparative and International Studies in the Department of Political Science at the University of Central Florida in Orlando. She received her Ph.D. from the Graduate School of International Studies at the University of Denver. Born in Austria, she has focused her research on the Third World and Latin America, especially Bolivia and the Andean region. Her publications include *Bolivia: Land of Struggle* (1992) and numerous articles on sustainable development, revolutionary change, "drug war" policies, humanitarian intervention, and global gender issues. She serves as the editor of the *Political Chronicle,* the journal of the Florida Political Science Association.

Leon Rappoport is Professor of Psychology at Kansas State University. He is the author of numerous research articles and a textbook on personality development, and is the coauthor with George Kren of *The Holocaust and the Crisis of Human Behavior.*

John K. Roth is the Russell K. Pitzer Professor of Philosophy at Claremont McKenna College, where he has taught since 1966. In addition to service on the United States Holocaust Memorial Council and on the editorial board for *Holocaust and Genocide Studies,* he has published more than twenty-five books and hundreds of articles and reviews, including *A Consuming Fire: Encounters with Elie Wiesel and the Holocaust, Approaches to Auschwitz* (with Richard L. Rubenstein), *Holocaust: Religious and Philosophical Implications* (with Michael Berenbaum), *Different Voices: Women and the Holocaust* (with Carol Rittner), and, most recently, *Ethics after the Holocaust,* as well as major contributions to the *Holocaust Chronicle.* In 1988, Roth was named U.S. National Professor of the Year by the Council for Advancement and Support of Education and the Carnegie Foundation for the Advancement of Teaching.

David Norman Smith is Associate Professor of Sociology at the University of Kansas. He is the author of several books, including *Marx's "Kapital" for Beginners* and *Who Rules the Universities?* and is the editor of the first English-language edition of Karl Marx's *Ethnological Notebooks* (forthcoming).

Roger W. Smith is Professor of Government at the College of William and Mary. He has written about the nature and history of genocide, language and genocide, ratification of the Genocide Convention by the United States Senate, and denial of the Armenian Genocide. He is currently writing a book on women and genocide.

Joseph A. Tainter is Project Leader of Cultural Heritage Research, Rocky Mountain Research Station, in Albuquerque, New Mexico. Research on the evolution of sociocultural complexity led to the publication of his book, *The Collapse of Complex Societies.* In addition to authoring many articles and monographs, he is the coeditor of the books *Evolving Complexity and Environmental Risk in the Prehistoric Southwest* (with Bonnie Bagley Tainter) and *The Way the Wind Blows: Climate, History, and*

Human Action (with R. J. McIntosh and S. K. McIntosh). Tainter's work has been used in the United Nations Environment Programme (Kenya), the European Joint Commission and the National Nutrition Institute (Italy), the Beijer Institute (Sweden), the Center for International Forestry Research (Indonesia), as well as throughout the United States and Canada. He has been invited to present his research to the Getty Research Center and the International Society for Ecological Economics. Tainter's biography is included in *Who's Who in Science and Engineering*, *Who's Who in America*, and *Who's Who in the World*.

Ted Trainer lectures on sociology within the School of Social Work at the University of New South Wales. His most recent publications include *The Conserver Society: Alternatives for Sustainability* and *Towards a Sustainable Economy*.

Isidor Wallimann is professor of sociology, economics, and social policy at the University of Applied Sciences in Basel, Switzerland, and an international faculty associate at the University of North Texas. He has published numerous books in English and German on a wide range of subjects. *The Coming Age of Scarcity* and *Genocide and the Modern Age* (both edited with Michael Dobkowski) were recently published by Syracuse University Press.

Introduction

On the Edge of Scarcity

Michael N. Dobkowski and Isidor Wallimann

THIS BOOK ADDRESSES one of the most pressing and significant issues that humanity has been confronted with so far. Yet, despite the compelling nature of the problem, only few attempts are under way to analyze the dangers we face and to develop strategies designed to avert the looming catastrophe. We would like to maintain that world industrialization and urbanization and its associated social system and techniques—such as the universal market system or centralized planning bureaucracies—cannot be sustained except for a relatively few privileged people and at the cost of increased mass death, which may include genocide. The alternative, namely, to abandon the global industrialization project and to begin a move away from industrial society as it is known today, equally entails a risk of mass death on a tremendous scale.

It is true that modernization and industrialization have confronted us with many great problems before while millions have been forced into deprivation, poverty, wars, and premature death. In the course of modernization worldwide, however, the world population has nevertheless grown significantly. Therefore, one might be tempted to conclude that the social and economic systems that have laid the paths and been the engines for industrialization will again respond in time to avert the anticipated mass death and increasing spiral of human self-destruction on a scale never witnessed so far. However, this attitude would indeed be fateful to assume.

As social scientists and humanists, we are thus well advised to speedily reconsider our priorities and to increasingly engage in a kind of scientific praxis that is *explicitly* directed toward the preservation of life, at home and elsewhere in our global society. But what exactly is the problem that confronts us? What are the anticipated bottlenecks based upon which one could say that traditional modernization will come to an end? What are the bottlenecks that could lead to mass death? In an attempt to address these questions, let us first turn to a short discussion of industrialization.

Industrialization

It is important to recall that the great transformation from agricultural to modern, urban, and industrial societies has always been financed on the backs of peasants both in the nineteenth century, in the area that is now known as the center, and in the twentieth century, in the area now known as the periphery. Whether this transfer of value from the agricultural sector has been achieved with political and bureaucratic means or through the indirect and anonymous coercion of market systems, the truth remains that the surplus value produced in agriculture alone financed industrial production and made urban and industrial life sustainable. This statement is not to deny that agriculture simultaneously became more productive owing, in part, to the very growth in the urban-based sciences and industrial production it had financed. However, much of this "great transformation" has always been associated with immense hardship on the peasantry, be it for the many who remained in rural areas or for those people who migrated as wage laborers to the growing cities. Much premature death because of poverty, disease, and lack of medical attention went hand in hand with drastic improvements in the life expectancy, particularly for infants. Thus, the age structure of the population was shifted to a median age of twenty, or even below, whereas life expectancy at birth rose to about sixty years.

Population Growth

All industrialization has been associated with significant population growth. The world's population roughly doubled from 1750 to 1900 and again from 1900 to 1950. In 1800 it still took far more than a hundred years for the world population to double. Today it takes only thirty-eight years. Some 1.7 billion people inhabited this planet in 1900. In 1990 it was 5.3 billion, and in the year 2025 we shall have 8.5 billion. Only about one-fifth of the world's population lives in the fully transformed and industrialized part of the world, including Eastern Europe. About two-fifths alone live in India and China, giving China a slightly larger population than India. Sixty percent of the world's population lives in Asia, about 9 percent in Latin America, and about 12 percent in Africa. The reasons for the ever faster population growth are well known. Although birthrates have tended to decline, they have not decreased fast enough to compensate for the gains owing to lower infant mortality and the general increase in life expectancy. These gains have been made possible not by high-tech medicine, but by relatively simple techniques, such as an improved diet, better control over bacterial environments (general hygiene, water supply, food storage, and antibiotics), and by vaccinations against various contagious and other diseases. The worldwide knowledge of these techniques, the possibility for their widespread deployment at a low cost, world information on social and medical problems, political pressure, the need for social control, and human compassion have been major causes for the ever accelerating population growth. Presently, it is not expected that AIDS or diseases such as cholera or tuberculosis, although growing, will significantly alter the rate of population growth in the near future.

One of the correlates of modernization has been that birthrates decrease with increased urbanization and a higher standard of living. Experience in the fully transformed industrial countries generally has shown that population growth tends to stabilize at a low positive rate and that some countries even have slightly negative growth rates. This experience leads to the notion that, once the world will be transformed into modernity, industrialized, and economically developed, the world population too will be stabilized in its growth. Of course, the crucial assumption made here is that it is possible to provide the world with the standard of living of industrial countries, irrespective of the economic systems—particularly capitalism, which chronically tends toward overproduction and crisis—and ecological considerations.

Experience shows that most campaigns to more swiftly reduce the birthrate are successful only in societies with a sufficiently high standard of living. However, they can also be successful in relatively poor societies with a low standard of living if, and only if, social and economic justice is simultaneously given a high priority. The more vulnerable people become economically, and the more they are threatened by modernization and industrialization, the more they are inclined to adhere to birthrates that enhance population growth. This pattern is often seen as an example of irrational behavior. Allegedly, it prevents families from accumulating the human, social, and financial capital needed for the family's economic improvement, and it is said to annul all productivity gains made on the macrolevel to improve the standard of living. However, as is well known among development workers and agricultural specialists, when people must live at the margins of existence, they tend to *minimize risks and not to maximize profits and accumulation.* By adhering to higher birthrates, they aim to spread severe existential risks to more people, which from their point of view is a reasonable thing to do.

However, it is also true that women often give birth to more children than they desire, and that the children are required for the family's survival and successful reproduction. Because this condition is usually induced by gender inequality, it follows that birthrates can also be reduced in part by strengthening the position of women in society. In sum, without sufficient equality on the micro—and macrolevels, there is little hope to reduce the birthrate sufficiently for population growth to level off.

Migration and Employment

Because the transformation reduces the percentage of the population employed in agriculture, and because insufficient alternative employment is available in rural areas, people have migrated to cities. The nineteenth-century transformation of agricultural society channeled migrants into industrial work—to the extent that they found employment at all. The tertiary, mostly service, sector was developed later. Today, just the opposite is true. The formal economy favors the expansion of services. In addition, the huge informal economic activity belongs itself more to the tertiary than to the secondary sector. This pattern seems to confirm the notion that we are far from growing into a true world industrial society. Displaced from agricultural occupations, people end up with few perspectives and no vision that can make them feel part of a new era, involving such things as the creation of nation-states, industrial production, and mobility, which were characteristic of the nineteenth century.

Energy and Other Resources

Thus far, all industrialization and urbanization have been associated with an increased use of energy, directly and indirectly replacing the human and animal energy used in production and distribution, expanding the sphere of unnecessary consumption, and allowing for world markets and their corollary, the world division of labor. This expansion of world trade and the world division of labor is, of course, again a precondition for world industrialization.

World energy consumption, although increasing, remained relatively low until 1950. From 1950 to 1990, however, the use of energy increased sevenfold, far outpacing the population, which approximately doubled during the same period. Most of this increase came from the use of fossil fuels, of which oil and gas constituted the largest share. The contribution of atomic and hydroelectric power to the world's energy supply is only about 15 percent.

As the gross national product (GNP) per capita grows, so does the use of energy. Therefore, one-fifth of the world's population uses about four-fifths of the world's energy, most of it as industrial fuels. Traditional fuels (wood, peat, and dung) supply about 5 percent of the world's energy and are almost entirely (85 percent) used in peripheral countries. At the present rate of use, it is estimated that the world has oil for another 40–60 years, gas for another 60–80, and coal for another 660 years. Coal supplies about a third of today's energy.

It is not possible here to address the future supply of all resources such as minerals and water. It is important, however, to mention that the arable land available for the production of food and fibers tends to shrink. Any expansion will be possible only at the expense of forests or grasslands, jeopardizing other resources, particularly water and topsoil. Any increases in the agricultural output would, therefore, have to come from different growing techniques, pest controls, irrigation, the use of fertilizers and plant breeding.

Bottlenecks: A Historically Unique Constellation

Impending bottlenecks center in population growth, land resources, energy, and environmental constraints. What is most crucial is that we have never found ourselves in a situation in which all four factors are so closely linked. Sure, we have had a growing population and population pressures before, but there has always been more land to be cultivated. Sure, we have had large populations to care for before, but more energy-intensive agricultural production and improvements in plant breeding have always been possible. Sure, we have had the need for more energy before, but there has always been some new oil field just a few feet below the ground. Sure, we have had all these pressures before. But have we experienced them as impenetrable limits, as absolute deficiencies of land and energy? Have we experienced them all at the same time and as impenetrable limits? Certainly not. Have we ever simultaneously experienced such severe land and energy limits and also faced the real danger of an ecological collapse? Again, certainly not.

Today, this planet counts some 6 billion people. In 2025, it will contain 8.5 billion. Beyond 2025, we do not know how much the population will grow. Current opinion tends to assume that, as a result of economic development, the birthrate will "automatically" fall to about two children per family before 2050, a level now observed for transformed countries. This assumption is very unrealistic. But even if the assumption should prove correct, the population is expected to reach 9.5 billion in 2050 and to level off at about 10 billion in 2075. However, by then, we shall also have exhausted the presently known oil reserves, or about 30 percent of today's energy supply. And by 2075, we shall further have exhausted the presently known gas supply, or (together with oil) about one-half of today's energy supply, although owing to population growth, we shall also have reduced the per capita energy consumption by about 40 percent.

The energy crunch is made worse by environmental limits. The degree to which we have been using fossil fuels is changing our ecosystem and the human, animal, and plant reproduction and survival patterns that have for centuries been built around it. The lives of millions are increasingly at risk if sea levels begin to rise and glaciers melt. It is estimated that 30 percent of the world's population lives in a thirty-mile-wide coastal strip and is concentrated in Asia and Europe. Millions of people would have to be relocated as environmental refugees, their lives would be threatened by floods and tidal waves, more fertile arable land would be lost, and the erosion inland would be more severe owing to increased rains.

Finally, the tremendous food pressures must be reiterated. We can cultivate the land more intensively and turn our lawns into vegetable gardens, but how many millions more can be fed by such measures? We may resort to the oceans for protein, but oceans are already overfished. We may turn away from animal protein to feed more people with the same amount of grain, but this reserve applies only to the transformed world and becomes increasingly insignificant as the Third World population grows. We may resort to ocean farming, greenhouse and hydroponic production, but can we compensate for the destruction of agricultural lands because of overuse and overexposure to wind and water? Can we compensate for the loss in land because of urbanization and the increased demand for housing? Can we compensate for the loss in plant growth and crop yield because of increased ultraviolet radiation? We do not believe that these challenges will be met without bottlenecks that may cost the lives of millions.

It seems evident now that there will be a temporal conjunction of four sizable bottlenecks: population, land, energy, and environmental carrying capacity. All of them are so intricately related that they form a system complexity whose very balance has never been so delicate yet so important to our survival. Therefore, we must also distinguish between bottlenecks that present continuous but stable challenges and the ones that represent discontinuous and unstable challenges. Population growth, for example, is a challenge with great continuity. However, as we approach the question of energy and land, particularly if environmental pressures are included, we can increasingly expect challenges characterized by discontinuity. Even though energy resources may not be depleted, the supply of energy could for technological, political, or economic reasons become highly discontinuous. Agricultural land may increasingly go out of commission in a discontinuous way, be it because of events such as droughts, floods, erosion, or drastic overuse. As the system reaches an ever greater complexity, and as survival hinges ever more and with small margins on this complexity, any jolt to the system is bound to make survival more immediately a matter of life and death.

Furthermore, the jolts emitted by the economic system are also of importance, for production factors such as population, land, energy, as well as many environmental constraints are mediated and coordinated by markets. Markets, however, are also known to have a great deal of discontinuity owing to the anonymous number of their participants and the unforeseeable outcome produced by their myriad market interactions. Thus, the capitalist market, the *very* technique chosen to *manage* survival, is itself a *threat* to survival, as is exemplified by speculation, recessions, and depressions, booms and busts. Market dynamics themselves upset the delicate balance among land, energy, population, and the environment, and thereby directly determine survival and death rates.

Additionally, techniques to *ensure* continuity in a world of random but significant disturbances may break down. Already insurance companies suspect that a number of weather-related events may have ceased to be sufficiently random or insignificant or both to be insured. The private market insurance system may soon prove unable to ensure against certain ecosystem risks. The instability would thereby increase, leaving politics as the last potential guarantor of continuity and stability, as is already the case with atomic power plants, where no private insurer is willing to cover the entire risk, *nor could such risk be covered*. However, how many big risks, should the event and the scarcity associated with them occur, can the political system handle before solidarity breaks down, instability increases, conflicts grow, and massive death results?

In times of growth and system expansion, potential conflicts can more likely be ignored, for their resolution is relatively easy. Everybody can come up with Pareto-type conflict resolutions. The going gets much tougher, though, and more lives are at stake, when conflicts await resolution during system contraction, increased scarcity, and shrinking surpluses. First, the number and severity of conflicts tend to increase. Second, conflict potentials can no longer be as easily ignored, for, should they erupt, the disturbance would only augment the scarcity and make any resolution increasingly and unnecessarily more difficult. Third, resolutions to conflicts are politically and economically much *harder* to find in times of general scarcity and contraction.

Presently, our world still relies on expansion and Pareto-type conflict resolutions. International exchange and free trade are thus enhanced, as is evident by the North American Free Trade Agreement (NAFTA) and the World Trade Organization (WTO). Furthermore, Eastern Europe, once a highly self-sufficient economic and political system, is being dismantled and integrated with the world division of labor. China, though still self-sufficient, may because of its participation in international trade and communication also become more unstable and be pressured to further expand market relations.

Capitalism, which is now the world's dominant political and economic system, thrives on market expansion. However, how compatible is capitalism with the long-term zero—or negative-growth environment of the future? It is incompatible! Not only does capitalism have great difficulty in handling such conditions, economically and politically, but it also has, for the same reasons, difficulty in preparing for them. Thus, markets, if left to themselves, cannot factor in long-term scarcity. Has the price of oil, for example, signaled that oil will soon be very scarce? On the contrary, oil markets have, if anything, signaled an ever growing supply of oil. The same could be said for land, lumber, and many other natural resources in limited supply.

The ability of the capitalist market system to guide us through the next decades of increasing scarcity and downscaling of industrial production is very limited indeed, and if lives are to be preserved, the primacy of politics over markets will have to be introduced again, as was the case for practically all of human history, except its bourgeois phase.

Issues to Be Addressed

To enter an age of scarcity and downscaling is to enter an age of increased conflicts that contain a great potential for mass death and even genocide, depending on the mechanisms by which scarcity is channeled to affect only certain groups and the mechanisms by which conflict is resolved, managed, or suppressed. If the analysis given here is correct or even plausible, and if the goal is to help humanity survive this tremendous challenge with no or minimal human loss, then we must increasingly ask questions such as the following:

1. Based on our knowledge, where and how can we warn the larger public of impending bottlenecks, and thus make the bottlenecks a legitimate focus of high-priority discussion everywhere?

2. How does the capitalist system tend to react when it approaches a zero—or negative-growth environment? What are the economic and political mechanisms by which scarcity is disturbed? What is the likelihood for fascism and other authoritarian political systems to arise to deal with scarcity while preserving class relations? What might be the cost in human lives if the distribution of scarcity were left to markets or to authoritarian and fascist politics?

3. What could we learn from societies at war or in an environment of war? How did they experience and deal with scarcity? What forms of solidarity and other coping mechanisms (even under capitalism) did they adopt?

4. What conflict-resolution strategies can be pursued for conflicts in which all parties have something to *lose*? How can conflicts be moderated by a long-term increase in the price of fossil fuels at a steady rate that doubles the price of this energy in ten and triples it in twenty years, for instance?

5. What can be learned from the behavior of cooperatives and other mutual-help-type social organizations pertaining to the management of *scarcity*?

6. To what extent is the broad social control over the means of production a *prerequisite* for increased solidarity and a more equal distribution of scarcity (or surplus)?

7. To what extent can the impending bottlenecks be dealt with only by reestablishing basic self-sufficiency on a regional basis?

8. To what extent can basic regional self-sufficiency, if coupled with a democratic access to the means of production, inhibit migration, decrease the birthrate, and reduce the transfer of value from the periphery to the center?

9. What is the necessary kind and level of industrial production and modern cultural and social life that must be retained to effectively and efficiently downscale while simultaneously meeting growing bottlenecks and needs?

10. To what extent should social scientists become ethically engaged as catalysts and organizers of movements concerned with social justice and the preservation of human life?

Other important questions could be added. Moreover, the social science-theory repertoire must, in anticipation of the issues ahead, also be reevaluated. Many classic and modern social science theories have their origin in the late eighteenth and nineteenth centuries. Invariably, these theories are concerned with the dramatic social changes brought about by the opening, expansion, and differentiation of social and economic systems, and, as a consequence, will soon prove grossly inadequate. The severe bottlenecks that lie ahead will bring about an equally drastic social change owing to scarcity, system closure, and the downscaling in industrial production, world markets, the world division of labor, urbanization, and so on. This transformation of society will be not just a 180-degree reversal of the ongoing world industrialization, but one of another kind. This all-encompassing, fast, and drastic social change of the near future will ultimately also generate a new brand of "classic" social theory.

The Enlightenment of the eighteenth century bore two different and opposing conceptions of the human being. Hobbes argued that left to their own devices, people would descend to the level of the animal, so that without the proper ordering of society and civilization, human beings would be ruled by the law of the jungle. The contrary position is that of Rousseau, who argued that people are inherently good but society was the corrupting influence. Modernist faith has largely followed Rousseau's position: the self was thought of as ultimately good. What was needed was a societal revolution that allowed the natural goodness of the individual to emerge and flourish.

We have come to be highly skeptical of the belief in the inherent goodness of the self. Enlightenment, education, culture, and science will not necessarily produce individuals who will do what is right. The genocides of the twentieth century, spilling over into the twenty-first, have unveiled the true heart of humanity. At our center lies an ability to commit evil of an almost unimagined degree. We have seen the nature of human beings and found that the most ordinary among us can transport millions to their death, can fill the earth and sky with the victims of killing fields. The theory of the inherent goodness of the human being was daily disproved in Nazi Germany and in the other state-sponsored genocides and massacres. Therefore, if Rousseau's argument was shown to be naive, then so has Hobbes's been proved wrong.

As time passes, genocides of the twentieth century will recede into memory. From this moment on, however, fundamental assumptions about human behavior and about civilization can no longer stand unchallenged, for though the occurrence is past, the phenomenon remains, as well as the causes exacerbated by the political, social, and economic bottlenecks outlined above. The unthinkable has already happened; the idea of future catastrophes is therefore not unthinkable.

When we look at our young students, we tremble for their future. We would like to be able to tell them that despite endless violence and disillusionment, one must maintain faith in people and in humankind and in our ability to solve problems. Despair is no solution. The solution lies in analysis, in hard thinking and questioning, and in purposeful and informed action. To that goal this book is dedicated.

Part One

STATEMENT OF THE
PROBLEM

Introduction

WHY SHOULD affluent societies in Europe or the Americas care about the population explosion in the developing world, ecological disasters in the Mediterranean basin, and the spread of mass poverty and disease in the far-flung corners of the world? Of what practical concern is it for a banker in Tokyo, a businessman in Copenhagen, a farmer in Iowa, or a housewife in Alberta—who are busy trying to live their lives—that there are famine and civil war in Somalia, floods in Bangladesh, and genocide in Rwanda, Bosnia, or East Timor? There always have been enormous gaps between the rich and the poor nations. The reason people in the developed world should care is that it is absolutely in their self-interest to limit the exponential growth in population and resource depletion.

The demographic imbalance between rich and poor societies is producing a migratory flow from the poor to the rich societies that is challenging the ability of the rich societies to absorb the poor without devastating conflict. It is certain that people have always inflicted damage upon their environment. Human beings have cut down, burned, over-grazed, and polluted their habitats since ancient times. But the environmental crisis we now confront is quantitatively and qualitatively different from anything we have faced before, simply because so many people have inflicted so much damage to the world's ecosystem during the present century that the system as a whole—not simply its parts—may be in danger. We see this happening in world population growth, in increasing rates of resource depletion, in ecological damage, and in widening disparities of income and resource use between developing and developed nations. All of these tendencies strain the capacities of the world's ecosystem to sustain itself into the next century without regional or global disasters. That is the focus of the following section.

Globalization and Security

The Prospects of the Underclass

John B. Cobb, Jr.

The U.S. Situation

WE OFTEN SPEAK of upper, middle, and lower classes. The "lower" class in this analysis is composed of workers with limited skills. In industrial societies, normally, more workers are available than needed, so that wages set by the market are low. Indeed, if there is a shortage of workers in one country, then arrangements are made to import them from countries where they are numerous. The regular importation of farm laborers from Mexico into the United States is a case in point.

A certain percentage of the lower-class workforce, thus, is normally unemployed. This state of affairs is considered desirable by most economists, since full employment would put upward pressure on wages. Most economists believe that rising wages lead to inflation and that inflation is to be avoided. In the United States, the Federal Reserve Board raises interest rates to slow economic expansion when unemployment rates fall below a set figure—usually 5 to 7 percent.

When those people without work are thought of as temporarily unemployed members of the workforce, they can still be considered part of the lower class. But when many of them are unlikely ever to be employed, when they give up seeking employment in the regular market, their class status changes. We can define this group as the underclass.

When society recognizes that its policies generate permanent unemployment of potential workers and that, in addition, there are some who do not have the mental or physical abilities required to take part in the market economy, it may provide basic necessities for these people. In a welfare society, provisions are made for everyone. No one goes without food, clothing, and shelter. In such a society, the underclass is supported by the government.

In the sixties and seventies, many European nations became welfare states. The United States moved partway in that direction with numerous ad hoc programs of aid to the needy. This pattern puts an end to extreme poverty and has much to commend it from a humanitarian point of view.

There are also problems with this solution. The underclass generates a culture in which no responsibility is felt toward the broader society. Even when work is available, the habits and motivation needed to succeed in the market are lacking. Furthermore, the economic recompense for unskilled labor may be no more than welfare payments. In the United States, members of the underclass who are ambitious and want to escape from poverty are more likely to turn to crime. Today American prisons house 2 million people, most of them members of the underclass.

Whereas Marx thought of class conflict as between the lower and upper classes, in the United States today it is more often between the lower class and the underclass. The lower class resents working hard for modest wages when others receive almost as much for doing nothing. It resents the personal danger brought about by the street crime in which the underclass plays the major role.

Welfare "reform" designed to pressure the unemployed to work has been popular. Since it was instituted at a time of high employment, a good many of the unemployed, including some who were part of the culture of the underclass, have entered the workforce. On the other hand, there has also been growth in the number of the homeless and the hungry, and the prison population continues to grow. As the rules ending welfare payments come into effect, the situation of the underclass will become more desperate.

Projection of the consequences of current policies is gloomy. Withdrawal of support from the underclass while maintaining a considerable amount of unemployment in order to fight "wage inflation" can only increase misery. People who cannot survive within the law will seek to survive by breaking the law. Resentment toward the underclass on the part of the working poor will increase. Society as a whole will see this whole class not only as superfluous but also as a cancer. The role of the police will be increasingly defined as protecting the rest of society from the underclass. The prospects for the underclass are bleak.

The danger is even greater than indicated in class analysis alone. In the United States, class and race are closely intertwined. Although the underclass includes persons of all races, blacks dominate the image of the class in the minds of others. Racist feelings toward blacks on the part of whites, and often of other minorities as well, are mixed with class feelings, and make them worse. They also affect attitudes toward blacks of all classes. Blacks react with rage to this continuing racism of U.S. society.

The most promising response to this threat to the underclass would be a change of policy with respect to unemployment and wages. If the government seriously sought full employment, the major cause of the growth of the underclass could be eliminated. Every child could grow up with the expectation of being wanted and needed by society.

In addition, a full-employment policy would lead to rising wages on the part of entry-level workers. What is now called "wage inflation" and successfully avoided by slowing the economy with higher interest rates would be understood instead as allowing workers to participate in the nation's prosperity. Well-paid workers would not resent welfare payments at a lower level to those people who, for one reason or another, are unable to become members of the workforce.

Of course, this policy would not immediately eliminate the culture of the underclass. All that can be done is to begin a process of change that will take at least two generations to complete. But a reversal of direction of this sort would, in itself, immediately change the situation in beneficial ways.

The argument against this solution is that it causes inflation. That it does so is not evident from history. The data can be read in quite a different way. It is significant that the low unemployment of the late nineties was not accompanied by inflation. If inflation comes in the early 2000s, it will, no doubt, be blamed on too little unemployment and the accompanying rise in wages. But it is just as likely to be the result of the repeated raises in interest rates by the Federal Reserve Board imposed in order to increase unemployment.

The Global Context

The problem is far more complex on a global basis. To whatever extent economies are organized around national markets, a nation can establish its own policies. It can decide to aim at full employment and to allow wages to rise, even to encourage this outcome. It can choose to take care of those people who are unable to participate in the market. Because all employers will compete for workers on an equal basis, all will have an equal chance to succeed. Full employment at good wages means high demand for goods. A stable prosperity is possible.

In a global economy, however, serious problems arise. Producers in countries with high wages must compete with producers in low-wage countries. In labor-intensive industries, they are forced to shift production to the latter. Nations that have had high wages and have taken care of all their citizens are under pressure to change. Either they must accept high unemployment, as in much of Europe, or they must reduce the cost of labor, as in the United States. Both of these policies lead to the growth of the underclass.

It is often supposed that when the highly developed nations pay this price, the less-developed nations benefit. Certainly, many of them are recipients of far more industrial development than they would otherwise have received. As measured by the gross domestic product (GDP), these nations progress rapidly. Sadly, this growth is typically accompanied by the emergence within them also of an underclass.

Developments differ from country to country. Some countries in East Asia, following Japan, maintained tight national control over their industrial development. In these countries, there was little underclass. This underclass is appearing only now as they are forced to open themselves to global market forces. The situation in Japan, South Korea, Taiwan, and Singapore is more like that in Europe.

Other Asian countries, such as Thailand and Indonesia, have developed chiefly within the global market. This model has been typical in Latin America, and in Africa as well, insofar as industrial development has occurred there at all. A few sweeping generalizations will indicate how an underclass grows in these countries.

Preindustrialized societies are labor intensive. There is work for most people, with income sufficient to meet survival needs but little more. Almost everyone is poor, but almost everyone has a place in the economy.

Transnational corporations transform these economies with their investments. They may purchase the best land for agricultural production for export, which displaces the subsistence farmers. Some of the farmers are employed in the new agribusiness, but because of less-labor-intensive methods, fewer workers are needed. Similarly, retail chains introduce imported manufactured merchandise that undersells local handicrafts and small neighborhood stores. Some former artisans and merchants are employed as clerks, but many are not needed. These workers, now separated from the means of independent livelihood, are available as industrial labor.

Displacement from traditional economic life takes place more rapidly than absorption of labor by the new industries. Social changes also generate new needs as well as new desires. Women, especially young women, enter the workforce in large numbers. The population of unemployed and underemployed explodes.

There is a vicious circle here. Because so many seek work, wages are very low. Because one wage cannot support even a small family, more and more family members must seek employment. This move adds to the pool of labor and further depresses wages. Further, if wages begin to rise in one country, then there are other countries that attract industry by keeping their wages low. This process dominates the global scene at present and can be described as the "race to the bottom."

The problems of development in the global context are exacerbated by the extreme mobility of capital. Capital flows create apparent prosperity and even considerable indigenous economic development. But the withdrawal of capital, which sometimes occurs abruptly, undercuts this development, bankrupts indigenous businesses, and often leads to the takeover of productive facilities in a fire sale by transnational investors. Developing nations are left with large debts to be paid by further exploitation of their workers. Defenselessness against these movements of international capital contributes to the precariousness of the condition of the poor.

The description of the underclass used with respect to the United States does not apply well here. In much of the global economy, employment does not lift one out of the underclass. Wages far below subsistence combined with the precariousness of the employment do not turn one into a part of an authentic working class. Too often the only member of a family who can find work is an adolescent daughter. In favorable circumstances, this work is in a factory, where young women constitute preferred employees. Sad to say, millions of young girls work as prostitutes. The global underclass is constituted of the unemployed, the underemployed, and the grossly underpaid who have been separated from their traditional means of subsistence. In most cases, governments are unable or unwilling to provide them with the necessities of life.

The type of "development" that produces this underclass is not the only possible one. We have noted that Japan pioneered another model that was successfully followed by South Korea, Taiwan, and Singapore. In this model, national governments controlled development patterns by working closely with indigenous businesses.

A third model has been much less tried. It can be called the community-development model. In this model, the unit of development is not the globe or the nation but the village or local community. The goal is to improve the life of the community rather than to undercut it. Simple technology is used to increase the productivity of farmers and artisans. They are not displaced by agribusiness, imported goods, or large retailers.

Those people who favor the globalized economy repeatedly inform us that there is no option, which is an exaggeration. The assertion is intended to reduce interest in considering options such as the ones noted above. There are places where these other models still have practical relevance, and, if they gathered sufficient support, they could become far more important. Nevertheless, we must also consider whether the plight of the global underclass can be alleviated within the dominant global economy.

There are various movements to influence the policies of transnational corporations. Some leaders within corporations do what they can to help their employees. Corporations have adopted codes of ethics governing their operations in developing countries. Conscientious investors propose to their corporations that they adopt the policy of paying a living wage. Consumers organize to bring pressure on selected companies to the same end. The most effective group has been college students who have persuaded colleges and universities to cease purchasing goods with institutional logos from corporations that do not cooperate. A few companies have released information about the location of their factories and allow independent inspections. The publicity will help to alleviate some of the worst abuses. Conscientious U.S. investors and consumers also support labor organizers in developing countries. There has been some success here, too.

All of these efforts to humanize the global economy are worthwhile. They can improve somewhat the plight of millions of members of the underclass around the world. Nevertheless, their limitations are apparent. In general, meeting the demands of people of conscience increases costs. Companies that do so are at a competitive disadvantage with those businesses that do not. Stockholder resolutions and consumer boycotts cannot be effective across the board. The corporations that are most responsive become the most vulnerable. Labor-union success in one country is frequently followed by the removal of production to another country that is able to guarantee more passive workers.

Significant and secure gains require global rules somewhat like the ones that labor won in most industrialized societies in the past. The organization in best position to implement such rules is the World Trade Organization. Thus far its policies have been supportive of corporate interests in the free movement of goods and capital rather than in fairness to workers. But the latter issue has been raised. The development of labor standards on a global basis cannot accomplish for world labor what national standards once did within nations, but it can reduce the worst abuses of the present system.

Another proposal that could help is the Tobin tax. The suggestion is that international-exchange transactions be taxed one-half of 1 percent, with the proceeds going to the United Nations. These transactions amount to $1.5 trillion a day, of which only 5 percent are for trade in goods and services. Most is short-term speculation that makes little contribution to the economy but does contribute to the turbulence described above.

The tax would both reduce the turbulence of the financial markets and provide money to combat poverty around the world. It would provide sufficient funds to improve education and health throughout the world and create safety nets for the poor. There is considerable support for this proposal, especially in Europe.

A final proposal is debt forgiveness. The story of how most of the world has become indebted to the developed nations and the international financial institutions is too complex to rehearse here. But there can be no doubt that many have debts they can never pay and that the payment of interest on these debts reduces the ability of many nations to provide services to the poor. It also presses them to compete for investments by holding wages down.

A movement of citizens in many countries, Jubilee 2000, has gained considerable attention to the proposal to forgive the debts of the world's poorest countries. Many governments have agreed to take steps in this direction. When examined carefully, not all of these agreements go as far as the rhetoric suggests. Nevertheless, the idea has been accepted in principle, and progress toward its implementation has been made.

The Larger Context

Thus far we have considered the situation of the underclass in the United States and in the world as a whole as if it existed in a physical vacuum. The situation is more disturbing when we consider the larger context. It is the earth system as a whole.

The chief argument for the globalization of the economy is that it is the most efficient system for promoting overall economic growth. Many economists of goodwill recognize that in the early stages of transnational investment there is much suffering. The rich get richer and the poor get poorer. But they argue that in time, production increases to the point that all benefit. Patience is required. In the end, they believe, the underclass, and indeed all poverty, will be abolished.

There are many reasons to be skeptical of this scenario. But of them, the chief is that it ignores the physical limits of the planet. Viewed ecologically, the quantity of global economic activity is already unsustainable. If current production were equally distributed today, then it could overcome extreme poverty everywhere. But no one, certainly not the proponents of economic globalization, proposes redistribution. The argument is that as total production increases, all will gain proportionately.

An influential report prepared for the United Nations under the leadership of Gro Brundtland argued that, given population growth, the income for the poor of the world would need to increase at least sixfold to eliminate miserable poverty. This rise cannot happen, the authors assumed, unless other segments of society also enjoyed a sixfold increase in income. That means that, in a world in which economic activity is already pressing the ecological limits, production must be increased six times!

The authors were somewhat aware of this problem. The solution, they believed, was to become far more efficient in the use of resources and to greatly reduce the emission of pollution. There is no doubt that important gains can be made in these ways. Furthermore, some of the growth can be in services that do not stress the environment. Nevertheless, it is exceedingly doubtful, even theoretically, that the quantity of growth envisioned could take place without catastrophic ecological consequences.

In any case, there is little possibility that ideal procedures will consistently be followed, which has certainly not occurred thus far. Rapid recent industrial growth in China, for example, has already led to appalling pollution and to the exhaustion of water resources. An additional doubling or quadrupling of industrial production there is difficult to envision.

Among the most crucial forms of impact on the environment is global warming. That it is already occurring, with concurrent increases in storms and other disturbances in weather patterns, is now well established. That increased industrial activity will worsen the situation is almost certain. At some point, the damage will exceed the short-term gain even by the most crass economic calculations.

The implication is that the ideal of global economic growth encouraged by a global market is in contradiction to the physical realities of the planet. It cannot solve the problem of the underclass it creates.

Particularly disturbing is the prospect of what will happen to the underclass as the awareness of limits sinks in. Once the ruling class realizes that the amount of economic activity that the planet can sustain will never have need of the labor of billions of the earth's present inhabitants, interest in their survival will diminish. The world decision makers will find that a greatly reduced population would be preferable. The underclass will appear not only as superfluous but also as an impediment to the well-being of those people who are productive. If, in desperation, the underclass turns to violence, then the powers that be will have the excuse they need to eliminate many of its members.

Ways Out

Can we envision a less dreadful scenario? Yes, but it would require changes now that are barely on the political map.

First, the meaning of economic growth would require drastic rethinking. There are good reasons for rejecting the ways in which it is now measured. The GDP, whose increase is now used to justify economic globalization, is in no sense a measure of human well-being—not even of economic well-being. This fact has been shown in detail. When an alternative measure, such as the index of sustainable economic welfare or the genuine progress indicator, is used as a guide to economic activity, it turns out that growth as measured by the gross domestic (or world) product often fails to contribute to real economic welfare at all!

Second, we should recognize that economic well-being is only one contribution to total well-being. The domination of the world by economic thinking in the past half century should be reversed. We should evaluate policies by their contribution to the health of the earth, including all its inhabitants, with special attention to the human ones. This evaluation would lead, like the destructive prospects summarized above but by a different route, to the judgment that further population growth is harmful to the human prospect. But it would focus on shifting priorities in wealthy nations away from the consumption of goods to more important human values and to positive means of encouraging small families in developing countries as proposed by the UN Cairo conference.

Third, we should affirm that the economic sector of society should serve the people as a whole. This change would entail a shift of power from economic institutions, guided primarily by the goal of economic profit, to political, social, and cultural institutions through which people in general can express their will. This move would reverse the trends of the past half century, although it should not lead back to the extreme nationalism of the past. National power should both be qualified by international organizations such as a strengthened United Nations and devolve to local regions in which people can participate more directly in decision making.

Fourth, economies should become much more national and, within nations, more local. This suggestion is implied in the preceding points. If economic power is global, then it cannot be subordinated to political, social, and cultural powers that are national and local. Such global economic power as remains should be subordinated to global political power. We cannot avoid catastrophe unless people in general are able to feed, clothe, and shelter themselves and unless human communities, national and local, can order their lives for the benefit of all their members.

There is little doubt that, eventually, local economies will reappear. The globalized economy becomes more and more fragile. Its assumptions—that it is benefiting humanity economically and that it can continue to grow indefinitely—are both false. Such fundamental errors portend collapse. But can such a shift occur without disaster?

Recent events in Cuba provide hope. Cuba had bought into standardized global-economy thinking even though the United States limited its access. It became a part of the Soviet economic bloc, specializing in sugar production and importing many necessities. When the Soviet Union collapsed, Cuba was left to its own devices. It was forced to reorganize its economy so as to feed, clothe, and house its own people as well as meet their needs for education and health care.

The United States responded to Cuba's crisis by intensifying its economic isolation, hoping to bring it to collapse. Nevertheless, Cuba survived. And despite all the misery imposed on its people by its own mistakes and by the U.S. embargo, Cuba's condition overall is better than most Latin American countries. Because of the lack of oil, much agricultural production is now organic. In general, Cuba's current economy is ecologically sustainable.

Our topic is the prospects of the underclass entailed in the dominant policies in the United States and in the world. The condition of the underclass is already wretched. Its prospects are appalling. We are told that the globalized economy is the solution. It is not. Even now it is far more the problem than the solution. Continuing present policies leads toward unimaginable horrors for the underclass. Cuba has many problems. It is not to be romanticized. But in Cuba there is no underclass facing dire threats.

Cuba moved toward a sustainable economy under extremely difficult conditions. Perhaps the world can do better. Imagine that scores of nations around the world would seek self-sufficiency in food production, relying chiefly on organic means, not abruptly and out of painful necessity imposed by the hostility of the United States, but because they were seeking a secure and sustainable future. Suppose they undertook to meet most of their other needs as well without heavy dependence on imports such as oil. Suppose that this endeavor involved more labor-intensive methods of production. Suppose that at every stage, these countries gave serious consideration to the effects of their policies on the poor and on the natural environment. Suppose further that the international community supported them in making these moves. Global warming and other environmental threats would diminish, the underclass would cease to exist in these countries, and the prospects of the poor would not include unmitigated disaster.

The shift we need is not under discussion in the halls of power. On the other hand, elements in this shift are coming to attention in the nongovernmental-organization (NGO) movement. Since 1992, in connection with the Earth Summit UN conference, NGOs representing a wide range of concerns began to find a common voice. Human-rights groups, environmentalists, labor, community developers, indigenous people, and others all recognized the threat to their concerns in mainstream globalization practices. Since then they have begun to work together, as in this country in Seattle in 1999 and Washington, D.C., in 2000. It is not impossible that their influence will grow.

Suggested Reading

Buchanan, Patrick J. 1998. *The Great Betrayal.* Boston: Little, Brown.

Cobb, John B., Jr. 1994. *Sustaining the Common Good: A Christian Perspective on the Global Economy.* Cleveland: Pilgrim Press.

———. 1999. *The Earthist Challenge to Economism: A Theological Critique of the World Bank.* New York: St. Martin's Press.

Daly, Herman E., and John B. Cobb Jr. 1994. *For the Common Good: Redirecting the Economy Toward Community, the Environment, and a Sustainable Future.* 2d ed. Boston: Beacon Press.

Friedman, Thomas L. 1999. *The Lexus and the Olive Tree: Understanding Globalization.* New York: Farrar, Straus, Giroux.

Korten, David C. 1995. *When Corporations Rule the World.* West Hartford, Conn.: Kumarian Press.

———. 1995. *The Post-Corporate World: Life after Capitalism.* West Hartford, Conn.: Kumarian Press.

Raghavan, Chakravarthi. 1990. *Recolonization: GATT, the Uruguay Round, and the Third World.* Penang, Malaysia: Third World Network.

2

Global Industrial Civilization

The Necessary Collapse

Chris H. Lewis

> *Collapse is recurrent in human history; it is global in its occurrence; and it affects the spectrum of societies from simple foragers to great empires.*
> —Joseph A. Tainter, *The Collapse of Complex Societies*

WE ARE NOW witnessing the collapse of a globalized modern industrial civilization. Far from being inevitable, globalization, the movement toward a globally integrated, free-market capitalist economy dominated by First World nations and transnational corporations (TNCs), is undermining the very foundation of global industrial civilization. Global populist challenges in the late 1990s and early 2000s by First and Third World activists and peoples to the World Trade Organization, the World Bank, and the International Monetary Fund (IMF) and the crippling burden of Third World debt illustrate the increasing stresses and ruptures that are even now undermining global industrial civilization. Just like the Roman Empire, overexpansion and structural weaknesses are undermining this emerging global civilization at the very height of its power. Smug, arrogant arguments about the inevitability of globalization, such as Thomas Friedman's *Lexus and the Olive Tree* (2000), and the triumph of global industrial free-market capitalist civilization are symptoms of the very contradictions that are being exacerbated by "forced" globalization and will cause the collapse of global industrial civilization. The seeds of its collapse are even now being sown by First World elites' and TNCs' efforts to impose a globalized, free-market capitalist economy on the world.

The most prominent of these increasing structural contradictions that are tearing apart global industrial civilization are the increasing destruction of the global environment, increasing poverty and inequality between First and Third World peoples, and increasing threats to national and democratic governance by the World Trade Organization and by global financial markets. Global industrial civilization is collapsing because the very economic growth and global development that it promises will address these structural contradictions are only making them worse. Our hope lies in the creation of local and regional cultures and economies that can truly solve these problems by focusing on sustainable development, the health of local peoples and communities, and the redemocratization of everyday life. Globalization will fail because it supports TNCs over peoples and communities, bolsters corporate profits over human rights and the environment, and demands the reign of global corporations and markets over people and nature. Led and supported by First World governments such as the United States, Britain, Germany, and Japan, globalization is swamping nation-states and putting nothing in their place but global corporations and unregulated global financial markets (Athanasiou 1996, 173). The current debate over the WTO is really a debate about the future of global industrial civilization.

The Rise and Fall of Global Industrial Civilization

Globalization really began with the growth and expansion of a European market economy starting in the seventeenth century and the development of a global industrial economy in the twentieth century. This global economy has been dominated by European and U.S. imperialism. The goal of this global imperialism, which First World elites call "development," was to suck the wealth, labor, and resources out of their colonial dependencies to increase First World wealth, freedom, and opportunity. Any Third World peoples who stood in the way of this imperialist drive were either enslaved or destroyed. The plight of American Indians, African tribes, and Asian island nations illustrates the larger reality of this global imperialism. By 1914, according to Craig Dilworth, the nations of Europe, and their offshoots such as the United States and Australia, controlled 84 percent of the earth's surface (1998, 142). The major wars of the twentieth century have been about which powers, or military alliances, would dominate and control this global economy. With the collapse of Soviet communism in 1991, the First World, led by the United States, Europe, and Japan, was now freed to impose a global capitalist market economy on the world.

With the deregulation of global financial markets in the 1990s, the creation of the WTO in 1995, and increasing World Bank and IMF pressure on Third World nations to pay off their foreign debt in the 1990s and early 2000s, we have witnessed the drive toward globalization, the creation of a First World-dominated global capitalist economy that serves only to enrich the wealthy and large corporations of the First World at the expense of the Third World poor, the global environment, human rights, and democracy. Globalization is really an effort by First World elites and global corporations to impose their neofeudal rule on the world. President Clinton's chief trade negotiator, Carla Hills, all but said as much when she admitted: "We want to abolish the right of nations to impose health and safety standards more stringent than a minimal uniform world standard" (Athanasiou 1996, 177). The director of the International Forum on Globalization, Jerry Mander, argues,

> The central operating principle of the WTO is that global commercial interests supercede all other interests. WTO suppresses obstacles to the expansion of global corporate activity such as national, provincial, state, and community laws and standards that are made on behalf of labor rights, environmental protection, human rights, consumer rights, local culture, social justice, national sovereignty, and democracy. (Mander and Barker 2000)

Both First World economic powers and TNCs have "used the threat of WTO action to roll back, block, or chill countless rules designed to benefit workers, consumers, and the environment, and to promote human rights and development in the world's poor countries" (Wallach et al. 1999, 13). World Bank and IMF structural adjustment loans have been used to force Third World countries to cut workers' wages and government spending on education, health, and the environment; devalue their local currencies; and reduce government regulation of TNCs. This emerging globalized world order is exacerbating the global destruction of the environment, poverty and economic inequality, and the poor quality of life of billions of people.

Globalization is creating record global corporate profits, increasing wealth for a small global elite, and promoting corporate domination of First and Third World governments. Using their increased wealth, TNCs and the wealthy are buying and controlling First and Third World governments. Indeed, globalization is really the result of dominant U.S. and European elites creating a global capitalist economy after World War II. The cold war was actually an effort by First World elites to crush all opposition to the globalization of this free-market capitalist economy. With the collapse of Soviet communism and the increasing political and economic weakness of Third World countries, First World elites are confident that nothing now stands in their way.

Now let's look at the most important structural contradictions that are undermining global industrial civilization: (1) environmental destruction, (2) increasing poverty and global inequality, and (3) increasing threats to state and local democratic governance. All of these structural contradictions reinforce each other and are creating positive feedback loops that only accelerate the collapse of global industrial civilization. The best example of this positive feedback system is West Africa. Increasing deforestation and soil degradation are undermining rural economies, which forces rural refugees to swarm into exploding industrial cities, which in turn creates massive urban poverty and underdevelopment, which further stresses local and national resources, which often leads to the collapse of African states and untold violence, anarchy, famine, and suffering, which is now occurring throughout Africa. I agree with Robert Kaplan who warns that "West Africa's future, eventually, will also be that of most of the rest of the world" (2000, 7). Our global future will be like West Africa's unless this uncontrolled globalization and accelerating positive feedback loop are not ended with the collapse of global industrial civilization. The challenge for the emerging local and regional cultures and economies will be to close this positive feedback loop forever by creating local, sustainable economies that support all their people, protect the environment, and allow people to democratically control their lives and local communities. In such a new world order, the health of local people, communities, environments, and economies would be paramount, not the profit and power of First World elites and TNCs.

Globalization and the Destruction
of the Global Environment

With the growth and expansion of a European market economy since the seventeenth century and the development of a global industrial economy in the twentieth century, science has recorded the rapidly accelerating human destruction of the earth (Turner et al. 1990). Since the 1950s, with the aid of modern science and technology, the human population has doubled, and scientists predict that the enormous transformations of the earth in the last three centuries will be doubled, trebled, or more in the centuries to come (Kates, Turner, and Clark 1990, 14). In 1999, the world population hit 6 billion and is now growing at the rate of 80 million people a year. If we are to feed the world's projected 8 to 12 billion people by 2050, then we will need to increase agricultural production three to four times and increase energy consumption six to eight times (ibid.). Can global, modern industrial civilization sustain this rapid rate of growth without destroying itself or greatly endangering the well-being of future generations? How can we support growing populations in the Third World and increasing affluence in the First World without destroying the earth and undermining global industrial civilization? Tragically, the struggle to feed exploding populations and improve living standards throughout the world is only accelerating the global destruction of the environment.

Since its birth in sixteenth—and seventeenth-century Europe, the modern industrial First World, driven by the desire to accumulate wealth and control human and natural resources, has waged a brutal war against the earth. In *Extinction,* biologists Paul Ehrlich and Anne Ehrlich note that "never in the 500 million years of terrestrial evolution has this mantle we call the biosphere been under such savage attack" (1981, 8). In their 1993 "World Scientists' Warning to Humanity," signed by more than 1,680 scientists worldwide, concerned scientists warned that "human activities inflict harsh and often irreversible damage on the environment and on critical resources" (Union of Concerned Scientists 1993, 3). Tragically, the industrial world's relentless struggle to conquer and subdue the earth in the name of progress will bring its collapse and ruin. Its vain struggle to control and defeat the awesome power of nature will, in the end, destroy global industrial civilization.

Driven by individualism, materialism, and the endless pursuit of wealth and power, the modern industrialized First World's efforts to modernize and integrate the world politically, economically, and culturally since World War II are only accelerating this global collapse. In the early twenty-first century, global development leaves 80 percent of the world's population outside of the industrialized nations' progress and affluence (Wallimann 1994). When this modern industrialized world collapses, Third World peoples will continue their daily struggle for dignity and survival at the margins of a moribund global industrial civilization.

With the collapse of global industrial civilization, smaller, autonomous local and regional civilizations, cultures, and polities will emerge. We can reduce the threat of mass death and genocide that will surely accompany this collapse by encouraging the creation and growth of sustainable, self-sufficient regional polities. John Cobb has already made a case for how it may work in the United States and how it is working in Cuba. After the collapse of global industrial civilization, First and Third World peoples will not have the material resources, biological capital, and energy and human resources to reestablish global industrial civilization. Forced by economic necessity to become dependent on local resources and ecosystems for their survival, peoples throughout the world will work to conserve and restore their environments. Those societies that destroy their local environments and economies, as modern people so often do, will themselves face collapse and ruin.

Thus, the rapid expansion of global industrial civilization since the 1600s, which modern peoples understand as progress and development, is destroying the earth and threatening the human future (Hauchler and Kennedy 1994). Since the birth of the modern industrial world, we have witnessed accelerating global population growth; air and water pollution; destruction of forests, farmland, and fisheries; depletion of nonrenewable natural resources; loss of biodiversity; and increasing poverty and misery throughout the nonmodern world (Brown and Kane 1994). In her chapter in Worldwatch's *State of the World, 1995,* Hilary French concludes: "The relentless pace of global ecological decline shows no signs of letting up. Carbon dioxide concentrations are mounting in the atmosphere, species loss continues to accelerate, fisheries are collapsing, land degradation frustrates efforts to feed hungry people, and the earth's forest cover keeps shrinking" (1995, 171). And in his own chapter in *State of the World, 1995,* Lester Brown (1995) warns that eroding soils, shrinking forests, deteriorating rangelands, expanding deserts, acid rain, stratospheric ozone depletion, the buildup of greenhouse gases, air pollution, and the loss of biological diversity threaten global food production and future economic growth. How could this rapid growth in wealth, population, science and technology, and human control over the natural world have produced such catastrophic results?

Globalization and the Creation of the First and Third Worlds

Globalization, development, and progress are proving to be dangerous delusions, which modern peoples continue to support despite the overwhelming evidence that they have led to an escalating war against the earth. Ironically, the modern industrial world's relentless pursuit of victory in this centuries-old war against nature will be the principal cause of its defeat and collapse. In *The Vanishing White Man*, Stan Steiner argued:

> The ruins of the Roman Empire, and the Mayan and Byzantine and Ottoman and Incan and Islamic and Egyptian and Ghanaian and Nigerian and Spanish and Aztec and English and Grecian and Persian, and the Mongolian civilization of the great Khans are visible for all to see. Is it heresy to say that the civilization of the white man of Western Europe, which has dominated much of the Earth for 400 years, is about to become one more magnificent ruin? Not because it has failed to accomplish its goals, but because it has succeeded so well, its time on earth may be done. (1976, 277)

The paradox of global development is that the tremendous success of global industrial civilization will be the cause of its collapse and ruin. In order to understand this paradox, we need to understand how modern economic and political institutions are creating both the so-called developed and underdeveloped worlds, which I will refer to as the First and Third Worlds (Escobar 1995).

Indeed, most people in the world are living on the margins of development. Three-quarters of the world's population lives in the 130 poorer countries of Latin America, Africa, and Asia, and the majority of these people do not have either steady jobs or secure incomes (Barnet and Cavanagh 1994, 179). In *Global Dreams*, Richard Barnet and John Cavanagh argue that there is a growing struggle between "the forces of globalization and the territorially based forces of local survival seeking to preserve and to re-define community" (22). Barnet and Cavanagh conclude that "local citi-zens' movements and alternative institutions are springing up all over the world to meet basic economic needs to preserve local traditions, religious life, cultural life, biological species, and other treasures of the natural world, and to struggle for human dignity" (429). This increasing conflict between the demands of global industrial civilization and diverse peoples and cultures to protect their way of life and local autonomy is further evi-dence that the modern industrial world is collapsing.

By creating the specter of vast, untold wealth and freedom in the First World and massive, desperate poverty and despair in the Third World, global development is creating the contradictions that will undermine global industrial civilization. On the one hand, global economic integra-tion, which is known as globalization, is creating spectacular wealth and progress for the 20 percent who live in the developed world, but, on the other hand, it is creating massive poverty and social unrest for the 80 per-cent who live in the underdeveloped world (ibid.). Between 1960 and 2000, rather than shrinking, the income gap between the rich and the poor actually grew. According to the *1999 UN Human Development Re-port,* in 1960, the richest 20 percent of the world earned thirty times as much income as the poorest 20 percent, sixty times as much income in 1990, and seventy-four times as much income by 1997. This UN report also reported that the richest 20 percent of the world consumes 86 per-cent of the world gross domestic product, the middle 60 percent consume just 13 percent, and the poorest 20 percent consume just 1 percent of the world GDP. In 2000, according to the World Bank, a sixth of the world's people produced 78 percent of the world's goods and services and re-ceived 78 percent of the world's income, whereas three-fifths of the world's people in the poorest sixty-one countries received 6 percent of the world's income.

Instead of trickling down, global wealth and resources are being sucked out of the Third and First Worlds, creating only more poverty and underdevelopment. First World elites' answer to this poverty and under-development is more development, which the reader should now under-stand will cause only more poverty and underdevelopment.

In his book *When Corporations Rule the World,* David Korten argues that the world's money, technology, and markets are controlled and man-aged by gigantic global corporations (1995, 131). In 1999, worldwide corporate mergers reached a new record of $3.4 trillion. This global merger movement reflects the increasing concentration of corporate power into larger and larger TNCs. According to the *1999 UN Human Development Report,* the 1990s witnessed the "increasing concentration of income, resources, and wealth among people, corporations, and countries." Faced with this growing structural contradiction, First World elites are calling for even more development in the Third World, arguing that only development will improve the lives of underdeveloped peoples. Of course, as we have seen, more development increases the wealth of only the First World at the expense of Third World peoples, the global environment, and human rights and democracy. Moreover, more development leads only to the further concentration of wealth and greater global inequality. By the late 1990s, of the world's one hundred largest economic entities, forty-nine are nations and fifty-one are corporations. In 1970 there were seven thousand TNCs, whereas in 2000 there were more than sixty thousand TNCs. The five hundred largest corporations account for 70 percent of world trade. In the 1990s, according to the *1999 UN Human Development Report,* there was increasing concentration of income, resources, and wealth among peoples, corporations, and countries. By 1997, the richest 20 percent had eighty-two times as much income as the poorest 20 percent. By 1995, 358 billionaires enjoyed a combined net worth of $760 billion, equal to the net worth of the poorest 2.5 billion of the world's people (Korten 1995, 83).

The Withdrawal of the Third World
from the Global Corporate Economy

If sustainable development and the further integration of the global economy are not the answers to the increasing problems confronting both the First and the Third Worlds, then what is the solution? The answer, as John Cobb has already argued, lies in the remarkable ability of peoples and cultures to adapt to constantly changing local and regional environments. Thus, if Third World peoples find that development and their dependence on the global economy are creating poverty, suffering, and political turmoil, then it would, in fact, be very adaptive for them to withdraw from the global economy and refuse to accept First World efforts to develop them. Of course, this reaction would further undermine the myth of development, the myth that human progress can be achieved only through modernization. Whether we call it civilizing, progress, modernization, development, sustainable development, or now globalization, modern peoples have imagined that it is the developed world's "manifest destiny" to teach the rest of the world that modernity is the only course open to them. But this belief is simply not true. There are just too many diverse cultures, religions, and ways of life for modernization and global industrial development to finally triumph. By refusing to disappear into history, despite innumerable attempts to civilize and teach them to be modern, nonmodern peoples demonstrate the resilience and strength of their cultures and societies to survive and adapt in a complex and chaotic world.

I need to be very clear here. I am not arguing that human overpopulation and the resulting destruction of global resources will be the primary factors causing the collapse of global civilization. It is the rich, not the poor, who are destroying the earth. Tom Athanasiou argues that "if current patterns of consumption do not change, the 57 million Northerners born in the 1990s will consume and pollute more than the 971 million Southerners born in the 1990s" (1996). The global environmental crisis is the result of the expansion of global industrial civilization and the development of the First World and the underdevelopment of the Third World since the 1600s. In *Sustaining the Earth,* John Young argues that "people constitute an environmental problem, not because of their existence, but because of what they do, and the parts of the environment they use up or damage" (1990, 107). The culture of the modern world—its individualism, materialism, scientism, and faith in progress—and the global expansion of that culture are the central causes of the collapse of global industrial civilization (Ehrenfeld 1978). And surviving polities and nations must keep these facts firmly in mind if they are to avoid future collapses themselves.

The Collapse of Global Industrial Civilization as an Opportunity

The First World's failure to modernize and civilize the world should be seen not as a tragedy, but as an opportunity. With the increasing recognition of the inability of development to resolve the economic and political contradictions it creates, whether you call it sustainable or not, peoples and communities will be once again forced to draw on their own cultures, histories, religions, and intimate knowledge of their local environments to improve their lives and ensure a "reasonable life" for their children. For most of history, successfully adapting to changing local and regional environments was the fundamental challenge facing human societies.

The only alternative we now have is to recognize the very real, imminent collapse of global industrial civilization. Instead of seeing this collapse as a tragedy, and trying to put "Humpty-Dumpty" back together again, we must see it as a real opportunity to solve some of the basic economic, political, and social problems created and exacerbated by the development of global industrial civilization since the 1600s. Instead of insisting on coordinated global actions, we should encourage self-sufficiency through the creation of local and regional economies and trading networks (Norgaard 1994). We must help political and economic leaders understand that the more their countries are tied to the global economic system, the more risk there is of serious economic and political collapse. The First World's effort to impose the WTO and globalization on the rest of the world in the 1990s and early 2000s is a last-ditch effort to keep global industrial civilization from unraveling. Who knows, but the recent collapse of the WTO Third Ministerial meeting in Seattle in November 1999, the Jubilee 2000 movement to cancel all Third World debt, and increasing challenges to World Bank and IMF policies might be harbingers of this global collapse. Indeed, we are witnessing the increasing collapse of global industrial civilization. My guess is that sometime between 2010 and 2050 we will see its final collapse.

In the case of the collapse of Mayan civilization, those city-states and regions in Central America that were not as dependent on the central Mayan civilization, economy, and trade were more likely to survive its collapse. Those city-states who were heavily dependent on Mayan hegemony destroyed themselves by fighting bitter wars with other powerful city-states to maintain their declining economic and political dominance (Weatherford 1994). Like the collapse of Mayan and Roman civilizations, the collapse of global civilization will cause mass death and suffering as a result of the turmoil created by economic and political collapse. The more dependent nations are on the global economy, the more economic, political, and social chaos they will experience when it breaks down.

In conclusion, the only solution to the growing political and economic chaos caused by the collapse of global industrial civilization is to encourage the uncoupling of nations and regions from the global industrial economy. Unfortunately, millions will die in the wars and economic and political conflicts created by the accelerating collapse of global industrial civilization. But we can be assured that, on the basis of the past history of the collapse of regional civilizations such as the Mayan and the Roman Empires, barring global nuclear war, human societies and civilizations will continue to exist and develop on a smaller, regional scale. Yes, such civilizations will be violent, corrupt, and often cruel, but, in the end, less so than our current global industrial civilization, which is abusing the entire planet and threatening the mass death and suffering of all its peoples and the living, biological fabric of life on Earth.

The paradox of global economic development is that although it creates massive wealth and power for First World elites, it also creates massive poverty and suffering for Third World peoples and societies. The failure of global development to end this suffering and destruction will bring about its collapse. This collapse will cause millions of people to suffer and die throughout the world, but it should, paradoxically, ensure the survival of future human societies. Indeed, the collapse of global industrial civilization is necessary for the future, long-term survival of human beings. Although this future seems hopeless and heartless, it is not. We can learn a lot from our present global crisis. What we learn will shape our future and the future of the complex, interconnected web of life on Earth.

Ways Out: What You Can Do to Help Create a Better Future

1. Support groups challenging globalization such as the International Forum on Globalization, the People-Centered Development Forum, Third World Network, Fifty Years Is Enough, Focus on the Global South, and Public Citizen.

2. Support local businesses and local and regional economies through purchases and public support. Boycott global chain stores and transnational corporations, which are the driving forces behind globalization.

3. Simplify your life. Reduce your consumption, reduce your use of energy and material resources, and focus on the quality of life in your local community.

4. Support sustainable local economies and local farmers and businesses. Support your local farmers' markets and recycling programs. Reduce, reuse, and recycle materials in your local community.

5. Challenge the national and global rights of corporations. Work to

end the legal fiction that corporations should have the same rights as individuals. Make corporations responsible to their local and regional governments and economies.

6. Demand campaign finance reform and end the selling of local and national governments to the highest bidder. Get corporations and "big money" out of politics.

7. Recognize and restore the rights of local communities and peoples to control their lives, their environments, their economies, and their cultures. Challenge globalization's "race to the bottom" by encouraging local communities to set their own standards for human rights, environmental quality, and quality of life.

8. Support efforts to restore local and regional environments. Work to create what Paul Hawken calls "restorative economies" (1993), economies that protect, support, and restore the environment while at the same time supporting local communities.

9. Support solar and alternative technologies that reduce energy and material resource use. Try to find ways to support alternative technologies in your daily life and in your community.

10. Accept the collapse of global industrial civilization as an opportunity. Instead of focusing on the tragedy of this collapse, focus on what you can do to help your local community and economy survive and prosper in this emerging new world of small local and regional economies and cultures.

Suggested Reading

Athanasiou, Tom. 1996. *Divided Planet.* Boston: Little, Brown.

Danaher, Kevin, and Roger Burbach, eds. 2000. *Globalize This!* Monroe, Maine: Common Courage Press.

Ehrenfeld, David. 1978. *The Arrogance of Humanism.* New York: Oxford Univ. Press.

Friedman, Thomas L. 2000. *The Lexus and the Olive Tree.* Rev. ed. New York: Anchor Books.

Hawken, Paul. 1993. *The Ecology of Commerce.* New York: HarperCollins.

Kaplan, Robert D. 2000. *The Coming Anarchy.* New York: Random House.

Korten, David. 1995. *When Corporations Rule the World.* West Hartford, Conn.: Kumarian Press.

Mander, Jerry, and Debi Barker. 2000. *Beyond the World Trade Organization.* Sausalito, Calif.: International Forum on Globalization.

Ponting, Clive. 1991. *A Green History of the World: The Environment and the Collapse of Great Civilizations.* New York: St. Martin's Press.

Weatherford, Jack. 1994. *Savages and Civilization: Who Will Survive?* New York: Crown.

Part Two

SCARCITY AND CONFLICT

Introduction

IN THE LIGHT of the broad global trends discussed in the preceding section, we should not be surprised if there is a relationship between scarcity and internal and regional conflict. It is also appropriate to ask whether there is a gender component to this violence. Are women particularly vulnerable and targeted as victims? With population pressures building in various parts of the globe, the struggle for resources intensifies, and with the end of the cold war, we may expect to see old ethnic animosities and religious conflicts come to the surface with greater intensity, particularly in the poorer parts of the world. We have already seen this outcome in Central America, Southeast Asia, Afghanistan, the Middle East, the Balkans, Africa, and the rimlands of the former Soviet Union.

The optimists argue that natural resources are not a finite entity that is steadily being depleted; they see the creation of new or modified resources that are the result of human inventions and labor, and they believe technology has an infinite capacity for solving the earth's problems. They also have abiding faith in the resiliency of the earth itself and its human inhabitants. Just as Malthus was wrong in his predictions, so are today's doomsayers. If the optimists are correct, then the world will just be a more prosperous place with more "stuff" distributed to larger numbers of people. If they are wrong, as the contributors in this section argue, then the human race may be in for more conflict and suffering if it does not change its course of the relentless pursuit of growth, accumulation, and waste.

3

Biophysical Limits to the Human Expropriation of Nature

John M. Gowdy

AMONG PHYSICAL SCIENTISTS, and among biologists and ecologists in particular, the view is widely held that the current level of human activity is unsustainable. The human population has reached 6 billion and is still growing rapidly. Per capita incomes are rising exponentially in the consumption-driven nations of the North. And technological advances are allowing the ruthless exploitation of the earth's biological and mineral resources on an unprecedented scale. Thus, all three elements of Paul Ehrlich's environmental impact equation (Impact = Population x Affluence x Technology [PAT]) seem to be increasing with no end in sight. The environmental-impact side of the PAT equation seems to be reaching crisis proportions. According to prominent biologists, the current loss of biological diversity is reaching the level of the five other mass-extinction episodes in the 600 million-year history of complex life on earth. Best estimates are that the current rate of species extinction is between one hundred and one thousand times the pre-Homo sapiens background rate. The rate of loss is accelerating with the clear-cutting of the world's remaining tropical forests, exacerbated by massive forest fires in the Amazon Basin and Indonesia. Edward O. Wilson estimates that by the middle of this century, more than 20 percent of existing species will be extinct (1992).

Another widely reported potential environmental calamity, global climate change, also appears to be accelerating at an alarming rate. Atmospheric CO_2 is expected to increase from its preindustrial level of 270 PPM to 600 PPM by the middle of this century, raising average global temperatures from 3.5ßC to 7ßC and raising sea levels one to two meters by thermal expansion alone. Very recent indications are that the eventual degree of global warming may be in the high range of current predictions. Global warming is most pronounced in the polar regions, which may lead to dramatic shifts in climate. A particularly alarming piece of news is that the total mass of Arctic ice shrunk by 40 percent in the last three decades of the twentieth century. Like many other environmental perturbations, the ultimate effects of global climate change are unknown and probably unknowable until they happen. Some scientists warn that the Antarctic ice cap may be melting so fast that it could cause a sudden catastrophic rise in sea levels. Others predict that the melting of the Arctic ice mass could change the course of the North Atlantic current and paradoxically cause a sudden cooling of Europe and eastern North America. Whatever the ultimate consequences of global warming turn out to be, if they are sudden then a tremendous strain will be placed on the world's agricultural system, a system increasingly fragile because of its growing dependence on ever more complex technology.

Many other less-publicized environmental crises loom, including water shortages, disruption of ecosystems because of rising levels of atmospheric nitrogen, and disruption of endocrine systems of higher animals, including humans, because of rising levels of dioxin in the ambient environment. The adverse consequences of any of these phenomena may be overstated. The likelihood, however, that all the dire predictions are fundamentally wrong is virtually zero. From many different perspectives, it is clear that we are pushing the limits of the ability of the biophysical world to absorb the continued expansion of human activity. Evidence from many independent sources leads us to the conclusion that industrial production will be drastically reduced, either because of constraints on energy and resource use or because of the limits of the environment to absorb the by-products of economic growth. It is increasingly likely that sometime this century, the "industrialization project," to use Isidor Wallimann's term, will come to a halt with unforeseen but most likely negative consequences for the human species. What are the prospects for getting off the industrial-growth path before social disintegration and mass death occur?

We who are alive today are in a unique position in human history. Not only do we exist at a critical instant in the biophysical history of the planet, but we also have an unprecedented understanding of the details of our place in the history of our world. We are beginning to understand how the biophysical boundary conditions for human activity are irreversibly changing, and we are beginning to recognize the human role in that process. The advance of scientific knowledge in the past few decades has been staggering. Models designed to predict the pattern and consequences of climate change are being continually refined and are becoming increasingly accurate. Ecological research showing the value of biodiversity to ecosystem stability is also advancing rapidly. Even more important, perhaps, we are beginning to understand the connections among social phenomena, such as class stratification and the generation of economic surplus, and environmental degradation.

The Importance of Economic Growth within the World Sociopolitical System

It is now obvious that the promise of utopia through the creation of an ever more abundant array of material possessions is a hollow one. Not only is continued economic expansion impossible in a finite world, but opinion surveys in industrial societies also indicate that despite rapid economic growth, people are becoming less, not more, satisfied with the quality of their lives. Even the relatively small percentage of the world's population who have reaped the benefits of material abundance are increasingly unhappy, are less secure, and have less leisure time to enjoy their lives. Furthermore, the promise of extending northern prosperity to the poor nations of the South is a fading dream. An increasing number of countries are being added to the list of what are cynically termed *failed nations.*

If it is physically impossible for economic growth to continue for much longer without irreparably undermining the life-support systems of the planet, and if this growth is making its supposed beneficiaries less happy, then why is the goal of economic growth not only accepted but also relentlessly promoted by every existing government? Two answers to this question are: (1) economic growth does benefit the tiny minority who make the basic decisions about resource use and the distribution of economic surpluses, and (2) economic growth and expansion are an essential feature of the self-organizing market system that now dominates human cultures throughout the world.

From the international to the local levels, the leading proponents of economic growth are, not surprisingly, those people who directly benefit from it. These people are the ones most willing to sacrifice environmental quality and long-run social stability for economic expansion. The people making investment decisions that will inevitably degrade the environment and the quality of life are the ones who can best insulate themselves from the adverse consequences of those decisions. World leaders across the political spectrum must be assured that "development" can continue before environmental issues are even discussed. Any interference with national sovereignty on ecological grounds is met with a self-righteous declaration of the "right to develop." At the local level, economic growth at all costs is promoted by the most conservative growth-oriented segments of the economy, as represented by local chambers of commerce. The adverse side effects of growth at the local level—including increased congestion, sprawl, and higher taxes to pay for new services demanded—are borne by others. The blind march toward increasing "rationalization" of the economy through privatization of formally collective activities is eliminating the last vestiges of social control over investment and resource-use decisions.

Economic growth seems to be indispensable to the world economy as it currently functions. Economic growth makes it possible to reap the benefits of technological advance by ensuring a more rapid turnover of capital stock, by alleviating the need to deal with questions of unequal income distribution, and by allowing firms to increase productivity through increasing returns to scale. When worker productivity increases, the resulting higher incomes generate a need for new products to absorb the increase in demand. Expansion due to increased demand enables producers to capture economies of scale, resulting in more productivity improvement, higher incomes, and so on, ad infinitum. These positive-feedback mechanisms mean that economic growth perpetuates more economic growth and that socioeconomic and political institutions that promote growth are constantly reinforced. The points of conflict between the prerogatives of economic growth and the prerogatives of maintaining an environmentally stable planet and socially stable communities are clear:

1. Population growth is good for the economy because it creates new markets for goods, but the human population has greatly surpassed the level of long-term sustainability.

2. Increasing per capita consumption is good for the economy but requires increasing amounts of resources and generates increasing amounts of waste products.

3. Income inequality increases productivity and economic growth by

funneling resources into their economically most productive uses (cumulative causation), but the cost is increasing income inequality and social instability.

4. New technologies increase productivity and stimulate the expansion of economic activity, but many of these technologies have negative consequences for society and the environment.

5. The expansion of markets is good for the economy, but it brings new parts of the natural world as well as diverse human cultures under the peculiar and shortsighted logic of market exchange.

When economic growth slows, income distribution becomes more unequal, as it has within the northern countries and between the North and the South since the mid-1970s. When economic output actually declines, as in the global and local economic depressions of the twentieth century and currently in much of Africa and Latin America, the result is usually social upheaval and mass destruction. Within the present world economic system, economic growth is essential to keeping the incomes of the wealthy high and keeping the lid on those people at the bottom. The problem is that biophysical laws will, sometime this century, halt the expansion of this human-created system.

The Entropy Law and the Human Economy

In the past twenty-five years, the dominance of neoclassical economics has been challenged by a number of alternative schools of economic thought, including post-Keynesian, institutional, social, and ecological economics. A basic insight of ecological economics is that economic activity is possible only by extracting low entropy from the larger biophysical system. The pioneer of this approach to economic theory was Nicholas Georgescu-Roegen who published his monumental work *The Entropy Law and the Economic Process* in 1971. Georgescu-Roegen used the entropy metaphor to develop an economic theory based in historical time and grounded in the fundamental laws of physics and biology. He called his theory "bioeconomics." He argued that low entropy, bound energy and matter, is not only the taproot of economic value but also the ultimate source of social conflict. His great contribution was to use the entropy metaphor to show that the economic process is not a reversible, self-contained circular flow, as depicted in standard economics texts, but rather an irreversible system dependent upon and constrained by the laws of physics and biology. Not only is economic activity constrained by larger systems, but by degrading the biophysical systems that surround the human economy, we limit the future possibilities for human activity as well. Thermodynamic analysis shows clearly the potential for chaos in far-from-equilibrium systems such as the modern economy.

The history of the human species since the widespread adoption of agriculture some ten thousand years ago has been one of playing out a far-from-equilibrium process of expansion and collapse. The agricultural way of life became dominant within a few millennia after its inception about ten thousand years ago, and with it came a profound shift in human social evolution. Societies became increasingly hierarchical and based on religious beliefs centered on the necessity of mobilizing a large workforce for the agricultural enterprise. This new hierarchical organization of society and the emergence of religious and political elites favored the continuance of a way of life that benefited the dominant and controlling social group, regardless of the consequences for the majority of the population. The relationship between humans and the natural world also changed dramatically. The adoption of agriculture ushered in the age of human-dominated ecosystems. This move meant homogenization and control of nature, on the one hand, and destruction of that part of nature not useful to humans, on the other. It is true that a characteristic of early agricultural societies was the increasing capacity to buffer environmental disturbances. But this ability to anticipate and plan for environmental disturbance came at a price. A growing body of evidence indicates that a variety of cultures in very different climates, regions, and epochs temporarily escaped environmental constraints by tapping scarce low entropy, only to collapse as the boundary conditions invariably changed. As Joseph Tainter (1988) has documented, societies as different as the Sumarians, the Mayans, and the Easter Islanders have followed a remarkably similar pattern of colonization, rapid growth, intensification of resource exploitation, and collapse. For these early agricultural societies, technological advances proved to be poor long-run substitutes for the biophysical processes upon which they ultimately depended.

The second great divide in economic history is the Industrial Revolution, which began some 250 years ago. In the relatively short period of time since industrialization began, the human population has increased sixfold, from about 1 billion to 6 billion people. The impact of the human species has become truly global in nature. The Industrial Revolution not only drastically altered the relationships among people and between humans and nature, but also set in motion an ongoing process of economic change with an inner logic of its own. It is important to keep in mind, however, that the basic pattern of resource exploitation in industrial societies was established with the widespread adoption of agriculture, that pattern being input substitution and intensification of production through technological advance in the face of diminishing resources. This pattern is not one of a self-renewing circular flow but rather a one-way, irreversible path toward chaos and collapse.

An instructive example of the entropic process of resource exploitation in the global market economy is the Pacific island of Nauru. Little is known about the island's prehistory, but it was apparently settled by several groups of Melanesian and Polynesian peoples over a period of several thousand years. Traditionally, the small island supported a population of about one thousand people living on fish and a wide variety of native and domesticated plants and animals. Because of its geographical isolation, Nauru experienced little contact with Western cultures until the late 1800s. In 1900, it was discovered that the island was composed primarily of one of the highest grades of phosphate rock, an essential requirement for plant growth and an ingredient in fertilizer. Under various German, British, Japanese, and Australian colonial administrations, and under independent rule beginning in 1968, most of the island of Nauru has been severely degraded by phosphate mining. Today, most of the island is uninhabitable and unreclaimable, except for a narrow strip of land around the coastal perimeter.

As the natural resources of Nauru were degraded, the inhabitants came to rely more and more on trade with the outside world for necessities that were once plentiful locally. A diet of fresh fruit, coconuts, vegetables, and fish has been replaced with imported canned goods. Even water now has to be imported from the mainland. The once vibrant and self-sufficient culture, living within the constraints of a local ecosystem, has been transformed into one totally dependent on imports from the world market economy. Not only have the cultural traditions of Nauru suffered, but the increased consumption of highly processed foods has given Nauruans one of the highest rates of diabetes in the world as well. Very high rates of hypertension and heart disease are also present, and in spite of a high per capita income, life expectancy on Nauru is one of the lowest in the Pacific.

In return for selling their island, the people of Nauru, in spite of gross injustices perpetuated by colonial powers, received substantial monetary rewards. A trust fund was established to provide for the day the phosphate would be exhausted, and the value of the trust fund was estimated to be more than $1 billion in the early 1990s. Unfortunately, most of the trust fund disappeared because of bad investments and in the Asian financial meltdown of the mid-1990s. Today the people of Nauru are left with few environmental resources and no income flow to provide for their livelihoods. The Nauru experience can be interpreted as an isolated case or as yet another contemporary example of the pattern of intensification of production, overshoot, and collapse that has prevailed in complex societies for the past several thousand years.

Ghosts from the Past: Is It Possible for Humans to Live in Harmony with Nature?

Our species, Homo sapiens, is the last remaining member of a genus that first appeared some 3.5 million years ago in East Africa. For almost all the time humans have lived on earth, our economic and social institutions were based on a hunting-and-gathering lifestyle. People lived directly on the flows from nature with a simple material technology and, judging from historical accounts of hunter-gatherers, a complex set of institutions favoring environmental stability and social equality. The hunter-gatherer way of life has been dubbed by Marshall Sahlins as "the original affluent society" (1972, 430–43). According to Sahlins, hunter-gatherers were affluent because they had everything they wanted: not because they had more but because they wanted less. An examination of the characteristics of hunter-gatherers can illuminate the connection between social equality and environmental integrity and give some insights as to how we might alter our existing institutions and move to a path leading to a just and environmentally sustainable society.

James Woodburn, based on field studies of the Hadza, a hunter-gatherer culture of Tanzania, describes some of the characteristics of that society that promoted social equality:

1. Social groups are flexible and fluid.

2. Individuals are completely free to choose with whom they associate, reside, and trade and exchange.

3. Individuals are not dependent on specific others for access to the basic requirements of life.

4. All relationships stress sharing and mutuality without requiring long-term binding commitments.

In these types of societies, individuals have no real authority over one another. Furthermore, all of the above characteristics are consciously protected as part of what Woodburn calls an "aggressively egalitarian" social strategy (1982, 432). He distinguishes between "immediate-return" and "delayed-return" cultures (433–40). In immediate-return societies, people receive an immediate and direct return from their labor. Food is eaten soon after it is gathered or hunted, and material technology is very simple. In delayed-return systems, people hold some property rights associated with wild products that have been improved with human effort, such as selectively culled wild herbs or wild plants that have been cared for. Although both types of hunter-gatherer societies are much more egalitarian than agricultural—or industrial-based societies, the immediate-return cultures are the most egalitarian in terms of wealth, status, and power over others. Inequalities of wealth are not tolerated, and women have more independence than in delayed-return systems. In immediate-return systems, access to the means for making a living is free and open to all. Material technology is limited; the basic requirement to get along is not the possession of a collection of material objects but rather an extensive knowledge about the specific ecosystems within which each society operates. This knowledge is freely available and is given to all members of the group. In delayed-return hunter-gatherer systems, although they are still egalitarian, we see the beginnings of class differences based on access to technology and the resulting control of an economic surplus.

To the Western way of thinking, the most remarkable thing about the economic output of hunter-gatherer societies is that its distribution is independent of who produces it. In societies such as the Hadza and !Kung, most of the meat is provided by only a few hunters. It is reported that among the Hadza, there are healthy adult men who have scarcely killed an animal in their entire lives, yet they are provided for just like everyone else and suffer no ostracism. The !Kung have elaborate rules of behavior dissociating the hunter from his kill. For example, it is the owner of the arrow that killed the animal who is entitled to distribute the meat, not the successful hunter himself. A study of the Aché of Paraguay found that on average, about three-quarters of the food that individuals consumed came from nonmembers of the immediate family. Successful hunters actually received smaller portions for themselves than they would have if the distribution had been random.

The fact that there is no connection between production and distribution in some societies, nothing like the "marginal-productivity theory of distribution" of neoclassical theory, exposes the fiction of "economic man." There is nothing inherently selfish and greedy about our species. Humans are capable of a wide variety of behavioral patterns depending upon the material basis of their particular societies and the ideological beliefs necessary to support specific ways of living. Judging from historical records of hunting-and-gathering societies, the "natural" state of humankind may be much closer to Marx's "primitive communism" than to contemporary capitalism.

Another relevant feature of hunter-gatherer economic systems is that there frequently exist sanctions on the accumulation of personal possessions. The lack of possessions is not merely due to the nomadic nature of the hunter-gatherer life. Sanctions apply to even the lightest objects, such as beads or arrowheads. It appears that a central feature ensuring egalitarianism is that people are disengaged from property and thus from the potential for property rights to create dependency. This idea could not be more subversive to the standard economic way of thinking that equates "freedom" with an ever greater expansion of property rights.

Ways Out: Maintaining Options for the Twenty-First Century

What can be learned from the fates of past civilizations and the knowledge we have about the precariousness of our own global market economy? Can we use the concepts and scientific evidence gleaned from records of past successful and unsuccessful cultures to break the pattern of overshoot and collapse and prevent the collapse of our current civilization? First of all, two simple facts follow from the above discussion:

1. The economy is a subsystem of a larger social system that is, in turn, part of and dependent upon an enveloping biophysical universe. Past civilizations collapsed because their institutions ignored this basic fact.

2. Strong connections exist between power and distribution of economic surplus, environmental degradation, and social collapse. Past societies have collapsed because decisions about resource use were made by a

minority whose power and prestige depended on the unsustainable exploitation of people and nature.

Taking these two observations as a starting point, we can begin to formulate a minimal program for environmental and social sustainability. First we should begin with a clear objective of what it is we wish to sustain. Following the suggestion of Georgescu-Roegen, a reasonable objective is to ensure the existence of the human species for as long as possible, recognizing the fact that humans, like all species, will someday become extinct. With this in mind, the following steps toward sustainability seem reasonable:

1. Distinguish between ecological and economic sustainability and adopt a no-substitution rule between human-made capital and the life-support systems of the natural world. Ecological economists argue that economic and environmental accounts should be kept separate. This separate accounting should also include ecological systems and species that have no apparent economic use or even no apparent value at all to humans. It has become a dangerous cliché to say that there is no conflict between the market economy and environmental protection. The conflict, however, is clear. In the global market economy we have created, humans can improve their economic well-being by destroying parts of the natural world. In the long run, however, human survival depends on protecting other species and the ecosystems they inhabit. The basic argument of ecologists is that when we trade nature for economic growth, we are destroying the life systems upon which all human life depends to achieve a short-run gain. Destroying the basis for future human survival should be no more acceptable to help the poor than to help the rich. This view is consistent with the anthropocentric goal of preserving the human species for as long as possible despite its "biocentric" appearance. We should keep the biosphere intact because it is in our long-run interest of all humankind to do so.

2. Define (or describe) ecological sustainability in terms of preserving evolutionary potential. Life on earth depends on complex relationships and the ability to respond to changing biological and physical conditions. In ecosystems, seemingly redundant species play important roles in system resilience and may assume the role of existing keystone species when environmental conditions change. Preserving humans for as long as possible necessitates preserving the biological potential of ecosystems to adapt to

changing conditions. The long-run survival of our species depends on preserving the environmental boundary conditions under which we evolved, including the potential of ecosystems to adapt to change.

3. Define or describe social sustainability. What are the necessary conditions for a socially just, smoothly functioning society having the ability to adapt to changing environmental conditions? Just as humans evolved under rather specific environmental conditions, so too did our social systems (our varied cultures) evolve under specific local biological and environmental constraints. We are only just beginning to understand the relationships between human biology and human culture.

4. Define and delineate conditions for economic sustainability. The field of economics is changing rapidly, and long-held notions of the sanctity of the market are changing. Spurred by massive policy failures in Eastern Europe, Asia, and Latin America, economists are beginning to recognize that unregulated markets are not consistent with economic sustainability. The recognition of this fact has far-reaching implications for the sustainability debate because it calls into question the efficacy of market-based environmental and social policies.

These points call for policies that bring the way humans currently live in line with the biological and social requirements of long-run sustainability. This change will not be easy because some of these policies will undoubtedly conflict with ideas of progress, individualism, and materialism enshrined in the fundamental belief systems of the modern world. By recognizing the conflict between human well-being based solely on market output and long-run environmental integrity, we can begin to make policies for sustainability consistent with biological and physical reality. We must go beyond arguments for "limits to growth" and find "alternatives to growth." The difficulty of this task should not be underestimated, but by beginning to formulate ways to decouple human well-being from consumption and economic growth, we can be ready with workable alternatives when the majority is willing to consider them seriously.

Suggested Reading

Daly, Herman. 1992. *Steady-State Economics.* 2d ed. London: Earthscan.
Georgescu-Roegen, Nicholas. 1971. *The Entropy Law and the Economic Process.* Cambridge: Harvard Univ. Press.

———. 1976. *Energy and Economic Myths.* San Francisco: Pergamon Press.

Gowdy, John M. 1998. *Limited Wants, Unlimited Means: A Reader on Hunter-Gatherer Economics and the Environment.* Washington, D.C.: Island Press.

McDaniel, Carl N., and John M. Gowdy. 2000. *Paradise for Sale: A Parable of Nature.* Berkeley and Los Angeles: Univ. of California Press.

Ponting, Clive. 1991. *A Green History of the World: The Environment and the Collapse of Great Civilizations.* New York: St. Martin's Press.

Sahlins, Marshall. 1972. *Stone Age Economics.* Chicago: Aldine.

Tainter, Joseph A. 1988. *The Collapse of Complex Societies.* New York: Cambridge Univ. Press.

Wallimann, Isidor. 1994. "Can the World Industrialization Project Be Sustained?" *Monthly Review* (Mar.): 41–51.

Woodburn, James. 1982. "Egalitarian Societies." *Man* 17: 431–51.

Our Unsustainable Society . . . and the Alternative

Ted Trainer

IT IS WIDELY UNDERSTOOD that our industrial, affluent consumer society is ecologically unsustainable, unjust, and deteriorating fast. Almost all social and economic problems are getting worse, and measures show that the quality of life is failing. The argument below is that these problems cannot be solved in a society that is driven by obsession with high rates of production and consumption, affluent living standards, market forces, the profit motive, and economic growth. A sustainable and just world order cannot be achieved until we undertake radical change in our lifestyles, values, and systems, especially in our economic system. There are now many people in many groups around the world working for a transition to the Simpler Way.

There are two major faults built into our society that are causing the main problems we are facing.

Fault 1: The Market

Markets do some things well, and in a satisfactory and sustainable society there could be a considerable role for them, but only if they are kept under careful social control. It is easily shown that *the market system is responsible for most of the deprivation and suffering in the world*. The basic mechanisms are most clearly seen when we consider what is happening in the Third World.

The enormous amount of poverty and suffering in the Third World is not due to lack of resources. There is, for instance, sufficient food and land to provide for all. The problem is that these resources are not distributed well. Why not? The answer is that this way is how the market economy inevitably works.

In a market, scarce things always go mostly to the rich, that is, to those people who can bid the most for them. That's why we in rich countries get most of the oil that is produced. It is also why more than 500 million tons of grain are fed to animals in rich countries every year, more than one-third of the total world grain production, although perhaps 1 billion people are malnourished.

Even more important is the fact that the market system inevitably brings about *inappropriate development* in the Third World, that is, development of the wrong industries. It will lead to the development of the most profitable industries, as distinct from the ones that are most necessary or appropriate. As a result, the Third World has mostly had development of plantations and factories that will produce things for local rich people or for export to rich countries. Thus, the Third World's productive capacity, its land and labor, is drawn into producing for the benefit of others. These consequences are inevitable in an economic system in which what is done is whatever is most profitable to the few who own capital, as distinct from what is most needed by people or their ecosystems. Consequently, conventional Third World development can be seen as a form of legitimized plunder.

We in rich countries could not have our high living standards if the global economy was not enabling us to take far more than our fair share of world wealth and to deprive Third World people of their fair share.

It is likely that the Third World will accelerate into squalor and chaos from here on. The United Nations has reported that 1.6 billion people, almost one-third of all the world's people, are getting poorer. The market system is now giving the corporations and banks much more freedom and power than ever before to develop in the Third World only those industries that will maximize corporate profits. There is no possibility of satisfactory Third World development until we develop a very different global economic system.

Fault 2: The Limits to Growth

The most alarming mistake built into the foundations of our society is the *commitment to an affluent, industrial consumer lifestyle and to an economy that must have constant and limitless growth in output.* Our levels of production and consumption are far too high to be kept up for very long and could never be extended to all people. We are rapidly depleting resources and damaging the environment. We can achieve our present "living standards" only because a few rich countries are grabbing most of the resources produced. By consuming so much, we cause huge ecological damage. Our way of life is *grossly unsustainable.* Yet, we are obsessed with economic growth, with increasing production and consumption, as much as possible and without limit! Following are some of the main points that support limits to growth conclusions.

Rich countries, with about one-fifth of the world's people, are consuming about three-quarters of the world's resource production. Our per capita consumption is about fifteen to twenty times that of the poorest half of the world's people. World population will probably stabilize around 10 billion, somewhere after 2060. If all those people were to have Australian per capita resource consumption, then annual world production of all resources would have to be eight to ten times as great as it is now. If we tried to raise present world production to that level by 2060, we would by then have completely exhausted all probably recoverable resources of one-third of the basic mineral items we use. All probably recoverable resources of coal, oil, gas, tar sand and shale oil, and uranium (via burner reactors) would have been exhausted by about 2045.

Petroleum is especially limited. World oil supply will probably peak between 2005 and 2020 and could be down to half that level by 2025, with big price increases soon after the peak. If all the people we will have on earth by 2025 were to have Australia's present per capita oil consumption, world oil production would have to be fifteen times what it will probably be then. There are strong grounds for thinking that it will not be possible for renewable energy sources to provide sufficient energy for rich-world lifestyles.

If all 10 billion people were to use timber at the rich-world per capita rate, we would need 3.5 times the world's present forest area. If all 10 billion were to have a rich-world diet, which takes about 1 hectare of land to produce, then we would need 10 billion hectares of food-producing land. But there are only 1.4 billion hectares of cropland in use today, and this amount is likely to decrease.

Recent "Footprint" analysis estimates that it takes at least 4.5–5 hectares of productive land to provide water, energy settlement area, and food for one person living in a rich-world city. So if 10 billion people were to live as we do in Sydney, then we would need about 50 billion hectares of productive land. But that amount is *seven times all the productive land on the planet.*

These limits are some of the main reasons for growth arguments that lead to the conclusion that there *is no possibility of all people rising to the living standards we take for granted today in rich countries such as Australia.* We must accept the need to move to far simpler and less-resource-expensive ways.

Hence the Environment Problem

The reason we have an environment problem is simply because *there is far too much producing and consuming going on.* Our way of life involves the consumption of huge amounts of materials. More than twenty tons of new materials are used by each American every year.

The Intergovernmental Panel on Climate Change has concluded that in order to stop the carbon content of the atmosphere from rising any further, we must reduce the use of fossil fuels by 60–80 percent. If we did cut it by 60 percent and shared the remaining energy among 10 billion people, then each of us would get only 1/18 of the amount we now use in Australia per capita. Most people have no idea of how far beyond sustainable levels we are, and how big the reductions will have to be.

The Absurdly Impossible Implications of Economic Growth

The foregoing argument has been that the *present* levels of production and consumption are quite unsustainable. They are far too high to be kept going for long or to be extended to all people. But we are determined to *increase* present living standards and levels of output and consumption, as much as possible and without any end in sight. Few people seem to recognize the absurdly impossible consequences of pursuing economic growth.

If we have a 3 percent per annum increase in output, by 2060 we will be producing 8 times as much every year. (For 4 percent growth, the multiple is 16.) If by then all 10 billion people expected had risen to the living standards we would have then, the total world economic output would be *more than 100 times* what it is today! Yet, the *present* level is unsustainable.

(For a 4 percent per annum growth rate, the multiple is 220.) In the 1980s, Australia had a 3.2 percent per annum growth rate, which was not sufficient to prevent virtually all our problems from becoming worse.

Globalization

We have entered a period in which all these problems will rapidly accelerate, because of the globalization of the economy. Since 1970 the world economic system has run into crisis. It has become much more difficult for corporations and banks to invest their constantly accumulating volumes of capital profitably.

Thus, the big corporations and banks are now pushing through a massive restructuring of the global economy, the development of a more unified and deregulated system in which they have swept away most of the arrangements that previously hindered their access to increased business opportunities, markets, resources, and cheap labor. The pressure is on governments to remove the protection, tariffs, and controls that they once used to manage their economies; to sell government enterprises to the corporations; to cut government services; to reduce taxes on corporations; and above all to increase the freedom for market forces, that is, the freedom for corporations to operate. These changes are enabling *the transnational corporations to come in and take advantage of more business opportunities.* A huge critical literature now explains how these changes are devastating the lives of millions of people, especially in the Third World, and their economies and ecosystems, but they are a delight to the corporations and banks (see especially Chossudovsky 1997).

Conclusions on Our Situation

It should be obvious from the above discussion that our socioeconomic system is extremely unsatisfactory and cannot solve our problems. *There is no possibility of having a just and morally satisfactory or ecologically sustainable society if we allow the economy to be driven by market forces, the profit motive, and economic growth.* In a satisfactory economy, the needs of people, society, and the environment would determine what is done, not profit.

We have allowed ourselves to be misled into thinking that we need more production, more efficiency, more GNP, more science and technology, and harder work. But we already produce far more than would be necessary to give a high quality of life to all, and we work much harder than is necessary. We could easily develop a society in which we do much less work and producing and have much more time to enjoy life, without stress and insecurity, knowing that we are not damaging the environment or depriving the Third World. We do not need better technology or more GDP to solve our problems. We need radical change in systems, lifestyles, and values.

The Alternative: The Simpler Way

There are now many books and articles dealing with the general form that a sustainable society must take. If the foregoing limits to growth analysis are basically valid, then some of the key principles for a sustainable society are clear and indisputable.

Material living standards must be much less affluent. In a sustainable society, per capita rates of resource use must be a small fraction of the ones in Australia today.

There must be small-scale, highly self-sufficient local economies.

There must be mostly cooperative and participatory local systems whereby small communities control their own affairs, independent of the international and global economies.

There must be much use of alternative technologies that minimize the use of resources.

A very different economic system must be developed, one not driven by market forces or the profit motive, and in which there is no growth.

The alternative way is the Simpler Way; we can and must all live well with a much smaller amount of production, consumption, work, resource use, trade, investment, and GNP than there is now. Doing so will allow us to escape the economic treadmill and devote our lives to more important things than producing and consuming. Living more simply does not mean deprivation or hardship. It means focusing on what is sufficient for comfort, hygiene, efficiency, and so on.

We must develop as much self-sufficiency as we reasonably can at the national level (meaning less trade), the household level, and especially the neighborhood, suburban, town, and local regional levels. We need to convert our presently barren suburbs into thriving regional economies that produce most of what they need from local resources. They would contain many small enterprises, such as the local bakery, enabling most of us to get to work by bicycle or on foot. Much of our honey, eggs, crockery, vegetables, furniture, fruit, fish, and poultry could come from households and backyard businesses engaged in craft and hobby production. It is much more satisfying to produce most things in craft ways rather than in industrial factories. However, it would make sense to retain some larger mass-production factories.

Many market gardens could be located throughout the suburbs and cities, for example, on derelict factory sites and beside railway lines. This change would reduce the cost of food *by 70 percent,* especially by cutting its transport costs. More important, having food produced close to where people live would enable nutrients to be recycled back to the soil through compost heaps and garbage gas units.

We should convert one house on each block to become a neighborhood workshop, recycling store, meeting place, surplus exchange, and library. Because there will be far less need for transport, we could dig up many roads, greatly increasing city land area available for community gardens, workshops, ponds, forests, and the like.

There would also be many varieties of animals living in our neighborhoods, including an entire fishing industry based on tanks and ponds. In addition, many materials can come from the communal woodlots, fruit trees, bamboo clumps, ponds, meadows, and so on. They would provide many *free* goods. Thus, we will develop the "commons," the community land and resources from which all can take food and materials.

It would be a leisure-rich environment. Suburbs at present are leisure deserts; there is not much to do. The alternative neighborhood would be full of interesting things to do, familiar people, small businesses, common projects, animals, gardens, forests, and alternative technologies. Consequently, people would be less inclined to go away on weekends and holidays, which would reduce national energy consumption.

The alternative way must be much more communal and cooperative. We must share more things. We could have a few stepladders, electric drills, and the like, in the neighborhood workshop, as distinct from one in every house. We would be on various voluntary rosters, committees, and working bees to carry out most of the child minding, nursing, basic educating, and care of aged and handicapped people in our area, as well as to perform most of the functions that councils now carry out for us, such as maintaining our own parks and streets. We would therefore need far fewer bureaucrats and professionals, reducing the amount of income we would need to earn to pay taxes and for services.

Especially important would be the regular, voluntary community working bees. Just imagine how rich your neighborhood would now be if every Saturday afternoon for the past five years there had been a voluntary working bee doing something that would make it a more pleasant place for all to live.

There would be genuine participatory democracy. Most of our local policies and programs could be worked out by elected nonpaid committees, and we could all vote on the important decisions concerning our small area at regular town meetings. There would still be some functions for state and national governments, but relatively few.

There is no chance of making these changes while we retain the present economic system. The fundamental concern in a satisfactory economy would simply be *to apply the available productive capacity to producing what all people need for a good life,* with as little bother and waste and work as possible, and without ecological damage. The basic economic priorities must be decided according to what is socially desirable and democratically decided, mostly at the local level, not dictated by huge and distant state bureaucracies—what we do not want is centralized, bureaucratic big-state socialism. However, much of the economy might remain as a (carefully monitored) form of private enterprise carried on by small firms, households, and cooperatives, so long as their goals were not profit maximization and growth. Market forces might operate in carefully regulated sectors. For example, local market days could be important, enabling individuals and families to sell small amounts of garden produce and craft items.

One large sector of the new economy would be cashless, involving barter, working bees, gifts (in other words, just giving away surpluses), and totally free goods (for example, from the commons, such as the roadside fruit and nut trees).

Unemployment and poverty could easily be eliminated. (There are none in the Israeli Kibbutz settlements.) We would have neighborhood work-coordination committees who would make sure that all who wanted work had a share of the work that needed doing. Far less work would need to be done than at present.

Above all in the new economy, there would be no economic growth. In fact, we would always be looking for ways of reducing the amount of work, production, and resource use.

When we eliminate all that unnecessary production, and shift much of the remainder to backyards, local small businesses and cooperatives, and the noncash sector of the economy, *most of us will need to go to work for money in an office or a mass-production factory only one or two days* a week. In other words, it will become possible to live well on a very low cash income. We could spend the other five or six days working and playing around the neighborhood, doing many varied, interesting, and useful things every day.

We would have all the high-tech and modern ways that made sense, for example, in medicine, windmill design, public transport, and household appliances. We would still have national systems for some things, such as railways, telecommunications, and taxes, but on nothing like the present scale. We would have far more resources for science, research, education, and the arts than we do now because we would have ceased wasting vast quantities of resources on the production of unnecessary items, including arms. The quality of life in this very frugal and highly self-sufficient Simpler Way could be much higher than it is for most people now in consumer society.

It must be emphasized here that if the limits to growth analysis are basically correct, then we have *no choice* but to work for the sort of alternative society outlined here. In rich and poor countries, a sustainable society can be conceived only in terms of simpler lifestyles, mostly in highly self-sufficient and participatory settlements, and zero growth or steady-state economic systems.

The Way Out

I think our chances of making the transition to the sustainable Simpler Way are very slight. Since the 1960s, many have been attempting to get public attention given to the limits to growth, the gross injustice of the global economy, and the need for radical change. However, there is now even less willingness to face up to these issues than there was thirty years ago. Governments, economists, educational institutions, and the general public all flatly refuse to think about the viability of affluent living standards and the obsession with economic growth.

What then can we do? I think we must continue trying to get attention given to these issues, but the much more important thing to do now is *to work to establish good examples of alternative ways,* especially whole settlements, so that when industrial, affluent consumer society starts to run into really serious problems, people will be able to see here and there examples of settlements in which people are living well in just and ecologically sustainable ways.

Over the past twenty-five years, many small groups all around the world have begun to develop settlements of the required kind, within the Global Eco-village Movement. We who are within the movement live with the burden of knowing that our way is the sustainable way, that it is a highly satisfying way of life, that we must get the mainstream to see this fact, that doing so will be extremely difficult, and that there is not a lot of time left. We know that it would be easy to defuse the terrible problems now threatening to destroy civilization, that it would be easy to form highly self-sufficient and cooperative local economies in which people can live very simply but with a very high quality of life, while preserving the benefits of modern medicine and so on.

Governments will not, and indeed cannot, help with this task. It has to be done at the grassroots level, as ordinary people begin exploring how they can come together to build the new communities. Where the task is most urgently needed and difficult is not at the level of rural intentional communities, where the Global Eco-village Movement is making most progress. The main problem is to gradually transform existing towns and suburbs within cities into local self-sufficient communities. The most promising beginning point for doing so is the formation of small community cooperatives that begin gardens, workshops, small businesses, recycling, and organizing of services to enable their participants, especially unemployed people, to begin producing for themselves many of the things they need. In time, these cooperatives must work to integrate with the existing surrounding economy, and move it in more sustainable directions, for example, by helping to reduce imports.

The fate of the planet depends on whether these things can be done. For anyone concerned about the global crisis, there is nothing more important to do than to get more people to grasp these issues, and to help alternative ventures flourish.

Suggested Reading

Chossudovsky, Michel. 1997. *The Globalisation of Poverty: Impacts of IMF and World Bank Reforms.* London and Atlantic Highlands, N.J.: Zed Books; Penang, Malaysia: Third World Network.

Douthwaite, R. 1996. *Short Circuit.* Dublin: Lilliput.

Mander, Jerry, and E. Goldsmith, eds. 1997. *The Case Against the Global Economy.* San Francisco: Sierra Club.

Rist, G. 1997. *The History of Development.* London: Zed Books.

Schwarz, W., and D. Schwarz. 1998. *Living Lightly.* London: Jon Carpenter.

Trainer, F. E. 1995a. "Can Renewable Energy Save Industrial Society?" *Energy Policy* 23, no. 12: 1009–26.

———. 1995b. *The Conserver Society: Alternatives for Sustainability.* London: Zed Books.

———. 1998. *Saving the Environment: What It Will Take.* Sydney: Univ. of New South Wales Press.

———. 1999. "The Limits to Growth Case in the 1990s." *Environmentalist* 19: 329–39.

Wackernagel, N., and W. Rees. 1995. *Our Ecological Footprint.* Philadelphia: New Society.

5

Population and Immigration

Sliding into Tribalism

Virginia Deane Abernethy

INCIVILITY AND DISRESPECT for law appear to be taking root in the United States. Continuation of the destructive process that has led this far will be detrimental to people of every class and ethnicity. Disintegration of the society into competing groups could occur along ethnic, religious, class, or geographic lines where, already, an identity separate from the national identity is forming. The alternatives appear to be reversal of the destructive process, containment of separatism through repressive authoritarian government, or civil wars.

Disintegration and fragmentation of a society can be traced, minimally, to explosive population growth, diversity, and exceeding the environment's carrying capacity. The two parts of the present discussion are: (1) the demographic sources of social fragmentation, and (2) the carrying capacity. Especially if the cohesive forces of a society are weak, competition for shrinking shares of resources can escalate into violent confrontations.

Other factors, of course, have a role to play. A strongly pacific religious orientation might dampen or redirect public disorder. On the other hand, lethal attacks on both domestic and foreign civilian populations, ordered during the 1990s by the highest officials of the U.S. government, modeled violence that arguably became a source of culture change.

Scarcity, Diversity, and Conflict

The incapacity of natural systems to support the resident population in the manner to which they feel entitled is almost always an underlying issue in domestic and international conflict. Nevertheless, opposing factions in violent upheavals are often identifiable by class, ethnic, or religious grouping. Group identity and the lines along which a society fractures are salient to many analysts and commentators and to the participants themselves. In the present ideological climate, cleaving to one's group on grounds of loyalty and as the basis of discrimination against other groups is applauded or castigated depending upon the identity of groups involved.

But emphasis on how lines are drawn obscures the root cause—smaller shares of valued resources than people consider fair or adequate. Numerous authors show how population growth triggers conflict.

Journalist Robert D. Kaplan, who writes for the *Atlantic Monthly*, observes that environments collapsed by the "impact of surging populations" are the frequent root cause of political chaos (1994, 73–74). As overtaxed environments fail, Kaplan expects to see "re-primitivized man: warrior societies operating at a time of unprecedented resource scarcity and planetary crowding. . . . Crime and war become indistinguishable." Security of sorts is found only in private guards, armies, and alliances.

Some areas are further advanced along these lines than others. But Kaplan sees all as vulnerable. Collapsing or invaded nations on every continent are potentially threatened by sociopolitical disintegration, refugee migrations across international borders, ethnic mixing, and loss of a cultural center.

Conclusions of this ilk are usually avoided because they break a number of cultural taboos. They suggest limits, the almost "un-American" idea that economic growth and resource extraction cannot endlessly continue. They suggest that some people may remain "better off" than others. And they suggest that people might not give so freely if they saw that altruism materially reduced their own well-being.

A number of Canadian political scientists have taken note of attempts to deny the role of population and resource imbalances as the cause of conflict, and they explicitly *reject the denial*—seeing it as a misguided effort to foster altruism. Analyzing civil and international wars on several continents, they show how population growth aggravates resource scarcity and contributes directly to conflict. Shares become smaller as a result of population growth unless economic growth keeps pace—which is not always possible. Competition turns into resource grabs, often with alliances providing both manpower and legitimacy. The alliances, naturally, are formed along recognized criteria that may include ethnicity and religion. (One wit suggests football conferences as new regional political units after the coming dissolution of the United States.)

Population becomes a particularly uncomfortable subject when it suggests limitations of either family size or immigration. Family size is seen as a personal decision in Western culture, and certain means of limiting family size—such as abortion—are widely viewed as unacceptable. Similarly, limits on immigration are considered heartless in some political sectors and an impediment to economic growth in others.

Nevertheless, in many countries—especially the ones that are particular targets of immigration because of being wealthier than neighbors—large majorities of citizens and their representative governments want to end immigration. They perceive that they—or fellow countrymen whose welfare they value and for whose support they are ultimately responsible—are progressively impoverished by an influx of strangers who are mostly poor.

A common result of immigration, ethnic mixing, is a particular concern of political scientist Milton Esman. He focuses on the risks, sources of conflict or accommodation, and likely channels of protest that accompany the presence of several minorities together, or, alternately, a minority residing alongside a majority group within one territory. Esman's thesis is that the presence of minorities invariably creates strain, so the implicit or explicit goal of a vigorous society is the minimization of diversity. He writes that the "classic approach to depluralization is the encouragement of individual assimilation" (1994, 255). An example, cited by Kaplan, is Saul Bellow's description of his immigrant family in turn-of-the-century Chicago: "The country took us over. It *was* a country then, not a collection of cultures" (1994, 75–76).

Esman's perspective, his acute worry about ethnic diversity, is rejected by many U.S. so-called intellectual elites. This stratum professes to deny the reality of ethnicity. Sociologist Kevin MacDonald summarizes their apparent operating principle: "[E]thnic interests are simply delusions imposed by exploitative ethnic leaders."

Indeed, insistence upon the worldwide mixing of ethnic and religious groups has become a major item on the globalist agenda. This goal carries pure altruism—much applauded in UN and psychiatric circles—to its logical and ridiculous conclusion: ridiculous because it amounts to denial that ethnicity is an ubiquitous organizing principle within society, and denial that individuals and ethnic groups compete.

Rudimentary history shows that denial of the importance of ethnicity is dangerously misguided. Political scientist Milica Bookman describes the Balkan struggle as one relatively typical example of festering ethnic competition. The struggle began more than five hundred years ago when ancestors of the present-day Albanians and Serbs split over resistance or cooperation with the conquering Turks of the Ottoman Empire. A parallel split occurred within the Serbian community, leaving some as Christians whereas others converted to the Moslem faith of the Ottomans. She describes the former Yugoslavia, today, as engaged in "a dirty civil war, in which neighbor has turned against neighbor, and each group is trying to be the first to cleanse undesirables lest they cleanse him instead" (1997, 47).

The frequent absence of historical perspective and the double standard that sometimes characterizes discussion of ethnicity confuse the emotional issue of population growth. The fears and frustrations of native-born people who see their traditional homeland and ethnic group overwhelmed may be underestimated. Debate about differential birthrates (a factor in both Israel and the former Yugoslavia, for example) and immigration (a rising issue in Europe, the United States, and more affluent Arab and Asian countries) is sometimes stifled with indictments of "racism" that leave this explosive term undefined.

As it pertains to traditionally white populations in Europe and British colonies, "racism" appears to be a charge leveled at whoever objects to cultural or physical displacement by foreign peoples. On the contrary, those people who founded alien colonies within Western countries are given a moral pass. Newcomers are even commended and targeted for special assistance by nonprofit groups such as the Ford Foundation, despite the growing evidence that many of the people being displaced are the poor, including established minorities.

The match to the tinder of ethnic competition is shortage or perceived maldistribution of resources. Conflicts among groups seem not to escalate into dangerous confrontations so long as wealth is growing at a rate acceptable to large or powerful majorities, or even entitled-feeling minorities who believe that they have legitimate claims. Unfortunately, economies often do not have straight-line rising trajectories sufficient to satisfy all expectations. Boding badly as well, resources and the capacity of natural systems to cope with pollution have limits that, from time to time, also cause a hiatus in the general improvement of the human condition.

Poverty is sometimes noted as a cause of escalating competition, competition that sometimes turns violent, but the underlying causes of poverty tend to be brushed aside. The causal role of population growth is routinely omitted in discussions of poverty. This omission is particularly noticeable when the focus is industrialized countries, and the commentators are advocates for high levels of immigration.

Population Growth and Carrying Capacity

Carrying capacity refers to the number of individuals who can be supported without degrading the environment. Not degrading the environment means protecting its capacity to sustain the population at the desired quality of life over the long term.

A degraded environment produces less. Exceeding the carrying capacity today reduces tomorrow's productivity, so that the number that can be supported without doing further damage gets smaller and smaller. Population growth combined with the high consumption levels to which all Americans and immigrants aspire are the ultimate threats to the carrying capacity—the topsoil, forests, energy, clean air and water, and other resources—of our national home.

Technological and market adjustments alter pressure points in the system, which means that one cannot predict which of several factors will ultimately limit national well-being. Agronomist David Pimentel et al. have found that U.S. topsoil is being eroded fifteen to thirty times faster than its natural formation rate, and that each year 3 million U.S. acres are being paved over or made useless for agriculture (1995). If present trends continue, arable land will shrink from the nearly 1.8 acres per person now available in the United States to only 0.6 acres per person by 2050. That amount would be just half of what is needed to provide a diverse diet.

Major U.S. sources of underground water, aquifers, are also being depleted at an alarming rate. Their water is being used up 25 percent faster than the replenishment rate. It is expensive and difficult to transport water from distant sources, and remaining water is becoming a source of friction between competing urban and rural users. Agriculture in key areas, especially California, could lose out—with severe ramifications for the nation's supply of fresh fruit and vegetables.

A further threat to the food supply comes from agriculture's dependence on petrochemicals (for fertilizer and pesticides, and to run machinery). Indeed, agriculture accounts for 17 percent of U.S. petrochemical use. However, domestic oil (including Alaskan oil) will probably be effectively gone in thirty years (meaning that the energy recovered will be less than the energy used to get, refine, and distribute the oil). Moreover, a number of respected geologists expect that the worldwide production of oil will peak and then decline within the next seven to twenty years.

Already, 60 percent of the oil used in the United States is imported. Reliance on foreign sources could greatly impact food production, domestic food prices, the foreign exchange earned through food exports, and policy options vis-à-vis oil-producing nations, especially Iran, Iraq, Egypt, Libya, Kuwait, Venezuela, and Saudi Arabia.

Demography explains the U.S. growing thirst for oil and energy. Nearly all (93 percent) of a 25 percent increase in energy use between 1970 and 1990 was driven by population growth. That is, consumption per capita leveled off because of increased efficiency and conservation, but these gains were, and continue to be, overwhelmed by the growing population.

Population growth is also endangering whole U.S. ecosystems, primarily by infringing on the habitats of native species. Ecologists suggest that most species find a niche as some land converts to agriculture. The critical shift is from agricultural to more intensive uses of land as population density increases.

Biodiversity contributes more to our lives than just moral and aesthetic goods. Many species have economic value. Honeybees, for example, pollinate billions of dollars worth of crops, and we have no good substitute! (When a major die-off of honeybees occurred in the mid-1990s, major resources were committed to discovering the source of the problem and treating surviving hives—an expensive technological substitute for what had been a free good of nature.)

Other factors (such as deforestation, pollutants, the collapse of fisheries and infrastructures, traffic congestion, and park and recreational congestion) could be chosen to illustrate carrying-capacity limits. Resources are being depleted even at the present rate of use; more people demand more resources; in using them, people often create more pollution. Expensive remedial efforts certainly reverse much environmental damage, but some systems have no substitute, and once used up or degraded, the loss is irretrievable. Remedying man-made environmental problems, problems made worse by population growth, soaks up public and private funds that might otherwise be available for making net social and economic gains.

Population Growth in the United States

As natural resources dwindle, the hardship that citizens endure depends on the population-growth rate, the distribution of wealth, and economic competitiveness.

The United States has the fastest population-growth rate in the industrialized world. Estimated (before the 2000 census) at more than 1.1 percent per year, the U.S. rate approaches that of some Third World countries and puts the population on track to double in approximately sixty years. That is, the estimated year-2000 population of approximately 280 million would become 560 million (larger than China's population when the Communists took power) by 2060. In fact, a 1990 publication by two respected demographers foresaw this result. The 2000 census results will show how far along into this future the country has gone.

Historically, the U.S. Census Bureau projections have been too low. Their array of *projections* (not predictions, because they are couched in assumptions) was revised upward in 1989, 1990, and 1992 because assumptions about immigrant numbers and subsequent family size had been too low. A 1995 array of projections escaped revision by altering assumptions about departures from the United States each year. Moreover, asylum claimants (similar to refugees except that they are in the United States when they make their claim), which are estimated at about 150,000 per year, were overlooked. This omission resulted in a greater than 10 percent underestimate of immigration numbers in the "1995 Report of the U.S. Commission on Immigration Reform."

The distribution of wealth is second in importance for determining national well-being. How is the man-made as well as the (inherently limited) natural wealth divided up?

The question can become muddy if the possibly *desirable* distribution of wealth is confused with what is *probable*. Historical studies, sociobiology, and principles of market economics suggest that equality in economic results is incompatible with either freedom or shrinking resources per capita.

Governments can alter for a time the identity of "winners," but equality of results is not—and never has been—achievable. As an anthropologist, I conclude that every society where there is population growth without offsetting growth in resources arrives at an advanced state of stratification. Some people become very rich, but the middle class shrinks and most people are poor. For example, the later Mayan, Aztec, and Incan civilizations preyed upon their neighbors and developed elaborate class systems probably including slavery, which is especially well documented for the Incas. Neolithic peoples in Great Britain evolved from egalitarian to stratified social structures as their communities became more densely populated. Class structures became more visible in both India and Algeria about the time that these societies became significantly more crowded. Women became chattel property in Europe's overpopulated middle and late Middle Ages. The overpopulated New Guinea Enga tribe victimized women, unlike neighbors whose land-to-people ratio remained favorable. So it goes through the ancient and modern worlds. The gap between privileged and powerless appears to widen as overpopulation grows and resources dwindle.

Growth in the labor force is a principal mechanism by which population growth widens the gulf between rich and poor. In economic terms, labor is a commodity. Therefore, a large supply of workers relative to the availability of jobs (demand for workers) drives down the price (wages and benefits) that employers are willing to pay. The larger the supply of labor relative to jobs, the more that compensation for labor falls.

Historian Ronald Lee shows that, in Western Europe from 1260 A.D. until the Industrial Revolution, a growing labor force reduced wages. He found that wages fell by 16 percent, on average, whenever population shot 10 percent above its long-run trend line (1987, 448). That finding for the amount of wage depression is an average for Germany, Austria, Spain, and France. The population effect on working persons in preindustrial England was equally dramatic. According to Lee, "Reckoning in terms of agricultural goods, a 10% increase in population depressed wages by 22% and lowered labor's share of national income by 14%" (1980, 547). The part of society that suffered most from an increase in the labor supply was the workers themselves. Labor received less of the national income when the supply of labor was growing, and much more during periods of depopulation, for example, when Europe was being ravaged by epidemics. Wages fell by 60 percent in the century of rapid population growth after Europe was at last free of the Black Plague. Population growth appears to depress wages and benefits regardless of the source of growth. Economist Claudia Goldin's study of the 1897–1917 period during which 17 million Europeans immigrated to the United States shows displacement of less-skilled native-born workers by immigrants who would work for less. She concludes that a 1 percent increase in a city's foreign-born population decreased wages, for everyone, by 1.5 to 3 percent (1993, 21–22).

Effects were probably more far-reaching than Goldin imagines, because the large labor supply imported from overseas stifled internal migration toward jobs. Booker T. Washington's well-remembered "Put Down Your Buckets Where You Are" address at the 1895 Atlanta Exposition states the case. Washington pleaded for an end to immigration because it contributed to continuing unemployment in rural and small-town America. Indeed, it is a matter of record that African Americans began to take advantage of industrial job opportunities in the North only after immigration was effectively ended in 1924.

Computer-technology jobs are the modern-day equivalent of industrial jobs. Not surprisingly, older computer scientists and engineers and professional associations of black engineers are among those people who oppose bringing in more high-tech workers under an enlarged H1B visa program. Immigration is displacing both older men and upwardly mobile, young black Americans. It is setting back forty years of social policy designed to raise all Americans into the mainstream.

The plight of unskilled U.S. workers is arguably the worst, because the close match between their labor characteristics and those traits of many immigrants throws them into direct competition for jobs, education, housing, health care, and further social safety-net protections provided by local and federal governments. Opportunities for unskilled labor are very limited in the modern economy, and the numbers of unskilled are being swelled by immigration.

By 1990, immigrants were 10 percent of the total U.S. labor force and a quarter of all workers without a high school diploma. Cornell labor economist Vernon Briggs Jr. (1990) testified before the Congressional Judiciary Subcommittee on Immigration, Refugees, and International Law that immigration victimizes the lower end of the U.S. labor pool, including both citizens and established earlier immigrants whose labor force characteristics resemble those traits of newcomers. Frank Morris (1990) testified in the same hearings that "the black community . . . may find that any encouraging assumptions we had about opportunities for young black workers and prospective workers have been sidetracked by hasty immigration policies. . . . It is clear that America's black population is bearing a disproportionate share of immigrants' competition for jobs, housing and social services."

The late Richard Estrada, a respected Texan journalist who served on the Congressional Committee for Immigration Reform under the leadership of an icon of the African American community, Barbara Jordan, concurs. In 1991 he wrote: "Apologists for massive immigration appear to blame the large-scale replacement of black workers by Hispanic immigrants in the hotel-cleaning industry of Los Angeles on the blacks themselves, instead of acknowledging the obvious explanation that the immigrants depressed prevailing wages and systematically squeezed thousands of citizens out of the industry" (1991, 25).

Earlier immigrants also lose, even when newcomers are part of their own ethnic group. Estrada attributes unemployment among established Hispanics to new arrivals from Mexico and elsewhere who undercut wages, that is, they will work for less and with fewer benefits.

Harvard economists George Borjas and Richard Freeman (1992) also find that the economic position of high school-educated U.S. workers has deteriorated because of competition from immigrants who will work for less money and fewer benefits. High school dropouts are harmed still more. Immigration and the overseas-trade imbalance together raised the 1988 effective labor supply by 28 percent for men and 31 percent for women. This rise accounted for up to half of a 10 percent decline in the wages of unskilled labor between 1970 and the late 1980s, a loss that has not been recouped.

As a contributor to the National Research Council's 1995 study of immigration, Borjas quantified the income effect on U.S. workers. As part of its costs, immigration accounts for working Americans' loss of $133 million annually in job opportunities, depressed wages, and deteriorating conditions of work.

Not everyone loses from immigration. The other part to Borjas's findings is that the lower labor costs put $140 billion annually into the pockets of employers. A clear social cost of the net $7 billion added to the aggregate economy is the increasingly large gap between the incomes of the rich and the poor (1995, 49).

This analysis does not count taxpayer costs, as someone picks up the tab for the education and health care of mainly poor immigrants. Economist Donald Huddle (1995) estimates that K–12 education is the largest single cost of immigration. The school-age populations in states that receive large immigrant flows have exploded, with a corresponding increase in state and local budgets and taxes. In addition, an estimated 2 million Americans were unemployed in 1992 because of immigration, and the resulting $11.9 billion in social safety-net costs was borne primarily by state and local governments. This latter type of cost wanes and waxes with unemployment rates.

The National Research Council estimated in 1995 that "native-headed" households in California pay an additional $1,178 per household in state and local taxes in order to offset the deficit of $3,463 incurred in public services on behalf of each immigrant-headed household (Marshall 1995). California has the most extreme redistribution of wealth from native-headed to immigrant-headed households, in part because California is the principal target for immigration. In addition, many of California's immigrants are Mexican or Central Americans, whose average educational achievement is less than eighth grade.

Steve H. Murdock's testimony on March 22, 1995, before the U.S. Commission on Immigration Reform suggests that immigration adds to aggregate national income but without corresponding benefit to individual U.S. families. Jobs are systematically downgraded by cut-throat competition from the growing labor force so that the nostrum that "There are some jobs that Americans won't do" becomes a self-fulfilling prophecy. Bring in Third World labor, and the wage, benefit, and safety conditions to which jobs devolve attract neither native-born Americans nor established immigrants. Supply and demand operating in the workplace means that a surge in immigration guarantees that the less-skilled service-sector jobs remain low paid.

Black and white Americans flee states that are heavily affected by immigration, so data from local labor markets understate the extent to which Americans are displaced. Moreover, Donald Huddle surmises that the present ideology, which treats immigration as a win-win situation for all, limits press coverage of the negative effects of immigration and population growth (1993, 532).

Never to be forgotten as one heads down this road is the widening gulf between rich and poor, and the squeeze on the middle class. In a democracy, the benefit of cheap labor to employers may be transient because it fosters the rhetoric of class warfare and demagoguery. The electoral process can then spew up tax and regulatory policies designed to redistribute wealth, but these very policies penalize everyone because they stifle wealth-creating business activity.

Lower compensation for work and heavier taxation eat at the middle class, which is the bulwark of the domestic consumer market, political stability, and democracy. Not only dissatisfaction among ordinary Americans but also pathological behavior can spread. Despair of ever joining (or remaining in) the mainstream fosters crime, riots, vigilantism, intolerance, scapegoatism, and other signs of disappointment and anger. All erode civil society and generate instability.

Stability

Failing assimilation, ways to manage ethnic conflict depend upon the strength of the state that mediates between parties. The strength of a centralized government depends on multiple factors, including the citizenry's tolerance for authoritarianism. For example, Marshal Josip B. Tito held Yugoslavia together, in part through the force of his personality and his World War II record, in part through authoritarian police measures, and in part because the Soviet Union created an external threat that induced Yugoslavs of varied ethnicities to cooperate. Tito died in 1980. I visited Yugoslavia two years later; already it was being said that the country would soon disintegrate.

Ultimately, the viability and legitimacy of government ride on the health of the national economy and the environment, which is the life-support system for the economy. In the words of former U.S. senator and the founder of Earth Day, Gaylord Nelson, the economy is a "wholly-owned subsidiary of the environment." A state is fatally weakened by environmental collapse, seen, for example, if food production begins to fail.

The legitimacy of a state is further affected by whether majority or minority interests are in control. Analyst Benjamin Schwarz (1995) suggests that dominance by a single mainstream culture is a precondition of national stability. The argument is both logical and supported by case studies. Schwarz points out that claims made by diverse elements in a society cannot be resolved by "reasonable" divisions of resources and power, because minorities are seldom satisfied by distributions that do not entail significant (therefore unacceptable) losses to the dominant group.

Diversity becomes a more severe problem if a nation's institutions allow or even encourage the mobilization, in Esman's terms, of "ethnic entrepreneurs" (1994). For example, certain elites in U.S. society encourage not only "hate-crime" but also "hate-speech" legislation. Such legislation is strongly favored by some minorities in the United States, not surprisingly, because it is widely assumed that such laws would be used to punish only whites. In the turn-of-the-century political climate, they could be correct. But how long whites will acquiesce in their own dispossession remains an open question.

A unique type of problem arises when a minority regards shared territory as its homeland. Noel Malcolm suggests that "aggressive nationalism is typically a syndrome of the dispossessed, of those who feel power has been taken from them" (1995, 55). This description surely fits the minority Serb population in Kosovo, where as recently as post-World War I they had been a clear majority.

The description "aggressive nationalism" also matches the profile emerging among Hispanics in the U.S. Southwest. A typical incident occurred outside the Westwood (Los Angeles) federal building on July 4, 1996. Here, a multiracial and multiethnic gathering of U.S. citizens celebrating Independence Day, carrying American flags and demonstrating against immigration, was confronted, then physically attacked, by a much larger group of mostly Hispanic immigrants organized by *La Raza Unida* (The United Race). The attackers carried Mexican flags, posters showing severed "gringo" heads, banners with hammer and sickle, and words including "Fight for Communism; Power to the Workers" and "Este Puno Si Se [unreadable] Los Obreros Al Poder." This group chanted epithets against the United States and such slogans as "Viva, Aztlan." The Hispanic attack turned physical while several police looked passively on. A few elderly Americans with bloodied heads were carried away on hospital stretchers, and the episode ended soon after, with no arrests, although the scene had been captured on videotape.

Aztlan is the name of the irredentist nation that is to be formed out of present-day California, Arizona, New Mexico, Texas, and southern Colorado. The May 1995 issue of the *Voz Frontera* approvingly describes the intention of the "brown berets of Aztlan" to establish a "revolutionary people's government" that will prepare for armed struggle in order to oust "the pigs. . . . The revolution has begun. Which side are you on?" In the same vein, a February 6, 1998, seminar at the Southwestern University School of Law in Los Angeles featured an address by the Mexican consul general to the United States, Jose Angel Pescador Osuna. He declared, "We are practicing *reconquista* in California."

In California, Hispanics already make up one-third of the population, and demographer William Frey (1995) finds that both white and black native-born Americans are fleeing. Demographic projections for the United States, as a whole, suggest that Hispanics have almost overtaken blacks as the largest minority and will soon be a full 25 percent of the population. Immigration and differential birthrates will leave the white population as a minority by midcentury.

Esman warns that diversity and democracy are intrinsically antagonistic because "where the state loses control of ethnic relations, the result is likely to be protracted violence and civil war, as in Bosnia, Sri Lanka, and Sudan" (1994, 104). He might have added to his short list Kosovo, Ireland, Somalia, Burundi, Rwanda, Indonesia, Sri Lanka (Ceylon), the Philippines, and Mexico.

The response to fulminating hostilities between groups is often an increasingly authoritarian state. An embattled state prefers an unarmed citizenry because weak factions can be opportunistically sacrificed in order to maintain quiet.

Citizens may have a different interest. If the state is (1) unable to keep order, (2) captured by a hostile faction, or (3) itself poses a threat to liberty, self-defense may be the best remaining option. Individuals and groups who perceive growing interethnic tension rightly fear losing the capability for self-defense.

Esman's predictions seem, at first glance, to be contradicted by the example of the United States, which is sometimes called "a nation of immigrants." Yet, most of U.S. history has proceeded against a backdrop of growing wealth. The acid test of shrinking shares has only begun to strain its democratic institutions.

The importance of broad access to wealth as the basis of democracy can hardly be overestimated. In the early nineteenth century, Alexis de Tocqueville observed that the roots of American liberty are planted in the natural wealth of the continent. He wrote that "the chief circumstance which has favored the establishment and maintenance of a democratic system in the United States is the nature of the territory that the Americans inhabit. Their ancestors gave them a love of equality and freedom; but God Himself gave them the means of remaining equal and free by placing them upon a boundless continent."

Recent U.S. history bears out, unfortunately, the de Tocqueville-Esman-Kaplan-Schwarz analysis. In the early 1990s, Kaplan's *Atlantic Monthly* article (1994) described multiethnic riots in poorer sections of Los Angeles as "blacks v. brown," but, in addition, recently immigrated Koreans became a major target of attack. Shopkeepers who had the artillery for self-defense escaped being burned out, but others were not so lucky. Other major cities including Philadelphia and Miami also had multiethnic riots.

Esman's observation that authoritarianism becomes indispensable to control ethnic relations foreshadows several political currents in the turn-of-the-century United States. Calls for hate-crime legislation and criminalization of "hate speech" (an attack on the First Amendment), attempts to narrow the scope of the Second Amendment (which guarantees citizens' rights to keep and bear arms), and the use of the police and National Guard to quell disturbances are each, in their own way, an attack on constitutionally guaranteed liberties.

These developments were punctuated by questionable uses of federal forces against citizens by the Clinton administration. These events include the Federal Bureau of Investigation's (FBI) and the Alcohol, Tobacco, and Firearms' (ATF) fatal shooting of a boy, a woman, and a baby-in-arms at Ruby Ridge, Montana, and the incineration of more than eighty men, women, and children at Waco, Texas.

Without missing a beat, the year 2000 began with U.S. Attorney General Janet Reno ordering the FBI and Immigration and Naturalization Service (INS) to break into a Miami home in order to grab Elian Gonzalez, who was to be turned over (probably rightly) to his Cuban father. But Reno ordered this raid on the strength of a search warrant (an attack on the Fourth Amendment) instead of a duly sworn-to court order as required by the Constitution. Moreover, just twenty seconds elapsed between the FBI's 5:00 A.M. knock on the door and the break-in. Respected Harvard Law School professor Lawrence Tribe said that the raid "strikes at the heart of constitutional government and shakes the safeguards of liberty."

As a society slides into chaos and a disregard of law, warns Kaplan, democracy becomes "less and less relevant to the larger issue of governability. . . . It is not clear that the United States will survive the next century in exactly its present form. Because America is a multiethnic society, the nation-state has always been more fragile here than it is in more homogeneous societies" (1994).

Liberty, tolerance, and democracy are delicate flowers. Civic virtues may not survive population growth and shrinkage of the ordinary person's portion. But the unwanted trade-off between liberty and order can be resisted. Much of the population growth results from immigration, a de facto population policy. Many Americans think that an immigration policy that results in approximately 1 million legal, and possibly half that many illegal, immigrants annually is both arbitrary and unnecessary.

Conclusion

Many of the environmental, economic, and cultural problems that the United States faces are being worsened by population growth. Many Americans resent the changes, having believed almost since the founding of the colonies that the American legacy was abundance and liberty. In the modern context, the tradition teaches that the U.S. birthright is the opportunity for honest work that will produce a good living. Population growth is not alone in changing the environment in which most Americans work and play, but certain negative tendencies become visibly worse as more people press upon the environmental, social, and cultural carrying capacity.

Most Americans are far ahead of their leaders in trying to stop population growth. Native-born Americans limit family size to 1.8 children. (The average national rate of 2.1 reflects the significantly higher fertility rate of the immigrant sector.) Roper and other polls of a cross-section of Americans also affirm most Americans' dislike of high levels of immigration. Similarly, the 1988–1990 Latino National Political Survey—released by the Ford Foundation in December 1992, two months after passage of legislation that raised legal immigration by 40 percent—suggests that more than 75 percent of Mexicans and Puerto Ricans residing in the United States agree or strongly agree that "there are too many immigrants."

The general public is not xenophobic in its rejection of immigration. Nevertheless, a growing number perceive a link between the large inflow of aliens and population growth. Growth in the size of the national population is felt locally as crowding (for example, of schools, roads, and national parks), dilution of the traditional culture, higher numbers without health care insurance, and higher taxes. On the national level, one sees that the looming collapse of Social Security is brought nearer by the inflow of impoverished populations.

One should note that Social Security is a redistributive system. Low-income participants accrue much higher benefits (will receive more) than the lifetime contributions they make. The shortfall must be made up, now or later, by middle—and high-income workers. With continuation of the current trend, which favors family-reunification immigrants who are predominantly undereducated, poor, and rarely speak English, resentment among native-born Americans could rise sharply, redefining whom is unwanted and what is un-American.

The perception that natural resources are being used up or degraded, and that liberty is giving way to authoritarianism where a chief goal is management of ethnic relations, could give rise to a sense of being cheated out of what is commonly seen as a birthright. Mutual tolerance many not survive the realization that government and the media elite have governed in their own interests, in disregard for the well-being of the average loyal citizen.

In the declining phase of any economic cycle, less sophisticated sectors of the public will sense mainly their own alienation from society and a near-total absence of a stake in its peaceful continuance. Demagogic leaders could mobilize this mass in the usual way—scapegoatism, myths, promises—and the United States that has been so honored would become history. A descent into genocide as gangs, tribes, and factions war over spoils seems farfetched, it is true, but the lessons of history warn of the alarming potential.

The further tragedy of the present liberal immigration policy is that the sacrifice of the national interest is based on self-delusion. It is based on the persistent belief that open-arms immigration policies help countries from which immigrants come. Such policies do not help. On the contrary, holding out the promise of rescue often promotes harmfully false perceptions. Believing that local limits do not apply, foreign governments and people conclude that reproductive self-discipline can be disregarded. This misperception is devastating, because only by limiting natural increase can an overpopulated society come into balance with the carrying capacity of the environment.

Ways Out

Stopping the momentum of population growth in the United States is a daunting goal. Albert Bartlett and Edward Lytwak (1995) explain that attaining zero population growth means that the total of deaths and *emigration* must equal (or be greater than) the total of births and immigration. Given the 1992 estimates for the United States of 2.2 million births and 0.2 million emigrants per year, the total of births and immigration should not exceed 2.4—a problem to say the least because births alone were 4.1 million in 1992! Time is not making these statistics come out better.

The array of instant zero-population-growth scenarios can be represented by two extreme possibilities. One hypothetical arm would give the whole 1992 allowance to births (2.4 million) while placing immigration at zero. Doing so would entail a 42.5 percent reduction in the actual number of births in 1992 and, of course, a 100 percent reduction in immigration. The other hypothetical no-growth scenario would leave immigration at its estimated actual level for 1992, or 1.3 million immigrants, which would leave room for just 1.1 million births (a 73.2 percent reduction in U.S. fertility).

This exercise reveals the strength of the forces producing population growth. It also points up the risk of delay in formulating and implementing policy. Delay now could contribute to crisis later, a high-stakes gamble. Never (one prays) will individual decisions about childbearing be overruled by government, but China, of necessity, provides precedent.

Immigration numbers, unlike childbearing, are historically and appropriately within the public-policy arena. An all-inclusive cap of one hundred thousand annually would serve the national interest. Visas might be allocated, for example, by giving continuing priority to spouses of American citizens, although nowhere is it written that only the United States should accommodate family reunification—couples can reunite elsewhere. Perhaps twenty-five thousand places could be reserved for refugees and those immigrants seeking asylum, giving substance to America's valued role as a refuge of last resort. Beyond that, skilled immigrants and citizens' nuclear families (but not collateral relatives) complete the list of those people who might receive priority under a reformed immigration policy. Alternately, visas could be allocated according to a point system that preferentially counted skills, then family connections in the United States, and so on. The total is what counts, and it should take priority over negotiations to determine how visas should be allocated.

Americans could be proud of a policy that explicitly and rationally committed the nation to balancing population size with the long-term carrying capacity of the environment. It is sensitive and restrained, and designed to minimize friction among existing residents and citizens of the United States. Given the population growth to which we are unavoidably committed given the demographic base, moderation is especially needed. In the words of elder statesman George Kennan, it is essential to not violate "the interests, and limitations of our country" (1995, 116).

Present immigration policies are driving the United States to a population increase of approximately 1.1 percent annually. This rate of increase foretells a doubling time of about sixty-three years, yielding a population of 560 million shortly after the year 2060. At this rate, the United States reaches approximately one-half billion at midcentury.

On the contrary, an all-inclusive cap of one hundred thousand immigrants annually would produce a slight increase and then gradual decline in population size (through attrition) beginning in about 2050. It would come none too soon to mitigate the very likely social and political fallout from the crowding, multiculturalism, and alienation from the mainstream that seem increasingly upon us.

Suggested Reading

Abernethy, Virginia. 1979. *Population Pressure and Cultural Adjustment*. New York: Human Sciences Press.

———. 1993. "The Demographic Transition Revisited: Lessons for Foreign Aid and U.S. Immigration Policy." *Ecological Economics* 8: 235–52.

———. 1994. "Optimism and Overpopulation." *Atlantic Monthly* (Dec.): 84–91.

———. 1999. *Population Politics*. 1993. Reprint. Piscataway, N.J.: Transactions Press.

Bookman, Milica Z. 1997. *The Demographic Struggle for Power: The Political Economy of Demographic Engineering in the Modern World*. London and Portland, Oreg.: Frank Cass.

Campbell, Colin. 1998. *The Future of Oil and Hydrocarbon Man*. Houston and London: Petroconsultants.

Esman, Milton J. 1994. *Ethnic Politics*. Ithaca: Cornell Univ. Press.

6

Population, Technology, and Development

The Vicious-Circle Principle and the Theory of Human Development

Craig Dilworth

THE THEORY of human development is a conceptual picture that explains human development as distinct from the development of other life forms. Darwin's theory of natural selection explains the development of the world's various life forms, including ours, but it does not explain what is *particular* about the development of our species.

Though to the best of my knowledge no other theory of human development has ever been put forward, there is a good deal of "conventional wisdom" about how we got where we are. This conventional wisdom tells us such things as that we humans have been successful as a species, and that a large part of that success is thanks to our ability to find technological solutions to problems of survival. The idea is that through technological change, we have continuously been progressing toward a better way of life, and that human inventiveness can solve virtually every problem, whether it be an environmental problem or one of scarcity. Conventional wisdom also tells us that we brought about the agricultural and industrial revolutions in order to improve our living conditions, and that economic growth increases our welfare while at the same time being necessary for dealing with our environmental problems. It also tells us such things as that the consumption of goods and services is the *motor* of our economy, that having a surplus is a good way to avoid the full impact of

77

natural disasters, that ethnic differences are a fundamental cause of war, and that recycling goods should be part of a sustainable society. On the theory to be presented here, conventional wisdom will be seen to be wrong on all of these points.

Where Darwin's theory of natural selection is based on the principle of *evolution,* the theory of human development, which presupposes Darwin's theory, is based on the *vicious-circle principle.* And where the principle of evolution came to constitute the core of *biology,* the vicious-circle principle is intended to constitute the core of *human ecology.*

The vicious-circle principle is both easy to understand and in keeping with common sense. Briefly put, it says that *increasing population size leads to technological innovation, which allows more to be taken from the environment while leaving less behind, while at the same time promoting further population growth.* Or, seeing as it is a matter of a *circle,* it could, for example, be expressed as: *technological innovation allows more to be taken from the environment while leaving less behind, the increase promoting population growth, which in turn creates a demand for further technological innovation.* I describe it in more detail below.

The Vicious-Circle Principle
(or, What We Are Up Against)

Human *population growth*
increases *consumption,*
which leads to *scarcity,*
which increases the chance of *war* at the same time as it creates a demand
    for *new technology,*
which is *developed* and *employed,*
which allows previously inaccessible *resources*—renewable, nonrenewable,
    or both—to be drawn from the environment (or, in the case of military
    technology, allows the *destruction* of goods produced using resources
    drawn from the environment),
which *reduces* the quantity of resources remaining,
while allowing the production of a *surplus* of goods or services or both
    normally of *lower quality* than the ones they are replacing,
which can mean increased *work* for individuals, a worsening of their *quality of life,* and a lowering of their *standard of living,*

both the taking of resources and the production of a surplus of goods and
  services increasing the use of *energy* (itself a resource),
while the existence of the surplus leads to increased *trade,*
which is the same thing as *economic growth,*
while the goods and transformed energy become *polluting waste*
at the same time as the surplus supports further *population growth.*

Note that the vicious-circle principle constitutes a *paradigm* of human development, not a *law.* In other words, it is intended to capture the *main thrust* of human development *to date,* and is not a description of how all instances of human development always have been and always must be. Some societies have, for varying periods of time, not gotten caught up in the vicious circle. But at present, the vast majority of humankind *is* caught up in it. But seeing as we are rational animals (as they say), we should have it in our power to break the circle and get on to a sustainable path. In not being sustainable, the vicious circle will sooner or later collapse anyway. But if we wait until it collapses of itself, it could very well take us with it.

In order to investigate the viability of our theory, we will consider the extent to which actual human development to date can be understood in its light.

The Human Revolution (ca. 100,000 BP)

Our species, the Cro-Magnons, or *Homo sapiens sapiens,* first appeared in Africa around 150,000 years ago. From there, we gradually wandered northward, coming first to the Near East about 100,000 years ago, and eventually to Europe and as far east as Australia about 40,000 years ago. When we arrived in Europe, the Neanderthals *(Homo sapiens nean-derthalensis)* had already been established there for about 100,000 years.

Due to the many technological innovations occurring in the Near East about 100,000 years ago, many archaeologists refer to this time as that of the "human revolution." These innovations include the use of bone for tools, the making of tools with built-in handles, and probably the use of skin clothing. On the theory of human development as based on the vicious-circle principle, it is just this *innovativeness* of our species and its predecessors that is responsible for the ecological and demographic predicament in which we find ourselves today. What this statement means, unfortunately, is that the problem lies in our *genes,* which makes it all the more difficult to come to terms with.

Starting about 40,000 years ago, there occurred another spurt in human technological development. It included the systematic hunting of selected animals; the widespread use of blade tools; the ability to create fire; and the invention of lamps, needles with eyes, spoons, pestles, axes, the spear thrower, and, about 12,000 years ago, the bow and arrow. At the same time as these technological innovations were made, the human population started to increase noticeably, as is to be expected in the vicious-circle principle.

Note that in the vicious-circle principle, *all* of these technical changes contribute to the number of humans that the environment can sustain *in the short term,* whereas the innovations that allow for the greatest short-term increase in population are the ones most likely to *reduce* the possible population size in the long term. That is, such innovations are the ones that, due to their enabling a greater exploitation of the resource base, are most likely to diminish the environment's *carrying capacity* for humans.

Perhaps what is most notable with regard to human technological development during the last ice age (ca. 80,000 to 10,000 BP) was the improvement in *weapons,* particularly the development from the wooden thrusting spear, to the stone-pointed throwing spear, to the throwing spear that could be hurled a greater distance with the aid of a spear thrower, and finally on to the bow and arrow. It may in fact have been the case that the demise of the Neanderthals about 28,000 years ago was a direct result of the latter phase of this development occurring earlier with us.

The Neanderthals were not the only large mammals to go out of existence toward the end of the last ice age. Somewhat before 12,000 years ago, but after our arrival, all megafauna in Australia, including the giant kangaroo, became extinct. And shortly after 12,000 years ago, in Eurasia and America, such large mammals as the mammoth, the mastodon, the woolly rhinoceros, the giant deer, the saber-tooth tiger, the giant wolf, the native American horse, the gomphothere, and the giant ground sloth all became extinct. All in all, by 10,000 years ago, more than *fifty* genera of large mammals had become extinct over a period of a few thousand years. This number is greater than what had become extinct during the preceding *4 million* years!

We humans with our weapons were undoubtedly directly or indirectly responsible for virtually all of these extinctions. Primitive man's attitude to and effect on his environment have not been so benign as, for example, some Native Americans would have us believe. Here we see just how deep the ecological problem is. It did not start with the Industrial Revolution or later. It started when our ancestors began to fashion and improve tools.

The Horticultural Revolution (ca. 10,000 BP)

The horticultural revolution was *not* a response to the warming climate at the beginning of the Holocene leading to a focus on gardening rather than hunting as an easier way to obtain a livelihood. Archaeological evidence suggests rather that food production developed in response to *problems* caused by the undue success of the hunter-gatherers, which led to not only an increase in their numbers, but at the same time a reduction in the amount of available food. The development of horticulture was an adjustment that human populations were forced to make in response to this situation of scarcity.

Hunter-gatherers of our species had continuously increased in population right from their first appearance, fully occupying those portions of the earth, including Australia and the Americas, that could support their lifestyle with reasonable ease. After they had undermined their own food resources by eradicating so many genera of large mammals, they were forced to become more eclectic in their food gathering, to eat more and more unpalatable foods, and in particular to concentrate on foods that, though being of lower nutritional value, were more abundant. Human populations throughout the world were forced to adjust to further increases in their numbers by increasing not the food resources that they preferred, but the ones that responded well to attention, and could be made to produce the greatest number of edible calories per unit of land.

The form of agriculture that developed was swidden, or slash-and-burn, cultivation. This form was coupled with the domestication of animals, first in western Asia, starting with the dog some 12,000 years ago or earlier; and succeeded by goats and sheep around 9,000 years ago; then cattle, pigs, and bees; and then the horse and donkey about 6,000 years ago.

To explain the origin of food production (and economic change in general), many scholars now assume that the people most likely to adopt a new subsistence strategy are the ones who are having trouble following the common subsistence practices of their group. Societies that had no need of horticultural techniques resisted their introduction for centuries after first becoming acquainted with them. In the Middle East, it was those people who lived *outside* the zone where wild foods were most abundant that began to experiment with horticulture. Recent archaeological finds suggest that domestication began in marginal areas rather than in the optimal zones, such as the Hilly Flanks, where traditional foods were most abundant. Early cultivation began as an attempt to copy, in a less favorable environment, the dense stands of wheat and barley that grew wild in the Hilly Flanks.

Here we have a clear case for the application of the vicious-circle principle. Technological advance in the form of the invention of such weapons as the bow and arrow made sources of food available that were previously inaccessible, paving the way for an increase in population at the same time as it led to resource depletion. And the greater population coupled with the diminished resources created the need for new technology—in the form of horticulture—capable of extracting even more from the environment.

Regarding the idea that technological advance leads to an improvement in standard of living—as is suggested by "conventional wisdom"—both archaeological and anthropological evidences indicate that quite the opposite occurred in the case of the revolution from the hunter-gatherer period to the horticultural, as is in keeping with the vicious-circle principle. The horticulturists' diet, based on crops and dairy products, was less varied and nutritious than the foragers', which was higher in proteins and lower in fats and carbohydrates. Whereas foragers were relatively disease free, stress free, and well nourished, protein deficiency and dental cares increased with the shift to food production, whereas people's average height decreased and the physical well-being of the population declined. Human life expectancy at birth fell from around thirty years for hunter-gatherers to about twenty years during the whole of the horticultural era, in spite of the resultant change from hand-to-mouth feeding to the storing of food. Apart from the effects of war, the dependence on specialized food production meant a lack of flexibility that could lead to starvation when crops failed, for example, as a result of drought. Higher population density and trade links also contributed to the increase in the spread of infectious diseases, and the sedentary lifestyle led to more unsanitary conditions and the spread of parasites, all of which worsened humans' quality of life.

Other disadvantages accompanied food production. Social inequality increased, as elaborate systems of social stratification replaced the egalitarianism of the hunter-gatherer society. Slavery was invented. Poverty, crime, war, and human sacrifice became widespread, and the rate at which humans degraded their environment increased.

Another notable aspect of the lowering of the quality of human life with the coming of the horticultural lifestyle is the drudgery it involves. The development of the Neolithic culture that accompanied the revolution to horticulture meant an increasing division of labor and the beginning of actual *work*. Whereas women worked in gardens, a task involving a good deal of drudgery itself, men worked grinding, polishing, and boring holes in stone tools for use in the gardens: the beginning of *boring* work and the daily *grind!*

But this result is not all. Further in keeping with the vicious-circle principle, we see that not only did horticulture allow for the sustenance of a population that had overexploited its environment with the aid of weapon technology, but also the new technology it involved actually allowed the size of that population to *grow*. During the 5,000 years of the horticultural period, the human population, in spite of undergoing a lowering in its standard of living, grew from some 10 million to around 80 million. This growth was not solely thanks to the use of the hoe in horticulture, but further supported by such technological innovations as animal domestication, and such inventions as sickles, cloth, woven baskets, sailboats, fishnets, fishhooks, ice picks, and combs.

Here I want to emphasize an important aspect of the difference between humans and other species. Given no technological change to allow increasing environmental exploitation, the population sizes of nonhuman species are limited by external factors alone, and fluctuate about a mean determined by the carrying capacity of their environment. As mentioned above, some human population sizes have also been rather constant over relatively long periods of time. In such societies, it has virtually always been the case that there has been little or no technological development to fuel population growth. So you might think of such societies as being similar in this respect to nonhuman populations. But there is an important difference. Societies that have not experienced population growth over longer periods of time have almost invariably maintained this state of affairs through the use of *internal population checks,* more particularly, *cultural* ones, which other species never use. These checks can be *preventive,* as in the case of contraception and late marriages, or *positive,* as in the case of abortion and infanticide. As is clear, preventive checks reduce fertility, whereas positive checks lower life expectancy (from conception). Such *internal* checks can be contrasted with *external* checks, which are virtually the only sort that exist for other species and can never be totally eradicated from human societies. External checks almost always lower life expectancy, and can take the form of disease or famine, for example. Both internal and external checks may be normally operative even when the size of a population is increasing. But where nonhuman populations always fill their biological niches, some human societies, thanks to the greater intellectual sophistication of humans, have actually been able to keep their populations *below* the carrying capacity of the environment, thereby being able constantly to reap the benefits of *abundance*.

Another positive check to population size, which is external to a society, but internal to humankind, is war. With the accelerated population growth resulting from the horticultural revolution, when the previous internal checks of the hunter-gatherer period were no longer in play, warfare became one way in which the size of the population was restrained in its rate of growth. As the horticultural period advanced, and populations and population pressure grew, so did the amount of warfare, as suggested by the vicious-circle principle.

As has been pointed out by a number of authors, warfare was virtually impossible for hunter-gatherers, not only due to their small numbers, but also because of their not being able to accumulate sufficient food to see them through such engagements. (Not that hunter-gatherers did not manage to use their weapons to kill one another anyway, only on a smaller scale.) Thus, it was only with the horticultural era, when food could be stored, either as grain or livestock, that warfare became possible. Furthermore, it was the existence of *property,* which hunter-gatherers lacked, that constituted the immediate cause of war, as well as being a prerequisite for commerce.

Apart from the direct loss of life resulting from such conflicts, warfare also functioned as a check on population size through its giving rise to female infanticide. By reducing the number of girls in a society, the group could devote its resources to the nurture of its male soldiers-to-be.

The Agrarian Revolution (ca. 5000 BP)

In the vicious-circle principle, as is in keeping with the archaeological and historical record, the most important technical development after the beginning of the employment of horticultural methods was the invention and use of the plow. The only way the constantly growing human population of 80 million some 5,000 years ago could be sustained was by exploiting the environment more thoroughly, and the plow was the primary means of doing so. With the plow, seed crops could be grown on a large scale, largely replacing the hand-planted tubers of the horticulturists. The resultant harvest per unit land in terms of calories increased tremendously. The vicious circle of population growth, technological innovation, and resource depletion was about to be repeated on a massive scale.

Once again, technological advance was not the result of a search for a better life, but the response to need imposed by increasing numbers of people. Though the average age at death did not change notably in the transition to the agrarian period, remaining at about twenty years, such phenomena as the drought and flooding resulting from changing weather were more widespread in their effects. Similarly, the spread of infectious diseases had a greater impact due to increased population and greater interaction among groups, coupled with worsening hygiene. The most devastating instance was the Black Plague in the middle of the fourteenth century, which killed about a third of the population of Europe over a period of four years. And just as the human workload grew with the move to horticulture, it grew again with the move to agriculture. Though oxen were eventually used to plow fields, at the beginning of the agrarian era it was *humans* who drew the plows. Large areas of land became the property of kings, and the vast majority of the population worked as peasants or slaves to produce the foodstuffs that constituted the kings' wealth, to create the monuments that would stand as everlasting tributes to the kings' greatness, and to fight in the kings' wars. In this last regard, it may be mentioned that at the beginning of the agrarian era, the time of the year directly after taking in the harvest was known as "the season when kings go forth to war." War was just a part of life. With the amassing of greater amounts of property, society became more stratified, there was a greater division of labor, and the distance between the rich and the poor constantly increased.

While the standard of living of the vast majority of the people declined, so too did the quality of the land, both changes being in keeping with the vicious-circle principle. Farmers first moved into thinly forested regions with light soils, especially along river valleys. Later, as these soils became depleted and populations continued to grow, they cleared forests.

The clearing of forests—with iron axes—in itself caused the leaching of nutrients from the soil, as well as its erosion, which altered both vegetation and soil quality. And this situation was only exacerbated by the use of the plow, which exposed the topsoil to wind and rain. In areas that were too hilly or deficient in nutrients for agriculture, goats were left free to roam, in effect exterminating all but the hardiest bushes. The results of these activities remain with us today, and can be seen, for example, over the whole Mediterranean area. The use of irrigation to supply water to fields located in areas that were otherwise too dry to support agriculture led to salinization, leaving the soil unusable for cultivation for thousands of years—as can be witnessed today in the Tigris-Euphrates Valley. Wastelands developed around cities, where the area was picked clean of fuel and building materials, and vegetation disappeared due to the constant tread of human feet. The increase in the numbers of people not only made the move to agriculture necessary, but also made its ecologically disastrous effects more widespread. As regards other species, the spread of agriculture and the human population forced many from their natural habitats, and some, such as the wild ox, were hunted to extinction.

For the last 100,000 years, humans' adaptation to the environment has taken the form of cultural change rather than biological change. With the evolution of commerce and warfare, much of that cultural change has consisted in adapting to the activities of other humans rather than to nature. By the time we reached the agrarian period, we no longer had to fear other predators, and for the most part had a dependable source of food through the domestication of plants and animals. Major successes and failures consisted in the results of exchanges on the market or on the battlefield, rather than in the results of the hunt. Nature became less the "habitat" for the farmer and more a set of economic resources to be managed and manipulated by the controlling group. This effect was particularly true of cultures where the dominant class was urban based, as in early Greece and Rome. With the continual distancing of nature from humankind came a gradual change in our conception of the world, with reality increasingly being thought of in terms of other people and their actions, as though we were not ourselves animals dependent on the ecosphere for our survival.

As human population size and pressure grew due to a paucity of internal checks, coupled with the increased short-term productivity of the soil through the use of the plow, warfare also increased. In this regard, the development of bronze weapons played a key role. For the first time in history, people found that the conquest of other people could be a profitable alternative to the conquest of nature. Thus, beginning in advanced horticultural societies and continuing in agrarian, we expended almost as much energy in war as in the more basic struggle for subsistence. You could say that bronze was to the conquest of people what agriculture was to the conquest of nature: both were decisive points in our sociocultural evolution.

As in the horticultural period, in the agrarian era one of the reactions to population pressure was infanticide in the face of the threat of severe deprivation. When crops failed and famine was imminent, families often abandoned their newborn by the roadside, or left them at the door of a church or monastery in the hope that somebody else might raise them. Sometimes even older children would be abandoned by their parents. The story of Hansel and Gretel is based in the reality of scarcity. In some districts in China, as many as a quarter of the female infants were killed at birth—signs were put up near ponds, "Girls Are Not to Be Drowned Here."

The length of the agrarian period was extended by the discovery of America, which also allowed a continuing increase in the size of the human population, first through emigration from Europe. At the same time, however, population also increased in Europe.

By the end of the agrarian period, about 250 years ago, the vicious circle had taken a gigantic turn. The technologies involving the plow and other inventions such as the wagon wheel, animal harnesses, the crossbow, gunpowder, horseshoes, stirrups, the lathe, the screw, the wheelbarrow, the spinning wheel, printing, water mills, and windmills all supported an increase in the human population from about 80 million to 730 million, at the same time as agricultural techniques drastically reduced the productivity of the land. The only way such a huge population could continue to be supported were if a new resource could be mined. There was such a resource in the form of *fossil fuels*. And the innovativeness to devise the technology necessary to mine that resource was not lacking.

The Industrial Revolution (c. 250 BP)

With the Industrial Revolution began the largest of all turns round the vicious circle, giving rise to the use of vast quantities of fossil fuels, which have indirectly sustained almost an *eightfold* increase in world population in the last *250 years,* that is, in the last *1/400th* of our species' short existence! From an ecological point of view, this statement bodes very ill indeed.

Increasing population pressure in Britain around 1750 led to a shortage of both land and wood, the latter being used as both a building material and a fuel. The possibility of using coal as a substitute fuel for wood led to the development first of the Newcomen engine, and then Watt's steam engine, to pump water out of coal mines.

Coal is an inferior substitute for wood, a fact that required the invention of other devices and processes such as the use of coke (derived from coal) as a substitute for wood-charcoal in the iron-smelting process. With these changes and the implementation of Watt's engine, the use of coal increased tremendously, a result of the vicious circle moving from need (of an energy source for heating and manufacturing) to innovation (in the form of the invention of the steam engine, among other devices) and on to resource depletion (through the extraction and use of coal).

The next phase in the vicious circle followed directly, namely, greater economic activity, spurred by the profit motive of capitalists; with this greater economic activity came increased use of energy and production of waste. Here we have an excellent example indicating why economic growth, the goal of so many of today's decision makers, ought rather be seen as an integral feature of our present failure to live in ecological equilibrium with our environment. The inability to husband an ecologically viable resource in the form of wood led to the need to tap a non-ecologically viable resource in the form of coal. Due to the existence of coal only in particular places, it was necessary that a means of distribution be found. This means—again involving innovation—consisted in the construction of railways and canals, and the development of hard surfaces for roads. All this construction activity demanded the expenditure of energy and constituted economic growth, while at the same time it involved ecologically regressive changes in the landscape and increasing pollution.

In history, each major technological advance has made possible our digging deeper *and* faster into the barrel of natural resources, the accelerated rate of exploitation increasing the size of the human population at the same time as it manifests itself as economic growth. So although more and more people are becoming dependent on the contents of the barrel, our constantly increasing consumption speeds us ever faster to the day when we will be scraping its bottom. We have to learn to live in such a way that the contents of the barrel are being replenished at the same rate as they are being consumed. In other words, to live in equilibrium with our environment, we must create a *stable* economic system, and not continue trying to support a *growing* one.

The Industrial Revolution also brought with it a further decrease in the standard of living of the common people. Instead of working out-of-doors or in cottages and enjoying the many holidays in the medieval calendar, people had no alternative but to work in mines or factories for longer hours at even more specialized tasks and with virtually no holidays. Child labor also increased, with children being used, for example, in mines, where they could squeeze into spaces too small for adults. The quality of clothing also became lower, with cotton largely replacing linen, wool, and leather.

Also in keeping with the vicious-circle principle, *wars* have become larger and more destructive since the Industrial Revolution, partly due to the invention and use of more powerful weapons, the latest on the list being nuclear weapons. The twentieth century involved greater destruction and loss of life from war than any previous 100-year period.

What will make the aftermath of the Industrial Revolution so devastating is the fact that it has led to the use of such huge, yet finite, quantities of fossil fuels, the second of major importance being oil. Whereas coal began to be used in response to a scarcity of wood, petroleum began to be used in response to a scarcity of whale oil. At present, 88 percent of the commercial energy used in the world comes from fossil fuels, about 40 percent of the total commercial energy coming from oil. And the use of fossil fuels is almost five times what it was fifty years ago, and is increasing each year, in spite of international conventions intended to reduce carbon emissions into the atmosphere.

The technological innovations during the industrial era most directly responsible for supporting the huge increase in the size of the human population are related to agriculture, and almost invariably involve the use of oil. They include farm machinery, pesticides, and fertilizers. Other innovations that have supported population growth, though in a less direct manner, include all machines used in manufacturing, as well as such better-known inventions as the telephone, the electric light, radio, television, the automobile, and the airplane. Many of these innovations have been dependent on the prior invention of the internal-combustion engine.

And so the vicious circle continues, with the newly available sources of energy allowing a further increase in population, in the present case a truly

tremendous increase, one that is still continuing. But whereas the population of the world has increased by about a factor of five since the 1850s,
the world's consumption of energy, mainly in the form of fossil fuels, has
increased *sixty*fold. For the wealthy 20 percent of the world's population,
the Industrial Revolution has also led to an increase in leisure time, the
reason being that the fossil-fuel resources constitute not only a *tremendous*
surplus of energy, but one that is unequally distributed as well. And it is to
be noted that average life expectancy in the world has risen to as high as
sixty-five years. But even now we are seeing a change in these regards, as
the size of the population continues to grow while the availability of energy decreases. Whereas in our parents' generation a household could be
supported by only one working person, now two are required, and the
length of the actual working day and the stress involved in work are both
increasing. And life expectancy has now started to decline, the most prox-
imate causes having to do with economic failure and disease.

As pointed out above, virtually the whole of the eightfold increase in
the human population since the beginning of the Industrial Revolution is
being maintained by the use of fossil fuels. When these fuels are no longer
available, either because of the environmental effects to which their use
gives rise or because they become exhausted, or when agricultural production drastically drops due to the overuse of these fuels, the world will be
facing a situation in which billions of people will experience real need, a
need that there will be no way of satisfying.

Ways Out

The above considerations lead to the realization that it is imperative for
humankind that we get out of the vicious circle, and as fast as possible.
That this demand is *in principle* possible is clear from the fact that various
societies have existed that have actually managed to do so. Their preconditions, however, were better than our own: they were invariably less
densely populated, never had anything near populations that *doubled* in
less than a lifetime (as the *whole world population* has just done), and had
lifestyles demanding relatively little from the environment. Furthermore,
they were not dominated by a *growth* ethos, as the decision-making world
is today.

But given that that ethos can be broken, and that we have not already gone too far in the vicious circle, at what point or points should we attempt to get out of it, and in what way?

A key aspect of the vicious circle is *population growth*. We must drastically reduce the size of the human population, in both more—and less-industrialized countries, and begin to do so with the least possible delay.

One way this feat might be accomplished is through the implementation of *exchangeable birth licenses*. The idea is that each woman in a particular country is given the right by the state to have a certain number of children. This number is decided upon on the basis of ecological and other considerations, but it is the same for everyone of a certain age. It could be, for example, 1.4 children. In that case, if a woman wanted to have two children, she might buy or receive as a gift six deci-licenses from somebody else; or, if she wanted only one child, she could sell or give away her four extra deci-licenses—receiving them from or giving them to another person living in the same country. Such a system would, of course, have to be supported by a program of family planning and immigration, and be keyed with statistics regarding the degree of success of their implementation.

Similarly, human *consumption of resources* is far too great, and it too must be drastically reduced, independently of population reduction. What is needed is a fundamentally different economic system, operative in the less-industrialized as well as the more-industrialized countries, in which the idea of economic growth is replaced by one of economic *conservation*.

On the conception of economist Herman Daly (1992), the quantity of stocks in such an economy is to be held constant, while the throughput is minimized and the service maximized. Some of the actual changes in the present economy that are necessary to transform it to such a *steady-state* economy include: politically supervising and limiting the size and monopoly power of corporations, setting upper and lower limits on income and upper limits on wealth, implementing quotas for the extraction of natural resources, taxing resources higher than income, charging at least as much for nonrenewables as for their nearest renewable substitutes, stopping the subsidizing of energy production, and setting up tariffs to protect local industries.

One particular aspect of such an economy as Daly envisages may be its not allowing the accruing of *interest*. This topic has been developed by Margrit Kennedy (1988), according to whom a reduction of interest rates lessens the pressure for growth in an economy, zero interest being a precondition for the zero growth of a steady-state economy. In order that a zero-interest economy also be an ecologically sustainable one, however, there must be a land reform and a tax reform. The land reform would put ownership of the land in the hands of the local government, from whom it may be leased, thereby removing the threat of land speculation, and the tax reform would be similar to that recommended by Daly, whereby products rather than incomes would be taxed.

Suggested Reading

Cohen, M. N. 1977. *The Food Crisis in Prehistory.* New Haven: Yale Univ. Press.

Daly, Herman E. 1992. *Steady-State Economics.* 2d ed. London: Earthscan.

Dilworth, Craig. 1997. *Sustainable Development and Decision Making.* Uppsala: Department of Philosophy, Uppsala Univ.

Ehrlich, Paul R., and Ann H. Ehrlich. 1990. *The Population Explosion.* New York: Touchstone.

Ellul, J. 1964. *The Technological Society.* New York: Vintage Books.

Kennedy, Margrit. 1988. *Interest and Inflation Free Money.* Steyerberg: Permaculture.

Malthus, T. R. 1970. *An Essay on the Principle of Population.* 1798. Reprint. Harmondsworth, Eng.: Penguin Books.

Meadows, D. H., et al. 1992. *Beyond the Limits: Global Collapse or a Sustainable Future?* London: Earthscan.

Mumford, L. 1967. *The Myth of the Machine.* Vol. 1, *Technics and Human Development.* San Diego: Harcourt Brace Jovanovich.

Wilkinson, R. G. 1973. *Poverty and Progress: An Ecological Perspective on Economic Development.* New York: Praeger.

7

Scarcity and Its Social Impacts

Likely Political Responses

Kurt Finsterbusch

THIS ESSAY is an exercise in prediction. It predicts the societal responses of institutionally developed societies to two possible scenarios for the next half century: one of long-term economic growth and one of nongrowth or decline due to environmental constraints and problems. The latter I label *scarcity*. This chapter explores the scarcity scenario more fully, because much more is known about the impacts of economic growth on society than the impacts of scarcity. My analysis is based on a macrotheory of social change that I have developed over the years (Finsterbusch 1973, 1983). My conclusion is that economic growth tends to have far more beneficial impacts on society than does scarcity. Economic growth tends to increase equality, integration, democracy, the rule of law, and freedoms, whereas scarcity tends to increase inequality, conflict, authoritarianism, and repression. What is uncertain, however, is how nation-states will respond to these negative impacts of scarcity. It is conceivable that society's responses to scarcity will involve progressive reforms. More ominous responses, however, seem more likely.

Impacts of Economic Growth and Scarcity on Inequality

Until recent globalization weakened the power of labor relative to capital, economic growth has decreased inequality whereas scarcity has increased inequality, as empirically demonstrated in the painstaking work of Simon

93

Kuznets (1955).. Although economic growth may have had negative effects on equality up to the nineteenth century, as the majority of the people in many countries remain at a subsistence level and the new wealth goes mainly to a small elite, the longer-term impact of economic growth is to increase equality. The main reason, as expounded by Gerhard Lenski in *Power and Privilege: A Theory of Social Stratification* (1966), is that economic growth provides a positive climate for business that makes it worthwhile for elites to highly reward professionals and skilled workers as a means to enlarge their own incomes through the resulting increases in productivity. Put in economic terms, Lenski's thesis is that economic development after some threshold of industrialization results in diminishing and even negative returns to elites for their monopolizing the surplus. He also points out that educated workers are not as vulnerable to exploitation as unskilled workers who must compete with masses of other unskilled workers. Educated workers have a better bargaining position that translates into higher incomes for the middle class. Finally, he discusses how economic growth facilitates the rise of democratic institutions, and they in turn increase the political power of lower groups, which usually translates into more favorable policies and economic benefits for them.

The above arguments point to elite concessions for their greater absolute benefit and lower groups wresting benefits from upper groups through democratic mechanisms. Another equalizing force is the diffusion of education that greatly expands the middle class and upgrades the occupational structure so that it no longer is a bottom-heavy pyramid but bulges in the middle.

Economic growth also increases equality in terms of changes in the consumption system. The consumption gap between classes declines as the lower class gets medical care, electricity, indoor plumbing, refrigerators, telephones, television, and possibly even cars. The rich have more and higher-quality goods, but their lifestyles do not differ so markedly as elites and peasants in less-developed countries.

In contrast to the positive effects of economic growth, scarcity has negative effects. There is consensus among scholars that scarcity increases inequality. Five arguments support this proposition. First, because scarcity is the opposite of economic growth, it should have the opposite effects. Economic growth expands jobs and opportunities. This expansion generally allows lower groups choices between jobs and reduces the number who must accept truly exploitative wages. In contrast, scarcity shrinks the job market, especially for marginal, unskilled jobs, and greatly increases the competition among the unskilled for the remaining jobs that tend to be offered at depressed wages. Economic growth also provides an expanding pie that can finance concessions of various kinds made to lower groups, including welfare for the needy and training for the unemployed. Scarcity, on the other hand, limits society's ability to address the needs of the needy. In political terms, the demands of lower groups for better lives in times of scarcity cannot be satisfied without threatening the favorable circumstances of the upper groups. Because the upper groups usually have considerable political power, the demands and needs of the lower groups are not likely to be met. Furthermore, the lack of assistance for the lower groups can be justified by claims that such redistributive policies would divert resources from those people who would invest in economic growth; thus, these redistributive policies would harm the lower groups in the long run (the trickle-down theory). What about the times when welfare policies have been instituted in depressions? Gurr (1985) points out that these policies were always premised on the depressed times lasting a short period. He argues that a relatively permanent scarcity would greatly limit welfare policies.

The second explanation for scarcity's negative impact on equality is that scarcity translates into inflation, which more adversely impacts lower groups. They spend a greater percentage of their income than do upper groups on consumer goods that have high resource inputs and will inflate substantially with scarcity. Upper groups buy greater quantities of goods but less proportionally. They also spend more on quality, which increases the value of most goods without using much more resources. Quality goods need not inflate as much from resource scarcity as lower-quality goods. In addition, upper groups buy bigger homes and estates that will inflate with scarcity because they involve considerable resources, but as owners they will benefit when these properties appreciate in value. On the other hand, the poor pay rent and will experience a marked decline in their standard of living even if they manage to stay employed.

The third explanation of why scarcity increases inequality is that upper groups are better able to protect themselves from the negative effects of scarcity. They organize faster and more effectively to advance and protect their interests. The managerial and professional classes and unionized labor have some control over the terms of their remuneration and will try to keep them up to the level of inflation, which increases inflation even more for the politically and economically weak.

The fourth explanation is that the controllers of resources, who are predominantly the rich, will actually gain in times of scarcity while the rest of the population suffers. Just as home owners and renters profit from inflation and scarcity, so do those people who control the natural resources that are becoming scarce.

Finally, the fifth explanation is based on the few empirical studies connecting scarcity with inequality. They show that when resources become more scarce, they become more unevenly distributed. On the whole, the empirical linkage between scarcity and inequality is not strong. The consensus on this proposition, however, is largely due to the absence of a counterargument.

Impacts of Economic Growth and Scarcity on Integration

Economic growth increases integration, and scarcity decreases it. Economic growth does not eliminate group identities and intergroup conflict, but it does mitigate the conflict between groups, reduces its violent expression, and channels it into legal political actions and compromisable demands. Economic growth leads to expectations that each generation will be better off so the system will be perceived as relatively effective. Discontent will be low and the system of inequalities that becomes identified with rising standards of living will not be seriously challenged. Thus, class conflict will be low and system legitimacy high.

The effects of scarcity are the opposite. Although there is widespread agreement that scarcity is likely to reduce integration and system legitimacy, the empirical evidence is again not strong, because there has not been much long-term scarcity in industrializing countries in the past two hundred years. Scarcity decreases integration by increasing competition, conflict, and disturbances and decreasing regime effectiveness and system legitimacy. These impacts in turn tend to increase repression and undermine or weaken democracy. Five explanations have been advanced in support of this proposition. First, scarcity negates the positive functions of economic growth for integration.

Another problem with a shrinking pie is that the conflict between classes and groups becomes a zero-sum game in which someone must lose if someone else gains. When the contest results in big winners and little winners, as with the distribution of the expanding pie, the conflict is not as intense as when it results in winners and losers or big losers and little losers. Furthermore, scarcity removes the justification for inequality which is that the inequality is needed to produce economic growth. If economic growth is not possible due to environmental limits, then this argument loses force, gross inequality becomes less tolerable, and conflict increases.

The second explanation of why scarcity decreases integration is derived from deprivation theory as developed by Ted Gurr in *Why Men Rebel* (1970). Unless scarcity arrives very slowly to allow for gradual adjustments, scarcity will cause strong feelings of deprivation as reality falls far short of expectations. The deprivation-induced anger and collective action may at first be deflected away from political institutions toward competitors or opponents or into self-destructive and antisocial behavior. In the long run, however, the anger will be directed toward the polity, the powerful, and the system of inequality, and more radical demands and forms of political action will become more legitimate and prevalent.

The third explanation is derived from Charles Tilly's mobilization theory of collective action (see *From Mobilization to Revolution* [1978]). In times of economic decline, competition increases and groups that organize to protect or advance their special interests will do far better than individuals or weakly organized groups. Those people who act first will gain the most benefits, because scarcity will rapidly deplete the government's capacity to confer benefits. Furthermore, governments will increasingly respond to challengers with repression as it is less costly in the short term than concessions. Collective action, therefore, will become more costly, but the costs of inaction are likely to increase even faster. Scarcity, therefore, spurs interest-group organization and the intensification of conflict among groups. Tilly also uses the cost-benefit logic to argue that scarcity fosters conditions that greatly favor revolutionary conflict, particularly the withering of support for the government and the shifting of the previously uncommitted to support challengers of the status quo.

The fourth explanation focuses on the legitimacy problems of governments in times of economic decline. Unpopular governments can often stay in power and the public remain acquiescent in times of economic growth, but economic failure will likely facilitate a government breakdown and the growth of challenging groups. Established democracies generally have a reservoir of popular support and may survive economic decline for a while. Over time, however, scarcity erodes legitimacy, making even democracies vulnerable to growing unrest and authoritarian movements, as in the 1930s.

Another link between scarcity and eroding legitimacy is the type of government policies that scarcity requires. They will require sacrifice. People will have to bear costs and consume less to protect the environment and adjust to scarcity, and these policies will be unpopular, as evidenced by the public's rejection of President Carter's five-cent-a-gallon gasoline tax during the energy crisis of the late 1970s. A likely scenario is that the government will institute many relatively painless policies that will not deal adequately with the problem and allow the crisis to get worse and more costly to deal with. Its failure will decrease its legitimacy and spawn challengers.

Our attention has been mainly on the developed democracies. When we consider the Third World, the scarcity-induced declines in integration can lead to government collapse and anarchy. Robert Kaplan (1994) provides vivid images of current anarchic situations in West Africa that make societal breakdown seem a very plausible impact of scarcity in societies with weak institutions. He describes countries where the government cannot provide law and order over most of the country and not even in many parts of the capital at night.

The fifth explanation is that scarcity aggravates all fissures in society. The shrinking pie intensifies the class struggle as discussed earlier, but Paul Blumberg in *Inequality in an Age of Decline* adds that scarcity "will almost inevitably increase the overall level of social nastiness" and aggravate all fissures and cleavages, "creating social conflict amid a general scramble for self-aggrandizement" (1980, 220). He goes on to describe how racial, gender, educational, generational, and regional conflicts are likely to intensify in the United States.

Another common speculation is that war and international conflict will increase greatly under scarcity. Not only will the powerful nations use military power if necessary to obtain resources from weak nations, but also, according to Robert Heilbroner (1992), underdeveloped countries or terrorist groups might also make war on or terrorize rich countries, demanding a greater sharing of world wealth and resources. Nuclear weapons are spreading, and nuclear blackmail could occur at any time. As national and subnational identities heighten, they make nonviolent resolution to conflicts less feasible. If this analysis is right, then the prospects are terrifying. Nuclear materials have become widely available through leaks from the former Soviet Union, and nuclear bomb making is within the capabilities of many terrorist groups. Biological and chemical weapons are even easier to acquire, and their results can be far more destructive. Terrorist actions are predicted by experts to increase in number and in destruction, even if economic growth continues. With increasing scarcity, the developed world will be in great danger. Democracies may have to tread on civil rights and greatly increase police powers to deal with the danger of terrorism. This trend is likely to move the United States further in the direction of authoritarianism.

Impact of Economic Growth and Scarcity on Democracy

Economic growth strengthens democracy, and scarcity threatens it. The explanation, in part, is due to the positive effects of economic growth on equality and integration because both strengthen democracy. Economic growth also expands the middle class, the educated, and the percentage of the population that has a stake in the system, and, therefore, would be adversely affected by political instability. With the class pyramid bulging at the middle instead of polarized between a small elite and the poor masses, power holders have much less to fear from losing the reigns of government in an election as the change in policies would not be very radical. Democracy is usually well served by a large middle class that dampens conflict, supports moderate politics, and generally opposes extremists. Economic growth and the expansion of education also increase intermediary organizations and tolerance toward those citizens with different views, both of which are essential to the effective functioning of democracy. Finally, economic growth reduces the intensity of conflict, as pointed out above, and accommodates the resolving of issues and handling of demands through a democratic bargaining process.

There is widespread agreement that scarcity is a threat to democracy. I give five explanations for this view. First, as with equality and integration, scarcity cancels the positive effects of economic growth. However, it does not necessarily produce the opposite effects. For example, it does not necessarily shrink the middle class. On the other hand, it could stimulate radicalism, which a large middle class tends to inhibit. Scarcity also increases inequality and decreases integration, which in turn threaten or weaken democracy. The aggravated conflict and loss of legitimacy that scarcity is likely to cause are particularly troublesome for the survival of democracy.

The second explanation of why scarcity weakens or threatens democracy is that it creates problems and crises that are hard for democracies to solve. Then when a democracy fails and the problems deepen, the public is tempted to jettison democracy for a more decisive, forceful, active, and authoritarian government. The strength of democracy is its responsiveness to the will of the people. This strength becomes a weakness in times of scarcity. Dealing with scarcity problems requires sacrifice, restraint, regulation against ecologically harmful behavior, and coercion in enforcing ecologically helpful behavior. These requirements, however, are not likely to be popular. Politicians in democracies, therefore, to retain the support of their constituents, generally do not pass the tough legislation that is required. For example, the U.S. response to the oil crisis in 1973 was to lower the speed limit to fifty-five miles per hour and urge the public to voluntarily lower their thermostats in winter. Later the government gave tax deductions for some insulation costs and required better gas mileage for cars with a very leisurely implementation schedule. Great sacrifice, such as an increase of three dollars per gallon gasoline tax, was not even considered.

The third explanation is that scarcity generates many technical issues that lend themselves poorly to participatory decision-making procedures. Considerable scientific inputs are required for sound environmental policies, so many important decisions with significant distributional side effects are best handled by experts. We would expect, therefore, that some amount of democracy would be sacrificed to technocracy as a practical matter.

The fourth explanation is that scarcity can cause fear and potentially even panic that can undermine the confidence in democratic institutions, which is required for them to function without a strong show of force. This line of argument is more speculative than the others but still highly plausible. Heilbroner observes:

> As the historians of ancient and modern democracies illustrate, the pressure of political movement in times of war, civil commotion, or general anxiety pushes *in the direction of authority*, not away from it. . . . The

passage through the gauntlet ahead may be possible only under governments capable of rallying obedience far more effectively than would be possible in a democratic setting. If the issue for mankind is survival, such governments may be unavoidable, even necessary. (1992, 132–34)

The fifth explanation is that lower groups in times of scarcity are ineffective in getting their demands met by peaceful means, so some of them turn to more radical and even violent means. The state is likely to become more authoritarian and repressive to deal with the dynamics of the resulting civil conflict.

Scarcity would have many other impacts on society that I do not cover in this short article. I can report, however, that the literature on scarcity generally concludes that they will be quite negative as a whole. In sum, I have not come across any good news about the impacts of scarcity.

Societal Response to Scarcity

It goes without saying that predictions about how society will respond to relatively long-term scarcity are speculative. They are contingent upon many factors, including the nature and extent of the crisis, public readiness for change, degree of government autonomy from control by the economic elite, and the idiosyncrasies of the leader(s). Accordingly, I offer the following comments as an initial exploration of the topic for democratic capitalist societies.

It is safe to predict that society will respond to scarcity problems by collecting information on the issues, because there would be little opposition to such low cost and relatively nonthreatening actions. In fact, some people will call for research as a way to delay action. Individuals on their own would also produce information on the issues, so public and private actions should increase public awareness of and concern about scarcity. The result would be that environmental issues will be perceived as getting worse and requiring more collective action.

The second societal response that we predict is technological innovation to reduce the costs of depleting resources and to protect the environment. Businesses will respond to rising costs of resources by using resource-saving technologies and practices. Market forces should spur the development of new conserving technologies. Other innovations will be directed at protecting the environment in ways that do not threaten current lifestyles. Many of the innovations will be stimulated by subsidies or by regulations concerning pollution, recycling, conservation, and hazardous substances. Regulations that are politically feasible are likely to have relatively low costs to industry or be widely perceived as important enough to pass over industry resistance. Often regulations are necessary to make it worthwhile for industry to develop new technologies and practices for protecting the environment or more efficiently use and reuse resources. Another source for new technologies is the academic research community that is subsidized by government and foundation contracts and grants. As awareness of the crisis increases, it is likely that subsidies for research addressing relevant environmental issues would increase substantially.

The third response that I predict is a range of minor behavioral changes on the part of individuals. Increasingly, the public wants to do something to help solve the problems. They participate in recycling programs, buy "Save the Bay" license plates, and contribute in other relatively costless ways.

The crucial question is whether the above responses will be sufficient to improve the environment and set society on the course of sustainable development. One group of scientists judges environmental problems as less severe than the view developed here and has immense faith in the inventiveness and adaptiveness of humans. According to this group, such actions would go a long way toward solving any problems that actually exist. Perhaps a few new governmental policies that are not too disruptive to the economy might be helpful, but no dramatic changes would be needed. These scientists argue that environmental problems are often exaggerated by environmentalists and that there is considerable scientific uncertainty about their extent and potential impacts. They are sanguine on energy availability because fossil fuels could provide for the world's energy needs far into this century and because nuclear fusion could provide all the energy that will be needed when fossil-fuel production declines. Though this view is plausible, it is highly speculative and does not convince most people that the environment is not in crisis.

A second group of analysts views the environmental crisis as far more severe than the above optimists, but prescribes actions for dealing with it that minimize disruption to the economy and demand only modest behavioral changes from the public. Al Gore's recommendations in *The Earth in Balance* (1992) are called a "Global Marshall Plan" to indicate how daring it is, but it relies heavily on market adjustments, voluntary actions, and nonradical changes in government policies to remove subsidies for environmentally destructive actions and to provide more incentives for environmentally helpful actions. Gore also emphasizes information gathering and learning. His program is ambitious and unacceptable to the controllers of Washington today, but does not step hard on anyone's toes. Except for population control in the Third World, his plan avoids the really painful actions that will be necessary. In like manner, Lester Brown, Christoper Flavin, and Sandra Postel in *Saving the Planet: How to Shape an Environmentally Sustainable Global Economy* (1991) are cautious in their suggestions for saving the planet. Nevertheless, both books are rich in helpful policies and actions for addressing environmental problems.

A much larger group of scientists who write on the sustainable society does not think like the optimists that new technologies and minor behavioral changes will overcome environmental scarcity, nor does the group think like Gore and Brown, Flavin, and Postel that an ambitious government environmental program that avoids significant costs can do the job. Most scientists concur that more significant changes are needed to achieve sustainability. Following in this line of thinking, the crucial question is what additional responses are likely or even feasible. Will people make sacrificial changes in their lifestyles? Will businesses risk some profits to protect the environment? Will governments pass tough environmental legislation? The dominant answer provided by these analysts to all three questions is "No!"

This pessimistic view is based on four arguments: the public-goods and free-rider problem, the business of business is profits, special interests have the power to resist tough new policies, and the public will not support painful solutions. The public-goods argument is that it is not in the rational self-interest of individuals or nations to voluntarily sacrifice for the good of the environment or for the conserving of nonrenewable resources, because they will lose out to others who continue to exploit the environment or use the scarce resources. People will not voluntarily reduce their travel miles by automobile to preserve petroleum; they must be encouraged to do so by high gasoline taxes or forced to do so by gasoline rationing. Nations will not voluntarily reduce their use of fossil fuel to slow down global warming unless other nations do the same, because they would pay heavy costs without getting any more benefits than those nations that paid no costs.

The business-of-business-is-profits argument asserts that solutions to environmental problems will not come from businesses unless government policies change their incentives. On their own, they will conserve in order to save money and invent technologies that help them do more with less, but they will not stop doing harmful things from which they benefit, nor will they do rightful things that cost them. They must be made to do these things by government policies, but, according to the third argument, they will prevent the passage of such policies, and according to the fourth argument, the public will likewise oppose the policies. Most commentators, therefore, are pessimistic about the government's ability to take the necessary actions. They believe, therefore, that environmental problems will worsen until an acute crisis forces a change in direction. At that point, democratic societies are predicted to become much more authoritarian, as pointed out earlier.

Thus, the probable outcome of long-term scarcity is the weakening and ultimate demise of democracy. Under the right circumstances, however, democracies could survive. If the democracy has a fairly high degree of equality and justice and is lead by a charismatic leader in a crisis that is perceived as requiring radical change to avoid certain disaster, it could act decisively and with considerable unity to achieve sustainability. The high degree of equality and justice is necessary to avoid destructive polarization and conflict. The right kind of crisis is one that is dramatic and sudden, because democracies can act decisively in emergencies, such as in wars or economic crises. Normal politics that are conflictful, incremental, and relatively impotent would be temporarily suspended while the conflicting interests and parties suspend their ambitions and allow the leadership to save the nation (pursue the common good). The charismatic leader is needed to inspire the widespread belief that the painful remedy will be good medicine for the whole nation and that it will be fair (all will share in the hardship). Roosevelt in the 1930s and Thatcher in the 1980s are examples of such leaders.

In sum, the societal response to scarcity will include research on the issues, technological innovations, and minor behavioral changes. These responses are likely because they will face little opposition. I also predict (in line with most commentators) that these responses will fail to adequately deal with environmentally induced scarcity with the result that democracies will drift into severe crises, and the resulting political struggles will probably, but not inevitably, end in authoritarianism.

Ways Out: Social and Political Changes
Required for a Sustainable Democratic Society

I now offer some ideas about major institutional changes for creating a sustainable democratic society. Each would have many profound impacts that cannot be evaluated here, so these proposals are simply for discussion.

The first requirement for a sustainable democracy is to increase the capacity of government to macromanage the economy to the extent that it needs to be macromanaged, thus, a national industrial policy. A common suggestion for this purpose is a planning agency that would be a fourth branch of government. It would make long-term plans for America's future, recommend legislation to Congress to implement needed macro-constraints, and sponsor the research necessary for creating these plans and legislation.

The second requirement for a sustainable democracy is for corporate power over the government to be reduced and for the power of major corporations to be brought under some measure of public control. They present the greatest threat to pluralist democracy today and are responsible for much of the damage to the environment. Presently, they possess unaccountable power. Campaign finance reform is required to reduce corporate influence over government, and I suggest two reforms to make the corporations more accountable. These reforms, however, would encounter immense opposition from corporations. The first is the federal chartering of all corporations that do interstate business and exceed some minimal size. Presently, corporations are chartered by states, and the competition among states in courting corporations has led them to abandon the oversight function that is legally theirs. The resulting unaccountability of corporations can be reversed by federal chartering and making charters contingent upon their demonstration of service to the public. In this way, environmental impacts, plant closings, safety records, treatment of workers, and so on, could be monitored and the corporations disciplined more effectively than at present.

Another reform that is directed at the corporations is that corporations that are larger than some minimum size and conducting interstate business would pay government taxes in stock shares instead of money. This change would cause a gradual dilution of the company's stock until the government owns 50 percent of its shares. Then what is good for General Motors would be good for the United States. The board of directors would be restructured to contain representatives of the government, communities containing its facilities, and other interests. In this way, values other than profits would have to be honored, though profits would still be the corporations' main goal.

The above reforms have addressed the issues of the capacity and fairness of the political economy but have not included reforms that directly deal with environmental problems. The major recommendations have been developed by Herman Daly in *Steady-State Economics: The Economics of Biophysical Equilibrium and Moral Growth* (1977) and are included here (and in many other lists of proposals for sustainability). They are: (1) setting of minimum and maximum limits on income and a maximum on wealth to discourage excessive consumption and mitigate inequality, (2) transferable birth licenses allocated 2.1 per woman by the government in order to achieve zero population growth, and (3) depletion quotas for all nonrenewable resources, set by the government to regulate the annual consumption of each resource, and auctioned to resource buyers. The birth licenses allow every couple to have two children. If they wanted more children, they would have to buy a license from someone who will not use both their licenses. The quotas would slow depletion and lead to higher prices, which would encourage efficiencies and innovations. All three procedures provide macroconstraints but do not interfere in the microprocesses that are governed by free markets and individual choices within those constraints.

Because the major natural resource in a country is its land, the final recommendation is a national land-use plan that would synchronize with state land-use plans. Real-estate interests would provide formidable opposition to this policy in order to protect their financial interest in using or selling land for the highest price. Nevertheless, it is necessary to preserve agricultural lands, forests, and complex ecosystems and to deal with a wide range of environmental problems. Zoning is necessary in urban areas and now is necessary in other areas for many of the same reasons. A current land-use trend that the plan would try to contain is the increasing dispersion of population to low-density housing that causes high energy and transportation consumption, infrastructure inefficiencies, and greater ecosystem disruption.

The above recommendations are radical by current standards of political change. They could not be enacted except in an acute environmental crisis. Many other changes would also be needed for sustainability, including a major realignment of the culture and value system from an emphasis on material consumption and individualism to an emphasis on environmental vitality, inner development, and connections with others. I do not, however, specify further the changes required to attain the sustainable society, because the problem is not a dearth of knowledge about what needs to be done, but the current lack of support for the needed changes.

Suggested Reading

Blumberg, Paul. 1980. *Inequality in an Age of Decline*. New York: Oxford Univ. Press.

Brown, Lester, Christopher Flavin, and Sandra Postel. 1991. *Saving the Planet: How to Shape an Environmentally Sustainable Global Economy*. New York: W. W. Norton.

Brown, Lester, and Hal Kane. 1980. *Building a Sustainable Society*. New York: W. W. Norton.

Daly, Herman E. 1977. *Steady-State Economics: The Economics of Biophysical Equilibrium and Moral Growth*. San Francisco: Freeman.

Finsterbusch, Kurt. 1973. "The Sociology of Nation States: Dimensions, Indicators, and Theory." In *Comparative Social Research: Methodological Problems and Strategies,* edited by Michael Armer and Allen Grimshaw, 417–66. New York: John Wiley and Son.

———. 1983. "Consequences of Increasing Scarcity on Affluent Countries." *Technological Forecasting and Social Change* 23: 59–73.

Gore, Al. 1992. *The Earth in Balance: Ecology and the Human Spirit*. Boston: Houghton Mifflin.

Gurr, Ted Robert. 1985. "On the Political Consequences of Scarcity and Economic Decline." *International Studies Quarterly* 29: 51–75.

Heilbroner, Robert. 1992. *An Inquiry into the Human Prospect: Looked at Again for the 1990s*. New York: W. W. Norton.

Kaplan, Robert D. 1994. "The Coming Anarchy." *Atlantic Monthly* (Feb.): 44–76.

Milbrath, Lester W. 1989. *Envisioning a Sustainable Society: Learning Our Way Out*. Albany: State Univ. of New York Press.

Ophuls, William, and A. Stephen Boyen Jr. 1992. *Ecology and the Politics of Scarcity Revisited: The Unraveling of the American Dream*. New York: W. H. Freeman.

Schnaiberg, Allan, and Kenneth Alan Gould. 1994. *Environment and Society: The Enduring Conflict*. New York: St. Martin's Press.

Tilly, Charles. 1978. *From Mobilization to Revolution*. Reading, Mass.: Addison-Wesley.

8

Foundations and Context
of Contemporary Conflict

Joseph A. Tainter

WITH THE END of the cold war, culturally defined conflicts have seemed to spring up everywhere and come from nowhere. They have emerged with such sudden intensity, in so many places, that superficially they appear entirely novel. When journalists try to explain that these conflicts are not truly new, they typically reduce them to stock phrases, such as "ancient tribal feuds." Such terms conceal more than they reveal. In fact, the origins of today's conflicts lie in historical events and processes far removed in time and space.

History is substantially a chronicle of reactive processes. For most societies and many people, the primary context to which they must adapt is other societies and other people. Reactive processes have been responsible both for the formation of much of today's world political system and for what seems like its impending dissolution. Today's conflicts can be understood in the historical context of competition among European nations, their global expansion and colonization, and the reaction of much of the world to Euro-American domination. Politicians, diplomats, and international workers who confront today's violence are working with a great handicap if they do not understand the origins of these problems, nor their reactive nature. Historical processes have shaped contemporary violence and must be understood in order to comprehend that violence.

Two types of reactive historical processes clarify many problems that confront the world today. The first of these types is the competition that forms when polities with equivalent military abilities contend for dominance. The second is the pattern by which much of the world has reacted to 500 years of European expansion, and 150 years of Euro-American domination. These processes in combination have set the foundation for the disintegrative forces of contemporary world politics.

Competition in European History

For at least the past 4,000 years, one of the fundamental historical processes has been competition among societies organized at approximately equivalent levels of population, territory, technology, organization, per capita product, and military capability. Such societies have been termed *peer polities*. Examples include the warring states of post-Chou China; the Mycenaean polities; the city-states of classical Greece; the Italian city-states of the ancient, medieval, and Renaissance periods; the southern lowland Maya; medieval and Renaissance Europe; and our current era. It is characteristic of peer polities that their evolution is stimulated primarily by their own interaction, rather than by reaction to a dominant power or by relations between cores and peripheries.

The relations among peer polities typically involve both trade and competition. Where natural or fiscal resources are sufficient, peer polities may engage in conflict that stretches over generations or even centuries. Such conflicts may involve endless maneuvering for advantage, forming and dissolving of alliances, and continual striving to expand territory or influence at a neighbor's expense, or prevent the neighbor from doing the same. Peer-polity competition stimulates growth in the size and complexity of military systems; increases in the scale of warfare; innovations in technology, strategy, tactics, and logistics; and the reorganization of society to support competition.

Europe before 1815 was almost always at war somewhere. From the twelfth through the sixteenth centuries, France, England, and Spain were at war from a low of 47 percent of years in some centuries to a high of 92 percent in others. In the whole of the sixteenth century, there was barely a decade when Europe was entirely at peace. The seventeenth century enjoyed only four years of total peace; the eighteenth century, sixteen years.

The development of siege guns in the fifteenth century ended the advantage of stone-built castles, and required changes in the strategies and technology of defense. From the early fifteenth century, fortification builders designed walls that could support defensive cannons. A short time later, walls were built that could also withstand bombardment. By 1560, all the elements of the *trace italienne* had been developed: a fortification system of low, thick walls with angled bastions and eventually extensive outworks. It was effective but expensive. The city of Siena in 1553, for example, found it so expensive to build such fortifications that no money was left for its army or fleet. Siena was annexed by Florence, against which, ironically, its fortifications had been built.

To capture a place fortified in this way could take months or years. Offensive tacticians designed more complicated siege methods, and their costs rose as well. A besieging force of perhaps 50,000 had to be kept in place for weeks or months. Each day, such an army needed 165,000 pounds of flour and 2,500 sheep or 250 cattle. This amount was more than was required to feed all but the largest cities of Europe. Local lords could no longer afford to build and defend an effective fortress, nor to attack one. The resources for war were no longer found in the feudal countryside but in capitalist towns.

There were parallel developments in open-field warfare. In the fourteenth and fifteenth centuries, massed archers and the pike phalanx made the mounted knight obsolete. These innovations in turn were gradually superseded by firearms. As commanders maneuvered for battlefield advantages, tactics were developed to increase the efficiency and effectiveness of firing. Training and battlefield coordination became more important. Uneducated soldiers had to be familiar with what were, at the time, history's most advanced weapons. Ranks had to open and close on signal. Victory came to depend on the right combination of infantry, cavalry, firearms, cannons, and reserves, and textbooks of drill sprouted across the continent.

The naval powers of the time were England, the Netherlands, Sweden, Denmark and Norway, France, and Spain. From 1650 to 1680, the five northern powers increased their navies from 140,000 to 400,000 tons. This naval strategy also led to problems of increasing complexity and cost. In 1511, for example, James IV of Scotland commissioned the building of the ship *Great Michael*. It took almost one-half of a year's income to build, and 10 percent of his annual budget for seamen's wages. It ended its days rotting in Brest harbor, having been sold to France in 1514.

War came to involve ever larger segments of society and became correspondingly more burdensome. Several European states saw the sizes of their armies increase tenfold between 1500 and 1700. Louis XIV's army stood at 273,000 in 1691. Five years later, it was at 395,000, nearly one-fourth of all Frenchmen. Between 1560 and 1659, Castile lost about 11 percent of its adult male population in the constant wars.

As the sizes of armies continued to grow through the eighteenth and nineteenth centuries, new fields of specialization were needed. There was demand for skills such as surveying and cartography. Accurate clocks and statistical reporting were needed. In the eighteenth century, some armies carried their own printing presses. Organization became more complex. Staff and administration were separated. Armies no longer marched as a unit, but could be split into smaller elements that traveled, under instructions, on their own. Battles came to last up to several months. In France, the *levÇe en masse* was begun in 1793. In 1812, NapolÇon invaded Russia with an army of 600,000, including 1,146 field guns, on a 400-kilometer front.

Yet, for all these developments, land warfare was largely stalemated. There were few lasting breakthroughs. The new military technologies, and the mercenaries to use them, could be purchased by any power with enough money. No nation could gain a lasting technological advantage. When a nation such as Spain or France threatened to become dominant, alliances would form to counter its power. Major wars of the time were therefore long, and tended to be decided by cumulative small victories and the slow erosion of the enemy's economy. Defeated nations were soon ready to fight again. Land warfare had to be augmented by what amounted to global flanking operations. European wars turned into contests for power and influence overseas.

In 1499, as he was embarking on a campaign in Italy, Louis XII asked what was needed to ensure success. He was told that three things alone were required: money, money, and still more money. As all things military grew in size and complexity, the main constraint came to be finance. In the decades before 1630, the cost of putting a soldier in the field increased by 500 percent. Nations spent ever more of their incomes on war. In 1513, for example, England obligated 90 percent of its budget to military efforts. In 1657, the figure was 92 percent. In 1643, expenditures of the French government, mainly on war, were twice the annual income.

The major states came to rely on credit to finance their wars. Even with the flow of precious metals from her New World colonies, Spain's debts rose from 6 million ducats in 1556 to 180 million a century later, and bankruptcy often undermined Spanish military operations. The cost of war loans grew from 18 percent interest in the 1520s to 49 percent in the 1550s. Both France and Spain often had to declare bankruptcy, or force a lowering of the rate of interest. From the sixteenth through the eighteenth centuries, the Dutch, followed by the English, overcame fiscal constraints by gaining access to reliable short-term and long-term credit. They were careful to pay the interest on loans, and so were granted more favorable terms than other nations. They used this advantage to defeat opponents, France and Spain, that were wealthier but were poor credit risks.

In 1775, Frederick the Great expressed eloquently the futility of stalemated European conflict:

> The ambitious should consider above all that armaments and military discipline being much the same throughout Europe, and alliances as a rule producing an equality of force between belligerent parties, all that princes can expect from the greatest advantages at present is to acquire, by accumulation of successes, either some small city on the frontier, or some territory which will not pay interest on the expenses of the war, and whose population does not even approach the number of citizens who perished in the campaigns. (Parker 1988, 149)

Global Consequences of European Wars

European competition stimulated technological innovation, development of science, political and financial transformations, and global expansion. The development of sea power and acquisition of colonies became aspects of strategy in stalemated European warfare. European war ultimately affected and changed the entire world. By 1914, the nations of Europe, and their offshoots, controlled fully 84 percent of the earth's surface.

As land warfare in Europe produced no lasting advantages, the expansion of competition to the global arena was a logical consequence. Competition expanded to include trade, the capture of overseas territories, the establishment of colonies, attacking adversaries' colonies, and intercepting the wealth that flowed from them. Overseas resources were needed to sustain European competition. These societies were, until the nineteenth century, powered almost completely by solar energy. Sweden's support base in the seventeenth century consisted nearly entirely (87 percent) of renewable resources. Lacking colonies outside her region, almost half of Sweden's forest-based exports went to finance foreign wars. For societies powered by solar energy, and using that energy so heavily within the limits of their technology, the main way to increase wealth was to control more of the earth's surface where solar energy falls. It became necessary to secure the produce of foreign lands to subsidize European competition. New resources were channeled into this small part of the world. This concentration of global resources allowed European conflict to reach heights of complexity and costliness that could never have been sustained with only European resources.

Peer-polity competition not only forced Europeans to search for foreign lands and resources, but also virtually guaranteed them success in doing so. The stalemated conflicts stimulated continual innovation in technology, organization, strategy, tactics, and logistics. Any power that did not match its competitors in these areas risked defeat and domination. A nation that survives this process will be so proficient at making war that, outside of its group of peers, there may be no other military force that can withstand it. The inexorable pressure on European states to become ever better at making war meant that, when they ventured outside Europe, they usually had a competitive advantage over other peoples. Time and again over the past 500 years, comparatively tiny European forces have defeated much larger forces in the New World, Africa, and Asia.

European expansion set the stage for a continuing chain of reactive processes in the rest of the world. Understanding those reactive processes is the second historical ingredient to comprehending the ethnopolitical problems we now face.

Reactions to Global European Expansion

An epoch of more than 400 years of colonial expansion, followed by a century of Western economic and cultural penetration of all parts of the globe, has resulted in a world system in which most people must define themselves partly in reaction to Europe and North America. It was inevitable that many people would define themselves in opposition to Euro-American dominance. This reaction has led to the development of such movements as Islamic fundamentalism, *Sendero Luminoso,* and some cases of reactive ethnonationalism. What is not always so clear, and is typically misunderstood, is that European expansion has also caused violence *among* non-Western peoples.

These reactions began with the earliest phases of European expansion.

Europeans in many areas commented upon both the frequency with which indigenous peoples engaged in conflict (against Europeans or among themselves) and the ferocity with which they did so. The practice of war by such people led to much social speculation, from Hobbes to the present day, about the nature of war in nonstate societies, about the role of conflict in the development of state institutions, and even about the supposedly aggressive nature of our species. This violence has been misunderstood from the beginning.

European expansion transformed indigenous societies from the outset. The immediate consequences were disease, introduction of new plants and animals, and technological change. Such effects often arrived before Europeans themselves, so that even the very first descriptions of indigenous societies were sometimes of people who had already been significantly changed. Among these changes were the formation of pan-tribal confederations and ethnic groups. Both tribes and ethnic groups appear to have formed in response to expanding states, and may not have existed before the state.

In the era of European expansion, many episodes of conflict among indigenous peoples, and between them and Europeans, concerned access to European goods. The circulation of goods beyond state frontiers has long been an element of state-nonstate relations. With its capacity for mass production, European expansion magnified this factor. European goods were valued by indigenous peoples not only for utilitarian reasons, but also because they became part of social relations. Manufactured goods were used to validate claims to status and were intimately involved in wars and alliances. War among indigenous peoples, and between such peoples and Europeans, often had much to do with access to European technology.

The Yanomami of the Amazon Basin illustrate these points. Long noted in anthropology for the frequency and severity of their violent behavior, they have come to public attention with labels such as "the fierce people." The Yanomami are depicted as representing the Hobbesian state of anarchic war in which all nonstate peoples supposedly once lived. Yet, analysis by Brian Ferguson (1995) reveals that there is nothing pristine or intrinsic about their violence. To the contrary, every reported incident of Yanomami conflict is, directly or indirectly, about access to or control of manufactured goods. Yanomami with direct access to Western goods try vigorously to monopolize them. This action creates tension with outlying villages, and even within villages. The problem of access to goods manifests itself not only through violence, but also through changes in kin relations, relocation of villages, population aggregation, village alliances, feasting, economic specialization and exchange, the authority of headmen, and the treatment of the Yanomami as a cultural entity. Manufactured goods so significantly transformed Yanomami society that its recent configuration cannot be considered to represent accurately the precontact society. Ironically, some anthropologists who have taken manufactured goods on their visits to the Yanomami may have inadvertently stimulated episodes of the "pristine" violence that they described.

The Iroquois in colonial North America were a group of independent "nations" often noted for their fierceness and territorial ambitions. Although Iroquois conflicts may have originated in prehistory, in the historic era the Iroquois made war well out of proportion to their disease-reduced numbers. This result was closely linked to their need for European goods. With the new importance of muskets in warfare, and a reduction in the local supply of beaver pelts, the Iroquois in the seventeenth century faced marginalization and ultimate obliteration. Pelts had to be obtained to trade for muskets. At the same time, losses to European diseases were so high that the Iroquois nations had constantly to replenish their populations with war captives and refugees. The Iroquois took to ambushing canoe fleets in Canada for pelts, and concluded that the solution to the shortage of beaver was to expand their hunting territory. Their wars were ultimately about obtaining European goods.

As frontier encounters were transformed into colonial administrations, and ultimately into independent states, political and economic processes in much of the world were modeled on the European nation-state. Yet, the fundamental reactive processes did not change. Many of today's conflicts can trace their origins to the expansion, domination, and meddling of the great powers. Political and territorial arrangements in the areas of former colonies, and in what were the Ottoman, Austro-Hungarian, and Soviet Empires, have caused people to accentuate their differences as they compete to control state institutions. Peoples that have coexisted for centuries now stress the "traditional" nature of their conflicts. New cultural identities are emerging, as among the Maya of Guatemala and in Tâjikistân. Ethnogenesis was apparently a policy of the former USSR. The role of the state in ethnic formation can be seen in Bedouin resistance to Israeli attempts to assign them an ethnic classification. A Bedouin school principal once complained, "[I]f it was not enough what they [the Israeli administration] are doing to us, now they tell us we are an ethnic group" (Jakubowska 1992, 85).

Colonial policies have in many cases exacerbated cultural antagonisms, or even created them. When the British displaced the Moslems as rulers of India, for example, they used Hindus to run the colonial administration, and emphasized the differences between the religions. Hindus were sent to English schools and recruited as minor officials. Moslems largely attended Islamic schools, where the teachings concerned religious orthodoxy rather than secular advancement. In the postcolonial era, continued poverty, lack of access to power, and disillusionment with Western-derived models of "modernity" have contributed to the rise of Moslem, Hindu, and Sikh nationalism. Throughout South Asia, politicians are exploiting these intensifying cultural differences for personal advancement, provoking recent violence. In such a situation, an aura of antagonism can be rapidly created by unscrupulous leaders, and manipulated to further political ambitions.

The tragedy in Rwanda has deeply impressed itself on the world's consciousness. The true origins of this conflict are little known to the public. A century ago, according to Alex de Wall (1994), European colonialists found in what is now Rwanda a centralized kingdom consisting of numerous clans, and three groups largely defined by occupations. The European administrators transformed the occupational hierarchy into an imaginary racial classification. The minority Tutsi rulers were proclaimed by Belgian missionaries to have a cultural and racial heritage in Ethiopia—and thus closer to Europe. As the Tutsi converted to Catholicism, they adopted this new "history" to legitimate their continued rule. Hutu cultivators were consigned to a life of toil.

In 1959, on the eve of independence, the Belgians reversed both their policy and the order of Rwandese society. They assisted in eliminating the Tutsi monarchy and in the installation of a Hutu republic. The Hutu have since seized upon the myth that the Tutsis originated elsewhere, condemning them now as foreigners. The fact that Tutsi and Hutu "ethnic" and "racial" identities were recently created by an outside power is now irrelevant. As they persecute each other and fight to control the Rwandan state, survival now demands that they *must be* ethnic groups.

In the 1930s, the Belgians issued identity cards, categorizing people as Tutsi, Hutu, or Twa (low-caste hunter-gatherers who do not emerge in today's journalism). Unable to implement their racial typology in practice, the Belgian administrators classified people by the ownership of cattle. Those people with ten or more were Tutsi in perpetuity; the ones with fewer were Hutu. These identity cards still exist, and were used to categorize people in the recent massacres. Upon such a distinction, 500,000 people were killed.

Ways Out

There is no simple way out of problems that have taken so long to develop. The most important step is understanding. It is most realistic to talk not of immediate solutions, but of comprehending problems well enough that intervention does not make them worse. Each conflict is but the tail end of a long series of prior events and processes. In our historical arrogance, we fail to see the context of today's dilemmas. The first step toward a way out is to understand the long history that drives today's events. Once that understanding has been achieved, further steps can be based on the factors generating conflict, such as reactions to external forces, rather than on the simplifications of journalists or the illusions created by local leaders. This obligation to understand the historical context of violence extends not just to intervenors, but also to the participants. For the participants, understanding brings the opportunity to choose whether to continue to behave reactively.

There has been a persistent pattern of reaction to European expansion, consisting of tribalization and ethnogenesis, intensification of cultural identity, and violence. The reasons for conflict range from control of Western manufactured goods to control of Western-style governments. These patterns are seen historically among the Iroquois, in recent decades among the Yanomami, and today in both those conflicts that receive public attention and the ones that do not. In such places as the Balkans, Iran, central Asia, Rwanda, Burundi, Somalia, Liberia, and Sierra Leone, violence is shaped by cultural and political reactions to external forces. Though the forms of these conflicts differ, the factor that unifies them is that each is in part a response to former colonial, imperial, or other global powers. Where violence focused on resisting European or U.S. encroachment, the great powers have found it comprehensible if disagreeable. Yet, much of today's violence has seemed so incomprehensible because it is directed internally. Europeans and Americans have not understood that their own expansion has stimulated much of today's culturally defined conflict. There is a direct line of cause and effect from warfare in medieval and Renaissance Europe, to global expansion and colonialism, to today's events in places such as Rwanda, Peru, and India.

This discussion suggests two implications for understanding today's and tomorrow's difficulties. Grasping these implications is the first step toward seeing a way out. The first is the importance of knowing where we are in history. Historical patterns, which may develop over periods of generations or even centuries, are the context of today's violence. In the Balkans, for example, we see the legacy of the Ottoman Empire more than a century after the Turks ceased to rule there. In the division between Catholic Croats and Orthodox Serbs, we still see the legacy of the division of the Roman Empire in 395 A.D. Rarely can an individual in the experience of a lifetime come to understand fully the origins of an event or a process. Yet, to remain ignorant of the origins of today's problems is to condemn ourselves to manage them ineptly, and to condemn others to the consequences of that mismanagement. As for the future, it is folly to suppose that we can use present conditions to predict the twenty-first century if we do not understand how the present came to be. Managing political and cultural problems requires that we know where we are in history.

Western nations that attempt to ameliorate or manage conflicts need to understand how their own histories have stimulated many of these problems. If today's culturally defined conflicts are a response to European political and economic expansion, then interference carries the risk of provoking further reactions. On one level, it can be seen clearly. Video clips released, for example, by Moslem fundamentalists in Lebanon, by the government of Iraq, and by the Bosnian Serbs are clearly intended for Western news broadcasts. The Tutsi-dominated Rwandese Patriotic Front has legitimated its claim to rule Rwanda by asserting that its struggle is based on social transformation rather than ethnicity, that its troops are well disciplined, and that it has no wish for revenge against Hutus, only justice. These messages are meant for European and American ears. Beyond these obvious reactions to Western intervention, there is a likelihood of more subtle and far-reaching consequences. These repercussions include continuing ethnogenesis, further intensification of existing cultural identities, and the emergence of new culturally defined conflicts. Those countries who design interventions in world conflicts must do so with the realization that involvement by dominant nations *always* stimulates unanticipated reactions.

A second implication concerns Western perceptions of cultural conflicts. Many in Western nations (including, unfortunately, journalists) assume that cultural differences are innate and immutable, and lead automatically to violence. Both journalistic and some scholarly reporting tends to "explain" violence as the irrational but inevitable result of "ancient tribal feuds." It is assumed that contemporary expressions of cultural difference represent both actual history and the "natural" divisions of our species.

Cultural differentiation in today's conflicts is, to the contrary, flexible and shifting, and responds to history, external stimuli, and deliberate manipulation. Conflicts in central Asia are a clear example, where new cultural identities (such as Özbek) are emerging, stimulated substantially by the involvement of external powers. In places such as the Balkans, "ethnic entrepreneurs" (a term suggested by Airat Aklaev of the Russian Academy of Sciences) manipulate cultural identity as a means of political mobilization. This manipulation masks the underlying issues, sometimes deliberately. To a casual observer, it is easy to suppose that conflicts between cultural groups are conflicts *about* culture. Often the conflicts are actually about relations to the West, about the relations of local groups to Western-style central governments, or, as in Somalia and Liberia, really about the control of those governments. In such struggles, appeals to culture raise the moral authority of the political claim and tap profound emotions. This strategy is, unfortunately, effective in political assertion. If cultural assertions mask real issues, then to address only the cultural dimension of a conflict is to miss potential ways out.

The conflicts of the twenty-first century cannot be avoided or managed if we consider only conventional, short-term factors. This analysis suggests a complex picture, in which reactive historical processes may combine with scarcity, power, politics, and culture to provoke violence, or may operate independently of them. The implications for preventing violence in the next century are complex as well: nothing can be more difficult in the management of conflict than to know that intervention itself may generate further violence (as we see in Sierra Leone). No doubt, many who work in the crisis-laden world of international relations will be reluctant to accept the additional burden of learning historical context. Yet, if we accept the simple premise that problems can rarely be solved if their causes are not understood, then historical knowledge is the first step toward a way out. Diplomats, politicians, and conflict participants cannot hope to achieve lasting resolutions unless they first understand the importance of knowing where we are in history.

Suggested Reading

Ferguson, R. Brian. 1995. *Yanomami Warfare: A Political History.* Santa Fe: School of American Research Press.

———, and Neil L. Whitehead, eds. 1992. *War in the Tribal Zone: Expanding States and Indigenous Warfare.* Santa Fe: School of American Research Press.

Kennedy, Paul. 1987. *The Rise and Fall of the Great Powers: Economic Change and Military Conflict from 1500 to 2000.* New York: Random House.

Parker, Geoffrey. 1988. *The Military Revolution: Military Innovation and the Rise of the West, 1500–1800.* Cambridge: Cambridge Univ. Press.

Rasler, Karen, and William R. Thompson. 1989. *War and State Making: The Shaping of the Global Powers.* Boston: Unwin Hyman.

Sundberg, Ulf, et al. 1994. "Forest EMERGY Basis for Swedish Power in the Seventeenth Century." *Scandinavian Journal of Forest Research* 1 (supp.).

Tainter, Joseph A. 1992. "Evolutionary Consequences of War." In *Effects of War on Society,* edited by G. Ausenda, 103–30. San Marino, Calif.: Center for Interdisciplinary Research on Social Stress.

———. 1996. "Competition, Expansion, and Reaction: The Foundations of Contemporary Conflict." In *The Coming Age of Scarcity: Preventing Mass Death and Genocide in the Twenty-first century,* edited by Michael N. Dobkowski and Isidor Wallimann, 174–93. Syracuse: Syracuse Univ. Press.

Wall, Alex de. 1994. "The Genocidal State: Hutu Extremism and the Origins of the 'Final Solution' in Rwanda." *Times Literary Supplement* 4761 (July 1): 3–4.

9

Sustainable Development and Human Security

Can We Learn from Bosnia, Kosovo, Somalia, and Haiti?

Waltraud Queiser Morales

One possible alternative explanation for the rise in hostilities during past years is the cumulative effect of decades of unsustainable development, the consequences and pressures of which have begun to undermine the well-being and security of many countries.

—Hal Kane, "The Hour of Departure"

Resource Scarcity and Violence

RESOURCE WARS describe a phenomenon as old as humankind itself. Despite the biblical images of Adam and Eve partaking of unlimited bounty in the Garden of Eden, through the ages mankind has struggled with both absolute and relative scarcity. Historically, scarcity has been imposed by two dominant causes. The first cause relates to geographical, ecological, and climatic limitations over which humankind has had only partial control. The second cause relates to the social and political conditions of inequality and injustice that humankind has created and perpetuated in its struggle for power and dominance globally and within states. As the cold war began in the late 1940s, a noted North American statesman celebrated as the father of anticommunist containment, George Kennan, warned fellow policy makers of the coming age of scarcity and the fierce challenge that resource scarcity would pose for the foreign policy of the

121

United States. In a secret policy brief, Kennan bluntly advised: "We have about 50% of the world's wealth but only 6.3% of its population. . . . Our real task in the coming period is to devise a pattern of relationships which will permit us to maintain this position of disparity without positive detriment to our national security" (cited in Etzold and Gaddis 1978, 227). In short, the challenge was to devise a strategy of permanent global inequality whereby the people of the United States could continue to live in prosperity in a world of limited and shrinking resources.

Scarcity has proved to be the curse of both the cold war and the post–cold war generations for the majority of the world's developing nations. Indeed, with the beginning of the twenty-first century, intrastate conflict has supplanted interstate conflict as the pattern of warfare.[1] Much of this violence within states has been aggravated by economic deprivation and scarcity. Theories of revolution and instability have long emphasized the important role of economic scarcity as a prime facilitator of violence. Economic conditions of deprivation, inequality, and underdevelopment exacerbated the tribal, ethnic, racial, and nationalist divisions that characterized much of the conflict of the twentieth century.

Nation-states around the world have experienced severe social fragmentation, giving new meaning to the term *balkanization*. For example, the disintegration of the former Yugoslavia has led to intrastate conflict in Bosnia and Kosovo, and fears of a similar outbreak in Macedonia. Tribal violence and postcolonial power struggles continue to ravage Somalia. In Haiti, a postrevolutionary society struggles to establish democracy and economic viability. In the aftermath of intrastate conflicts, these countries seek to achieve a form of equitable and sustainable development that will break the brutal cycle of poverty, group rivalry, and violence.

Why are the states of the twenty-first century seemingly more vulnerable to internal disintegration and internal violence? Increased relative economic scarcity and deprivation clearly have been part of the answer. In societies from the former Soviet Union, former Yugoslavia, to the former colonial regions of Rwanda, Liberia, the Congo, Zimbabwe, Liberia,

---

1. Intrastate violence or conflict is understood as violence between or among one or more advantaged or disadvantaged minority or majority groups, and one or more of these groups and the political and juridical state, in order to gain either a greater share of limited resources or to secure control or autonomy or both over the territorial state. Violence may take on ethnonationalist, tribal, indigenist, or religious dynamics.

Ethiopia, Sudan, Afghanistan, Indonesia, East Timor, El Salvador, and Guatemala, to name but a few, increased pressure on scarce resources and the struggle to achieve sustainable development with justice and equity have contributed to bloody revolutions and civil wars. Scarcity, although downplayed by some theories of violence, has been a primary and secondary explanation for increased civil unrest. Moreover, whether relative or absolute, scarcity has activated the process of internal "balkanization" and social disintegration. Both "objective" and "subjective" increases in socioeconomic competition for scarce state resources have been essential preconditions of intrastate violence. Scarcity, especially when aggravated by inequality, has intensified the "us" versus "them" polarizations in most developing societies.

Therefore, this overview suggests that the socioeconomic scarcity that in large part unsustainable development has created and perpetuated is an important explanation of global wars, ethnic violence, and civil unrest within and among states. Recently, the importance of resource scarcity and socioeconomic deprivation has been obscured by an emphasis on the cultural, ethnic, and nationality factors as causes of violence. Additionally, the fixation with the technological and military-hardware dimensions of national security has ignored the fact that resource deprivation is closely linked to the global struggle for sustainable development. What is really at issue is the collective survival of mankind in an era of ever increasing scarcity and inequality, and it is this global struggle that has been mirrored in localized, intrastate conflict. A review of four cases of intrastate conflict in Bosnia, Kosovo, Somalia, and Haiti demonstrates that "no country is an island." In the final reckoning, resource deprivation and depletion among the world's poorest nations are integrally linked to global sustainability and human security.

Why Intrastate Conflict?

Because of rapid global changes, the twenty-first century has seen a proliferation in the causes of conflict and in popular theories that try to explain that conflict. An important part of the difficulty is that the traditional distinctions between revolution and war, interstate and intrastate violence, and internal and external conditions of strife have all basically collapsed. At the same time, theories of war, revolution, and intrastate violence have become closely linked to theories of racial, indigenous, and ethnonationalist resurgences and rebellions. Domestic and international dimensions of conflict have become tightly intertwined, and conflicts, such as the ones in Bosnia and Kosovo, not only have bridged the conceptual and actual barriers between internal and external war, but also have recombined intrastate and interstate violence in novel ways. Multilateral interventions around the world, especially the peacekeeping operations in Somalia, Haiti, Bosnia, and Kosovo, have further demonstrated the significant deterioration in state boundaries, authority, and sovereignty. Indeed, war and revolution in the twenty-first century have become two sides of a single coin.

In the search for explanations, "politicized ethnicity" has been isolated as a prime mover in both intrastate and interstate conflict. Among the competing theorists who attempt to explain intrastate violence, James Kellas (1991) and Ted Gurr (1993) emphasize the causal importance of minority-group relations with a dominant majority group and the presence of ethnic conflict. They identify various economic, social, psychological, and cultural mechanisms as key triggers that create or intensify antagonistic in-group and out-group perceptions, attitudes, and behaviors. Both argue that an important indicator of the potential for intrastate conflict is whether ethnic, racial, or nationality groups aspire to revolutionary political or territorial claims or both.

Another potential explanation of intrastate violence is found in sociobiology. Kellas concludes that although "identity and behavior are partly genetic," they are also influenced by context and choice (1991, 19). For example, politicians routinely manipulate group identities for their own ends. Indeed, such political manipulation by unscrupulous political leaders was an important element in the cases of Bosnia, Kosovo, Haiti, and Somalia. Human nature may provide the "necessary" conditions for ethnocentric or racist behavior, but politics converts them into the "sufficient conditions" for ethnic and racial violence. Gurr also emphasizes "politicized communal groups" formed against socioeconomic conditions of discrimination and deprivation. In his words, "treat a group differently, by denial or privilege, and its members become more self-conscious about their common bonds and interests" (1993, 3). The experiences of discrimination (economic or political) and the politicization of group interests provide the sufficient conditions for intrastate conflict.

Considering human nature and sociobiology, theorists Paul Shaw and Yuwa Wong propose a connection between violence and the genetic predisposition to kin selection. Over evolutionary time, kin selection and environmental forces have predisposed "genetically related individuals to band together in groups, oriented for conflict" (1987, 5). In short, intergroup conflict relates to successful reproductive fitness and survival of close relatives. Although controversial, of interest to an explanation of the causes of intrastate conflict and violence are the environmental, structural, and socioeconomic conditions that trigger violent behavior. According to their theory, the biological processes underlying human cooperation and aggression are "exacerbated under conditions of scarce resources or stress" (6).

All four theorists concur that socioeconomic mechanisms of scarcity, deprivation, competition, and economic discrimination are instrumental in causing in-group versus out-group conflict. Material deprivation (often extreme impoverishment) and systematic discrimination (by dominant groups and advantaged minorities) may threaten the group's physical survival. In this sense, resource scarcity activates group conflict and transforms it into intrastate and ethnonationalist violence. This convergence of grievances, according to Ernest Gellner, creates the volatile combination of "nation-classes" that define themselves ethnically, and "class-nations" that develop class consciousness and activism (quoted in Kellas 1991, 41–44).

This brief review of relevant theories of intrastate conflict indicates that conditions of regional and global scarcity are potentially devastating for the future of human cooperation and the delicate calculus between war and peace. At no time in human history does it seem more vital that both civil and global society function as a "collective survival enterprise." Certainly, a more supportive context for human behavior would reduce or eliminate the dehumanizing conditions of resource scarcity and inequality at all levels of social organization. A necessary step toward a comprehensive solution to global scarcity and intrastate conflict is the implementation of a global policy of sustainable development within a just international economic order.

Collective Survival of Humankind

A "new cold war" or North-South resource war directed against the developing world has replaced the ideological East-West cold war of old. The only way to "win" this new war is to resolve the global crises of poverty, scarcity, overpopulation, and chronic underdevelopment. Despite the professed policies of democratization, nation building, and sustainable development by northern governments, the goals remain elusive. Indeed, the rhetoric may mask a process that has been characterized as the "structural resubordination" of the developing world by the rich and powerful countries. This neocontainment of the developing nations intends to maintain the global disparity in resource distribution primarily through orthodox and free-market development policies. Narrow ideologies of economic individualism and growth undergird traditional development models and the inequitable global economic order. Can the egoistic development of global resources be replaced by a sustainable and communal model?

Sustainable development broadly means meeting present needs without destroying resources that will be needed in the future. However, agreeing on the what and how of sustainable development has been problematical and controversial from the start. In 1987, the United Nations World Commission on Environment and Development (the Brundtland Commission) interpreted sustainable development as "sustainable industrial development." In 1992, the UN conference on environment and development, the Rio Earth Summit, equated sustainable development with the "greening" of traditional development. Rio popularized the myopia that "clean growth" that minimized environmental and ecological damage and "eco-efficiency," or efficient growth, could resolve the scarcity crisis. The Earth Summit also legitimated transnational corporations as major global actors in sustainable development, rehabilitating them as part of the solution rather than the problem that they had partly helped create. At Rio the TNCs and mainstream NGOs recognized that their brand of environmentalism and sustainable development was profitable.

As long as sustainable development is defined by "unsustainable development models" that fail to question the traditional assumptions of unlimited growth and industrialization, the real global crisis and its solutions will be overlooked. The popular myth of development as unlimited growth dies hard. Nevertheless, we can no longer be seduced by the illusory promises of technocratic solutions to scarcity and underdevelopment, and the comfortable belief that everyone can attain First World lifestyles without limiting growth and consumption. Such thinking is itself a cause of global scarcity and conflict.

Learning from Cases of Intrastate Conflict

The country cases of Bosnia, Kosovo, Somalia, and Haiti demonstrate that the environmental and socioeconomic conditions of intrastate violence already discussed were generally shared. First, these diverse cases reveal uncommonly similar histories of internal economic, social, cultural, and political oppression and exploitation. Second, all four societies experienced colonialism and dependent (unbalanced and exploitative) development. Third, the imposition of traditional and unsustainable development policies aggravated conditions of resource scarcity, poverty, and ecological and environmental devastation. Fourth, ethnic and religious differences and nationalist sentiments were egregiously manipulated to intensify socioeconomic discrimination against out-groups. Fifth, radical shifts in the balance of power within states and among minority-majority group relations fostered instability. Sixth, localized instability and conflict threatened the continued prosperity of neighboring countries and regions, as well as global peace.

Above all, an important lesson that we must learn from the intrastate violence in Bosnia, Kosovo, Somalia, and Haiti is that societies do disintegrate under the strains of life-and-death competition for scarce resources. When economic deprivation is based upon hateful ethnic and group discrimination as in Bosnia, Kosovo, Somalia, and Haiti, multiethnic states can easily fragment into "politicized communal groups," and contentious "nation-classes" or "class-nations." With time, collective insecurities and fears for the very physical survival of one's group find release in bloody internal conflicts.

Bosnia and Kosovo

The Balkan wars have confused the experts and challenged traditional assumptions. Were these intrastate or interstate conflicts, civil wars, interethnic wars, religious wars, or international aggression? In a sense, intrastate conflict in Bosnia and Kosovo involved all of these possibilities; it challenged the sanctity of international borders and threatened proliferation from a Balkan to a wider European war. And with the swell of refugees fleeing genocide and "ethnic cleansing," both conflicts fed fears of global ethnic warfare. What were the causes of the Bosnian and Kosovo conflicts? And what was the role of unsustainable development and re-source scarcity in the outbreak of the devastating intrastate conflicts in the Balkans?

The first stage of the recent Balkan crisis began in 1991 when the for-mer Communist state of Yugoslavia, comprising six component republics and regions (Bosnia, Croatia, Macedonia, Montenegro, Serbia, and Slove-nia), disintegrated. After the death of Tito in 1980 and the demise of com-munism since 1987, the multiethnic state could not withstand the resurgence of ethnic divisions and fears. In 1991, Milosevic's attempts to make Greater Serbia the dominant nationality of the new post-Communist Yugoslavia precipitated the secession of Slovenia and Croatia and the outbreak of war. Soon ethnic Serbs living in the newly independ-ent Croatia sought to secede, create their own independent republic (Kra-jina), and reunite with Serbia proper. The new Croatian government violently repressed the secession, but in the end lost 30 percent of its territory.

By 1992, Bosnian Moslems also voted to secede from Yugoslavia, but Bosnian Serbs boycotted the vote and began a resistance war against the new government. Nevertheless, the United States and European Commu-nity recognized the secession of Slovenia and Croatia in 1991, and of Bosnia-Herzegovina in 1992. Slobodan Milosevic, leader of what was left of Yugoslavia, armed the local Bosnian Serb resistance and escalated the conflict into a trilateral Yugoslavian war of Croatia, Serbia and Bosnian Serbs, and Bosnian Moslems. UN peacekeeping troops were dispatched to contain the conflict in early 1992. Despite some twenty-five thousand peacekeepers, largely from Western European countries and the United States, there were hundreds of thousands of deaths and 3 million refugees before a precarious status quo was imposed by the Dayton Peace Accords in December 1995.

A similar violent and disastrous scenario unfolded in Kosovo, a region heavily populated by ethnic Albanian and Moslem people but dominated by Serbia. The political and economic crises of the 1980s and renewed Serbian nationalism led the majority Albanians (90 percent) in Kosovo to also demand more autonomy and ethnic rights. But Milosevic, unwilling to lose control of Kosovo, part of the historic heartland of Serbian nation-hood, ordered the army to crush Albanian demonstrations. Clearly, Kosovo was not Bosnia. Despite a similar disintegration of state and soci-ety, ethnic rivalry, and fears of a wider war, Kosovo was basically an intrastate conflict between Yugoslavia (mainly Serbia) and its province (Kosovo). Unlike Bosnia, the international community opposed Kosovar independence and sent in UN and NATO forces on a limited mission to prevent humanitarian atrocities and end Serbia's brutal ethnic cleansing. This time, Milosevic's genocide in Kosovo branded him an indicted war criminal instead of an equal partner in a peace process as in the Bosnian war. In the end, the NATO bombings (which lasted seventy-eight days and included forty thousand missions) and the protracted humanitarian intervention have meant more suffering and casualties among the refugees.

In both Balkan conflicts, disadvantaged minorities and majorities were subject to economic, social, cultural, and political oppression. The realignment of internal and external borders destabilized the relationships among minority and majority ethnic groups. For example, in an independent Bosnia, the Bosnian Serbs feared becoming a disadvantaged minority (31 percent of the population) in a state controlled by Moslems (44 percent of the population). Similarly, in an autonomous or independent Kosovo, the Serbian population (less than 10 percent) would become a potentially disadvantaged minority in the 90 percent Albanian-dominated state rather than retain the advantages of the Serb majority in Yugoslavia.

Also behind the Balkan crises were depressed and discriminatory economic conditions that systematically disadvantaged the weakest and poorest ethnic groups and regions. Uneven economic development and internal colonialism reinforced scarcity and inequality. Thus, the economic downturn in the 1980s had a greater impact in Kosovo, one of the poorest regions of Yugoslavia, and in the less-developed Bosnia. Misconceived and unsustainable development models promoted wasteful industrialization and reinforced existing inequalities and resource scarcities. At the same time, because economic discrimination against Kosovo's Albanians and Bosnian Moslems was popularly rationalized by hateful racist and nationalist prejudices, ethnic resentment and mistrust among ethnic groups festered and ultimately exploded in violence.

Somalia and Haiti

Although in two very different parts of the world, these two black nations have experienced some of the worst conditions of resource competition and scarcity. In Somalia and Haiti, severe environmental degradation contributed to massive social disruption and both class and ethnic conflict. In Haiti, intrastate violence escalated with the genocidal revolution of 1986 that overthrew the corrupt and brutal dictatorship of the Duvalier family. In Somalia, a major regional war (the Somali-Ethiopian war in the Ogaden in 1977–1978) and a protracted civil war (1988–1991) that deposed the longtime dictator, Siad Barre, devastated the land, created a massive refugee crisis, and reinforced a cycle of mass famine. In both cases, intrastate conflict was precipitated and aggravated by conditions of deprivation and unequal and unsustainable development.

The 1992 humanitarian intervention in Somalia was initially precipitated by mass starvation that threatened 2 million people, but the underlying problem was intrastate violence among some fifteen warring tribal clans and the resource competition and environmental destruction that chronic civil war caused. In times of extreme scarcity, food and resources were divided along tribal and class lines with the dominant clans discriminating against the out-groups. Therefore, in Somalia, once tribal identities were reinforced by socioeconomic and class differences, and aggravated by scarcity and famine, the key preconditions of instrastate violence were in place. The overthrow of the Barre dictatorship also destabilized the balance of minority—and majority-group relations and created a political vacuum that quickly disintegrated into social and political chaos.

Somalia, like Haiti, is one of the world's poorest countries, chronically dependent on food imports, and with scarce arable land, subject to misuse by farmers, overgrazing by nomadic herdsmen, and desertification. The economic development model, again like Haiti's, relied on foreign aid (largely from the United States), and cash crop–primary exports. Both countries suffered from extreme trade imbalances with imports greatly exceeding exports, foreign debts, and severe IMF structural adjustments (imposed economic belt-tightening). Much foreign aid, as in Haiti, was food aid, which served to undermine local farm prices and impede agricultural sustainability. Northern focus on "growth" areas for development assistance in Somalia and Haiti ignored the importance of sustainable development and left the poorest of the poor few alternatives than humanitarian assistance or the destruction of their environment in their desperation to survive day to day. In short, Somalia (not unlike Haiti) was a hapless victim of both cold war and post–cold war politics and shortsighted and exploitative northern models of unsustainable development. The years since the 1992–1993 humanitarian intervention have seen few solutions to the endemic causes of hunger, scarcity, and conflict that continue to wrack Somalia. Somehow it seems that the $3–4 billion that were expended on the UN humanitarian operation could have been used more effectively to promote sustainable development.

In Haiti, the conditions after the 1986 revolution and the 1994 humanitarian intervention have not improved significantly either. The peasantry, the dispossessed of Haiti, continue to suffer desperate poverty, political repression, and systematic violence. Haiti's economic and social history has been one of internal and external colonialism: exploitation by dictators and Creole elites from within (François "Papa Doc" and Jean Claude "Baby Doc" Duvalier) and by foreign interests (the United States) from without. Haiti's unsustainable development model relied on the export of primary commodities and assembly products to U.S. and global markets, and on foreign assistance from the United States. Haitian peasants have served as a large, cheap, and nonunionized labor pool for U.S. industries. This development model has not only been unsustainable environmentally but also contributed to an absolute poverty level of $60–100 per capita yearly income for more than 60 percent of Haitians. Cultivation of land for food was shifted to export crops, forcing the starving peasants to denude the island for cheap firewood to sell and exhaust the sparse and depleted arable land. Haiti's soil and resource depletions portend a major environmental and ecological disaster.

In the ten years since the 1986 revolution, Haitians experienced terrible violations of human rights and outright genocide by the state's military and security forces. The 1994 U.S.-UN humanitarian intervention served to moderate some of the worst abuses, but the ultimate result has been the shift of power to a more conservative minority ruling class—a new Creole elite—and through them the containment of Haiti's popular revolution. In the process, sustainable development has yet to be achieved; until it is, internal conflict and violence are unlikely to end in Haiti.

Ways Out

More global conflicts of the twenty-first century will be rooted in the convergence of resource scarcity and environmental depletion. Scarcity intensifies human degradation and deprivation, and ethnopolitical and religious hatreds. Unless action is taken, these conditions will provoke more violent intrastate conflict and ultimately threaten the collective survival of humankind. What can and should be done to avoid such catastrophe? As in all problem solving, the logical and vital first step is to identify the problem correctly, because a mismatch between problem and solution invites failure. Therefore, this investigation is the first step in systematically identifying and addressing the causes of intrastate conflict.

The challenging second step is the search for solutions and comprehensive policy changes. Among the actions that can be taken to prevent more intrastate conflict and further social and political disintegration are changes in our fundamental attitudes and loyalties. It is critical to define state and national security in more humane terms, so that the peoples whom governments claim to protect come first and their political and economic human rights are fundamentally respected and preserved. State security must also be understood in more comprehensive and holistic terms. Survival is inherently indivisible. And in the absence of sustainable development, exhaustive resource competition will promote resource scarcity and speed environmental collapse. In the end, humankind will no longer have homes or societies to protect. Thus, human security must be accepted as the only real security.

Global interdependence and globalization in the twenty-first century mean that distant crises of famine, disease, environmental degradation, and ethnic strife cannot be ignored, isolated, or confined within national borders. No longer can any individual, group, nation, or state remain an island unto itself. Collective interests must replace narrow self-interests. Each one of us must take to heart and act upon the clear lesson revealed in this examination of the theories and cases of intrastate violence. Unless the survival of the few means the survival of all, future intrastate conflict is inevitable. The future portends immense challenge. If it is to be met successfully, then citizens must support national and international policies that will achieve the goals of sustainable development, equitable and limited resource consumption, and the elimination of poverty and scarcity. The collective survival of humankind demands radical and immediate changes in how we think and act today.

Suggested Reading

Bello, Walden, with Shea Cunningham and Bill Rau. 1994. *Dark Victory: The United States, Structural Adjustment, and Global Poverty.* London: Pluto Press, for Institute for Food and Development Policy, or Food First.

Chatterjee, Pratap, and Matthias Finger. 1994. *The Earth Brokers: Power, Politics, and World Development.* New York: Routledge.

Etzold, Thomas H., and John Lewis Gaddis, eds. 1978. *Containment: Documents on American Policy and Strategy.* Vol. 2, *1945–1950.* New York: Columbia Univ. Press.

Gurr, Ted Robert. 1993. *Minorities at Risk: A Global View of Ethnopolitical Conflict.* Washington, D.C.: U.S. Institute of Peace.

Human Rights Watch. 1995. *Slaughter among Neighbors: The Political Origins of Communal Violence.* New Haven: Yale Univ. Press.

Kane, Hal. 1995. "The Hour of Departure: Forces That Create Refugees and Migrants." *World Watch Paper* 125 (June): 5–56.

Kellas, James G. 1991. *The Politics of Nationalism and Ethnicity.* New York: St. Martin's Press.

Morales, Waltraud Queiser. 1998. "Intrastate Conflict and Sustainable Development." In *The Coming Age of Scarcity: Preventing Mass Death and Genocide in the Twenty-first Century,* edited by Michael Dobkowski and Isidor Wallimann, 245–68. Syracuse: Syracuse Univ. Press.

Shaw, R. Paul, and Yuwa Wong. 1987. "Ethnic Mobilization and the Seeds of Warfare: An Evolutionary Perspective." *International Studies Quarterly* 31, no. 1 (Mar.): 5–31.

United Nations Development Program. 1995. "Redefining Security: The Human Dimension." *Current History* 94, no. 592 (May): 229–36.

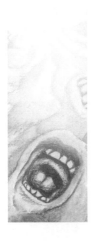

Part Three

CASE STUDIES OF SCARCITY AND
MASS DEATH

Introduction

THE TRAGIC VIOLENCE we have witnessed recently in Bosnia, Somalia, East Timor, and Rwanda has some common roots. Resource scarcity is a necessary precondition that apparently activates group conflict and transforms it into the virulent ethnonationalist violence we are seeing with greater frequency. It may be a precursor of genocidal incidents and tendencies that will be only more pronounced as resource-scarcity problems and population pressures continue to intensify in the coming decades. If current ecological and demographic trends continue apace, particularly population growth combined with resource depletion, this situation will put added pressure on already fragile social and political systems in the affected parts of the world. These areas, as Roger Smith, David Smith, and Waltraud Morales point out, are the very places where much of genocide since 1945 has occurred. To forestall what may be likely, if not inevitable, as Leon Rappoport argues, we need major paradigm shifts in values, psychology, politics, and economic organization. The authors in this final section begin to address the threat of proliferating genocides and offer some possible solutions.

10

Scarcity and Genocide

Roger W. Smith

GENOCIDE IS NOT INEVITABLE; it is a political choice. But political choices, including genocide, are effected by many different forces, internal and external. Scarcity will increasingly be one of those forces in the not-so-distant future.

The question of the relationships between scarcity and genocide is an important one, both in terms of understanding the causes of genocide and in anticipating the prospects for genocide in the twenty-first century. If current trends continue, a combination of environmental degradation, loss of agricultural land, depletion of fish stocks, dwindling of fuel resources, and a doubling of population to around 11 billion persons in the latter part of the century will lead to conditions of extreme hardship, even disaster, in many parts of the world. These areas, mainly in the Third World, are the very places where much of the genocide since 1945 has taken place.

The genocides that have occurred in Bangladesh, Burundi, Cambodia, Indonesia, and Rwanda, however, have not been brought about by material scarcity. In fact, genocide, with some exceptions to be noted later, has seldom been the result of material scarcity; on the contrary, material scarcity has often been a direct result of genocide. Nevertheless, in a world that in the twentieth century displayed an unparalleled capacity for mass slaughter, it would be surprising if severe shortages would not exacerbate existing tendencies toward resolving social and political problems through elimination of the groups thought to constitute the problem.

"Scarcity" is a concept that includes both the relative and the absolute. For those people used to affluence and abundance, a mild reduction in goods available to them will be perceived as a matter of scarcity; similarly, they may feel worse off if other persons improve their material condition while they remain at their previous level. Scarcity, in these instances, is not only relative, but also psychological: desire is confused with need. Psychological scarcity is an important facet of the "developmental" genocide that indigenous peoples have faced, and, most likely, will face. Although many philosophers have seen "desire" and its control as a crucial problem, the modern view, one that underlies ideas of progress and development, is that the expansion of desire and continual efforts to satisfy its expectations thereby created are the principal reasons for social existence. It is this artificial scarcity, a scarcity created by desire rather than need, that in large part drives the development projects that have destroyed the lives of indigenous peoples in the name of "progress." Scarcity may also be both absolute and material: without food and water for a certain period, we, of course, die.

Considered in material terms, scarcity can take at least two different forms. First, there may be a scarcity of resources—little usable land, forests that have been depleted, minerals long ago extracted from the soil. Some of these resources can be renewed, whereas others are simply no longer there. Whether resources are renewable or not is itself an important dimension of overcoming scarcity and any role it may have in prompting murderous conflict. Second, resources may be scarce because of the size of the population: even if all goods were distributed equally, there would still be generalized poverty. In order to overcome this kind of scarcity, either the material resources would have to be increased (the green revolution in agriculture, for instance) or the population would have to be decreased.

In addition to psychological scarcity and the material scarcities described, there is a kind of scarcity—political scarcity—that includes both material and political deprivation. Where political scarcity exists, there may be sufficient resources to meet everyone's needs, but the allocation of resources favors certain groups and discriminates against other groups. In practice, there will often be a scarcity of resources and an expanding population, both of which may contribute further to policies of unequal distribution of goods. Such situations frequently exist in ethnically divided ("plural") societies and help to drive demands for equal treatment, demands that may be met with repression and, if the conflict persists, with an attempt at partial or total genocide. Power sharing, protection of basic rights, and equality of treatment could go a long way in overcoming the difficulties otherwise exacerbated by deteriorating resources and expansion of population.

The relationships between genocide and scarcity fall into four broad patterns. First of all, genocide typically produces scarcity: it creates social chaos; disrupts the economy; destroys the lives of hundreds of thousands, even millions, of persons who possess skills and productive capacities; and diverts the perpetrators themselves from their role in economic life, turning them into persons who destroy rather than produce and create. In extreme cases, such as that of Rwanda, economic production may cease altogether. Moreover, in many instances, disease may sweep through the society, facilitated in part by famine, water sources contaminated by the dead, and lack of sanitation. Where the genocide occurs in the context of war, as in Bosnia, human habitations, production facilities, and the environment itself may all suffer significant damage, creating additional material scarcities.

If genocide falls most heavily upon the intended victims, the perpetrators are not immune to the scarcities it induces. In Cambodia, for example, hundreds of thousands of people whom the Khmer Rouge tried to turn into the foundation of a peasant society died from malnutrition brought about by its agricultural policies. Although humanitarian aid in the form of both food and medicine was available, the Khmer Rouge would not accept it for ideological reasons: its vision was of a self-sufficient peasant society; moreover, if food was scarce, the regime maintained it was due to sabotage by "enemies of the revolution," not any failure of the revolutionary design itself.

Perpetrators may be so intent upon destroying a group that they fail to calculate the effects that their actions will have on themselves. Or there may be a recognition of this consequence, but the calculus used to assess costs and benefits is one that stresses ideology, revenge, or power rather than the material well-being of the perpetrator group.

There is one type of genocide in which scarcity falls almost entirely upon the victims. In developmental genocide, it is the indigenous peoples' land that is taken and their sources of food eliminated. The perpetrators, on the other hand, gain land, gold, timber, or cheap electricity from the hydroelectric projects erected on the indigenous peoples' territory.

Scarcities that stem from genocide may be either short-term (a temporary shortage of food, for example) or long-lasting (where much of the existing housing is damaged or destroyed, as in Bosnia). In some cases, the damage to the economy will continue for generations: eighty-six years after the 1915 genocide of the Armenians, lands that were once highly productive lie barren in eastern Turkey.

Direct conflict over scarce resources is another recurrent theme. It is likely to occur in three situations, each of which is compatible with genocidal actions. The first is the result of migration into areas occupied by other groups. A well-known example of this occurrence is the Israelite exodus from Egypt, their migration into Canaan, and the ensuing wars over resources that the early books of the Bible invariably depict as wars of extermination. Migration may itself result from lack of adequate resources, but more commonly in the modern world from persecution, war, and genocide.

Direct conflict over material resources is also likely where resources held by indigenous peoples are slated for "development." Much of the scarcity perceived by the ones who set development into motion involves a lack of abundance rather than economic hardship. The other form of scarcity involved here is the maldistribution of resources, particularly land, within the perpetrators' territory, rather than a lack of resources. One of the reasons that development appeals to political and economic elites ("progress" is another) is that it offers a kind of safety valve to release the frustrations of the landless and the impoverished without requiring any redistribution of resources held by the elites. The costs of development will be borne instead by those people whose lands are taken. There are currently some 200 million indigenous peoples around the world, most of whom are already vulnerable to existing pressures for greater and more productive utilization of resources. Given an age of scarcity in the twenty-first century, the future of indigenous peoples would appear to be bleak.

The third basis for direct conflict over resources occurs when a state collapses, followed by fragmentation, with no group capable of gaining overall power or control. When a state fails, with the consequent breakdown of security for life and property, scarcity can be expected to increase, leading to a struggle over basic resources.

In principle, a dominant group may arise out of the "state of nature" and impose a repressive order. But it is possible that a variety of groups will sustain the low-level conflict for many years, with repeated genocidal attacks being made by all sides. Genocide, rather than being exceptional, would become part of an equilibrium of destruction. Under these conditions, life would almost certainly be "poor, nasty, brutish, and short." In this situation, any distinction between war and crime, and war and genocide, would blur or disappear.

The history of genocide also provides many examples of the act being carried out primarily through depriving the victims of food. Ancient warfare was synonymous with genocide; when a walled city offered resistance, the perpetrators would resort to siege warfare, cutting the inhabitants off from fresh supplies of food and drink. Eventually, the people within the city would starve or would capitulate and then be killed or enslaved. During the Spanish "conquest" of Mexico, Indians were forced into submission or died by starvation when their supplies of food were confiscated and their crops burned. A modern example is the Stalinist man-made famine of 1932–1933 in Soviet Ukraine that led to the death by starvation of some 5 million Ukrainians, most of them the very peasants who had produced the grain that was confiscated. A calculated policy to force peasants into collective agriculture and to crush a rising Ukrainian nationalism led, in two years, to the death of almost 20 percent of the population.

Scarcity, particularly in its psychological and political forms, has played a role in genocide for centuries; material scarcity has less rarely been a source for mass killing. Other motives have included conquest, retribution, dominance, and, where certain ideologies were involved, the total remaking of society to achieve salvation and purification. Although many of the motives and pressures for genocide that have existed from ancient times to the present will likely continue, it may be that we are entering an age in which scarcity in its various forms will increasingly contribute to the decision to resort to genocide. In this context, "scarcity" includes degradation and depletion of natural resources, fewer goods per capita due to population growth, and unequal resource distribution. It also includes the psychological and political scarcities that play a role in the genocide of indigenous peoples and minorities in plural societies. Each form of scarcity can contribute to the conditions that make genocide more likely: they include conflict over resources; population displacement and ensuing conflict between groups; allocation of resources along racial, religious, or ethnic lines, resulting in demands for autonomy or independence; and weakening of the legitimacy of the state, followed by either revolution, an attempt at secession, or a growing authoritarianism that seeks to solve social and political problems by force. New ideologies may also arise, and are likely to be formulated along lines of ethnicity or religion. In some instances, states may fragment into warring groups, with no group able to achieve dominance, but able to decimate other groups in intermittent combat. Finally, genocide itself begets new, especially material, scarcities, laying the basis for further violence in the future.

To spell out one example of the possible effects of scarcity contributing to genocide: where the legitimacy of the state or the ruling group in a plural society is challenged, it is likely that the old regime will resort to authoritarian solutions to hold onto power. But in so doing, it will further alienate the minority groups that it has previously excluded from power. This alienation will provoke further challenge to the elite's authority, which will be met with greater force, including massacres. This example is, in fact, the classic case of what leads to genocide in ethnically divided, plural societies. If there is also the problem of material scarcity, which is likely to be accentuated in the future, then increasing demands will be made on those people in power. These demands, due to lack of resources, competence, or fairness, will not be met, resulting in further erosion in the legitimacy of rule by the dominant elite. In such a situation, the tendency is to crack down on the ones making the demands, but also to allocate scarce resources even more decidedly along ethnic lines, favoring members of the dominant group. This result is in part a matter of what might be called a politics of identity, in which one favors one's own group, but also in part a strategy to reward those citizens thought to be loyal to the people in power. The end result will be that in times of scarcity, the regime will move from its usual pattern of discrimination to a policy that increases hardship and, at the extreme, leads to destitution. If the destitute have the means to resist, then this violence will in turn generate a new spiral of repression, beginning with massacres, which are a way of keeping a group in its place, and possibly ending with genocide, which attempts to eliminate the group itself.

In this scenario, a type of society (plural), a type of regime (authoritarian), a type of policy (unequal allocation of resources), a challenge to that policy (by the group that is viewed as inferior and excluded from power), and material scarcity (whatever its sources) come together in a mix that is fatal.

Preventing Genocide

Those people who study genocide do so in order to understand why such extreme violence takes place and why it is directed at particular groups.

The quest to understand, however, is a desire not only to know, but also to find ways in which that understanding can be used to prevent future acts of genocide. As previously mentioned, there is nothing inevitable about genocide; nevertheless, there are certain predisposing elements, and the likelihood of preventing genocide is enhanced if they can be overcome. The chapter will conclude with some reflections upon possible means of removing the links between genocide and scarcity.

The means fall into two broad patterns. First, there is the question of how "scarcity" can be dealt with so that it does not put pressure on regimes to commit genocide. Second, there is the more general question of how genocide can be prevented, even if such pressures cannot be wholly removed.

Reducing Scarcities

As we have seen, "scarcity" takes a number of different forms: psychological, political, and material. Let us consider each in turn.

The psychological expectation of ever increasing material satisfaction is deeply embedded in the modern worldview, but instead of attempting to dominate nature, we could respect and work with it, seeing ourselves as part of nature, and dependent upon it for our very existence. Another approach would call attention to the fact that cutting down rain forests, for example, is not the best use to which they can be put, and that many large-scale development projects in indigenous areas have been failures at great cost in terms of lives, money, and damage to the environment.

Deprivation, on the other hand, is the hallmark of political scarcity. It contains three elements: deprivation in terms of power, material well-being, and respect. Plural societies often display these forms of deprivation, prompting challenges to the structure of authority, and leading in turn to repression, renewed demands for equality or autonomy, and, without outside intervention, genocide. In fact, the most frequent source of genocide in the twentieth century was that which sprang from the political scarcity imposed by domination and exclusion. The question, then, is not only of divided societies, but also of authoritarian government.

The conditions for averting genocide that arises in part from political scarcity are reasonably clear. Some form of power sharing would be necessary. The precise form it would take could vary from society to society, but it might involve, for example, federalism, a degree of autonomy, or certain offices, or a percentage of offices in the military, bureaucracy, or parliament, being reserved for members of the previously subordinate group. It would require justice in the allocation of goods. And finally, it would require some degree of acceptance of the minority group as persons, and the repudiation of stereotypes and prejudices that had served as justifications for exclusion from equal treatment.

The conditions are easily stated, but societies have their own histories, and their social arrangements are not accidental. The alternative to changing the existing arrangements is outside intervention.

The third form of scarcity is the most obvious and the most difficult to overcome. Material scarcity has two possible sources: resources either are not available or have been degraded in ways that make them less productive, and there may be fewer goods per capita due to population expansion. The solutions to resource scarcity and population explosion are both technical and political. Further, these two sources of scarcity are so entangled that it is not possible to solve one without the other.

High growth rates in population tend to occur precisely in societies that can least afford them, those places that are already resource scarce or whose government allocates resources in ways that favor some groups and deprive others. Given the existing strains in such societies, rapid population growth will lead to increased scarcity, violence, and possible genocide. The spiral of scarcity will increase both because goods now have to be divided among more people and because attempts to increase production (especially of food and shelter) often produce severe ecological damage, undermining further the capacity to meet material needs.

Populations in the past have been reduced within a specific territory by migration, disease, famine, war, and genocide. These factors may operate in the future; less apocalyptic visions, however, are possible, though they are not without their own difficulties in terms of implementation. High birthrates will tend to fall where four conditions are present: a low mortality rate, a relative improvement in earnings, the availability of family planning and birth control, and an equal status for women. Where these conditions are not met, the surge in population will most likely continue, leading both to increasing impoverishment and to long-term environmental damage.

Solutions to the problems of resource scarcity are likewise difficult to implement, but some progress can be made if the size of the population can be stabilized. Too often, however, the response to growing population has been to adopt means that may offer some temporary relief, but lead to even more resource scarcity in the future.

Institutional and Political Means

Scarcities exacerbate the conditions that favor genocidal choices, but they do so within societies already divided along racial, religious, or ethnic lines and governed by authoritarian regimes. This realization brings us, then, to the more general question of how genocide can be prevented, even if not all of the pressures exerted by scarcities can be removed.

There are numerous steps that can be taken to prevent genocide. A carrot-and-stick approach might be adopted by states and international organizations to support social and political transformation in divided and repressive societies. Societies that are likely to resort to genocide can be identified and closely monitored. Early warning systems can be devised to forecast the likelihood of genocide, allowing governments and international bodies time to decide upon appropriate responses. Publicity and the mobilization by nongovernmental organizations of a human-rights constituency to pressure governments to act are also important in this context. International law can be strengthened through the creation of a standing, permanent tribunal to sit in judgment of those people who commit war crimes, crimes against humanity, and genocide. Also, the right of humanitarian intervention must be both recognized and made effective. At present, individual states have the capacity to intervene, and the United Nations is capable of putting together a coalition of forces, as in Bosnia and Somalia. But far more effective, and most likely a precondition for preventing genocide, is a permanent, standing international force that can be rapidly deployed. What is also crucial, for it is unlikely that the other steps will be undertaken to any extent without it, is for states to enlarge their definition of national interest to include the prevention of genocide. Here morality and realpolitik largely coincide.

Conclusion

Many, if not all, of the strategies for preventing genocide and reducing the scarcities—psychological, political, and material—that can contribute to it could be effective, *if implemented*. The prevention of genocide, however, is less a matter of knowledge than of political will. Two related questions thus hang over the future: Will the states and international organizations of the world continue to be bystanders to genocide, looking on and doing little? Or will a human capacity to resolve political and social problems in a manner befitting humankind finally assert itself in this century?

Ways Out

There are neither simple nor guaranteed solutions to the problems of scarcity, genocide, or the increasing likelihood that the material scarcities of the twenty-first century will exacerbate the pressures toward genocide already exerted by scarcities rooted in politics and modern expectations. But there are possible solutions, and even if not completely effective, they could mitigate or even reduce the incidence of genocide.

If scarcity contributes to the decision to commit genocide, then it is plausible to attempt to reduce scarcity. But as we have seen, there are several forms of scarcity. A reduction in material scarcity will require above all a decrease in population growth. Raising the status of women and providing family planning are crucial here. To prevent the continued assault on the lives of indigenous peoples will require a change in attitudes toward the environment, greater concern by international lending agencies for the environmental and human effects of "development," and restraint by global capitalism. Political scarcity could be reduced by power sharing and the replacement of authoritarianism by democracy. An economy adequate to meet needs is also crucial.

On the international plane, many steps could help to prevent genocide. But the most important of these methods is for governments to redefine "national interest" to include the prevention of genocide. Until there is political will to take effective steps to prevent this crime against humankind, genocide will remain a distinct possibility.

Suggested Reading

Arens, Richard, ed. 1976. *Genocide in Paraguay*. Philadelphia: Temple Univ. Press.

Conquest, Robert. 1986. *The Harvest of Sorrow: Soviet Collectivization and the Terror-Famine*. New York: Oxford Univ. Press.

Fein, Helen. 1993. "Accounting for Genocide after 1945: Theories and Some Findings." *International Journal on Group Rights* 1: 79–106.

Hirsch, Herbert. 1995. *Genocide and the Politics of Memory: Studying Death to Preserve Life*. Chapel Hill: Univ. of North Carolina Press.

Hobbes, Thomas. 1960. *Leviathan; or, The Matter, Forme, and Power of a Commonwealth Ecclesiasticall and Civil*. 1651. Reprint. Oxford: Blackwell.

Homer-Dixon, Thomas F. 1991. "On the Threshold: Environmental Changes as Causes of Acute Conflict." *International Security* 16: 76–116.

Kuper, Leo. 1981. *Genocide: Its Political Use in the Twentieth Century*. New Haven: Yale Univ. Press.

Smith, Roger W. 1987. "Human Destructiveness and Politics: The Twentieth Century as an Age of Genocide." In *Genocide and the Modern Age: Etiology and Case Studies of Mass Death*, edited by Isidor Wallimann and Michael N. Dobkowski, 21–39. Westport, Conn.: Greenwood Press.

———. 1998. "Scarcity and Genocide." In *The Coming Age of Scarcity: Preventing Mass Death and Genocide in the Twenty-first Century*, edited by Michael Dobkowski and Isidor Wallimann, 199–219. Syracuse: Syracuse Univ. Press.

Van Crevold, Martin L. 1991. *The Transformation of War*. New York: Free Press.

11

Globalization and Genocide

Inequality and Mass Death in Rwanda

David Norman Smith

THE SCALE and intensity of the Rwandan genocide of 1994 took the world by surprise. More than eight hundred thousand people were killed in just one hundred days, capturing the attention of a global audience that, until then, had barely heard of Rwanda. Soon, however, surprise yielded to clichés. The problem was said to lie with the Rwandan people, whose hatreds could not be contained. The genocide, we were told, was the result of incorrigible "tribal" and "ethnic" tensions that had existed since antiquity.

Ultimately, this way of thinking led many pundits to conclude that the only hope for Rwanda lies with external forces: the international lending agencies, once they learn the "policy lessons" of the genocide; the Rwandan state, duly reformed; global free trade; and perhaps even a "return to colonialism," if all else fails.

This perspective, I will argue, rests on a misreading of history—and finds hope in the very forces that spurred the genocide in the first place. Far from being an engine of genocide, the Rwandan people are in fact the only force with a realistic chance of preventing future genocides. Rwanda's many ailments—political, ethnic, military, cultural, economic, and environmental—require popular solutions that existing states and global agencies are likely to oppose.

◆   ◆   ◆

Before 1990, many observers regarded Rwanda as an oasis of progress in east-central Africa, in striking contrast to nearby Zaire, Uganda, and Burundi. The ruling party had been in power since 1973, and the human-rights situation, though classified as "poor" by outside monitors, was demonstrably better than in many neighboring countries. Indeed, fleeing terror elsewhere, many schools, missions, and NGOs had relocated to Rwanda. Rwanda also appeared to be economically sound. Since 1965, Rwanda had reduced its reliance on agriculture more than any other sub-Saharan country except Lesotho. In the 1970s, when population growth outstripped food production elsewhere in sub-Saharan Africa, Rwanda enjoyed better luck. In the mid-1980s, only one other sub-Saharan nation boasted a faster growth rate in agricultural exports (which, in the Rwandan case, consist mainly of coffee).[1]

Although still very poor, Rwanda was evidently on an ascending curve. In the 1980s, the European Community acknowledged this progress by inviting Rwanda to participate in its Food Strategies program, along with just three other African countries. The World Bank, reviewing nearly a decade of African development, gave Rwanda its highest accolade.

Few observers in 1962, when Rwanda won its independence, would have predicted such a promising future. Rwanda was tiny (about the size of Vermont), landlocked, crowded, and almost entirely rural. Of modest geopolitical significance, Rwanda had been an afterthought even for its conquerors. Germany, which ruled Rwanda from 1899 to 1916, valued the country mainly as a path for a railway (which was never built). Even Belgium, which seized Rwanda and Burundi during World War I, initially hoped to trade "Ruanda-Urundi" for territory elsewhere in Africa. When this action failed to materialize, the Belgians forced Rwanda to supply food to the copper miners in the Belgian Congo. In 1929, when the copper market collapsed, the Belgians forced the peasants to grow coffee for the export market. During World War II, as forced coffee production rose to new heights, a famine of epic proportions killed three hundred thousand people—one-tenth of the entire population.

Other problems sprang from the growing polarization of Rwandan society. Precolonial Rwanda had been divided into two major social

---

1. Coffee is the most widely produced agricultural export commodity in sub-Saharan Africa. Almost half of the forty nations analyzed in a 1992 study specialize in coffee production, whereas more than 25 percent specialize in cotton production.

classes, the Tutsis (a warrior nobility) and a "Hutu" peasantry. The key to Rwandan history is the fact that the term *Hutu* refers not to a pristine ethnic group, as many assume, but rather to a modern peasant class, drawn from a variety of conquered peoples whose shared identity as "Hutus" (literally, "subjects") reflects their common subjection to Tutsi nobles. The Rwandan empire, which grew rapidly in the late precolonial era, was the joint product of both classes. When this empire fell to Europeans, the delicate balance of Rwandan class relations was upset. The Tutsi lords became hated labor bosses, who were driven by the Belgians to "whip" the peasants to grow coffee for the world market.

In 1962, upon the departure of the Belgians, a "Hutu" regime surged into power on a wave of anti-Tutsi emotion, leaving thousands of Tutsis dead or in exile, the victims of a movement that showed many signs of racism (because many Hutus accepted the Belgian myth that Tutsis, as "Bronze Caucasians," were their racial enemies). The cycle of violence that climaxed in 1994 had begun.

Act Two in this tragedy unfolded in Burundi, where another "Tutsi" nobility retained power even after Belgium withdrew. In 1972, a flicker of revolt served as a pretext for one hundred thousand murders. Similar massacres ensued in 1988 and 1993. Act Three took place in Uganda, where more than a million Rwandans had migrated since the 1920s, fleeing famine or persecution. In 1982, the Obote regime responded to a revolt with vicious repression in the Luwero District, in which Rwandans were singled out for attack. About three hundred thousand people were killed, including about sixty thousand Rwandans.

After Obote fell in 1986, several Rwandans assumed leading roles in the new Museveni regime—but even so, anti-Rwandan bias remained rife. Many Rwandan exiles sought to return home, but they were consistently rebuffed by the Rwandan government. In October 1990, Rwandan soldiers from Museveni's military, organized into the "Rwandan Patriotic Front" (RPF), entered Rwanda to replace the one-party "Hutu Power" state with a multiparty, multiethnic regime. In April 1994, shortly after signing a peace treaty, the Hutu Power regime made a final effort to cling to power by massacring domestic Tutsis (most of whom were peasants) and dissidents. The RPF resumed fighting, won the war, and halted the slaughter. The former government and its supporters fled into exile.

Rwanda's oasis of progress, in other words, had become a vast killing field. Why? What forces plunged Rwanda into this vortex of murder and mass death?

◆   ◆   ◆

Africa has long been plagued by exceptionally high levels of civic violence. From 1960 to 1987, 4.5 million sub-Saharan Africans were killed in civil wars, revolts, and other internal conflicts—far more than in Asia or in Latin America.[2] Since 1987, the death toll has continued to spiral, as fighting has engulfed Sierra Leone, Liberia, Somalia, the Sudan, Rwanda, Burundi, Eritrea, Ethiopia, and Congo. The ultimate reason, most observers agree, lies in the internal contradictions of the postcolonial regimes. These contradictions are, at times, "ethnic" in nature. But ethnicity is not the whole story. Nor are the divisions in Africa as simple as many outsiders imagine. In Rwanda, for example, what appears to be "ethnic" conflict is, in many respects, class based, with only a partly or residually ethnic character. And there are also powerful global forces that have wreaked havoc with African societies.

To grasp these points, we must look briefly at Rwandan history. What, to start with, is the reality of Rwandan ethnicity?

In the earliest phase, the Tutsi-Hutu nexus was far more "ethnic" in nature than in any later period. The first "Tutsis" (literally, "newcomers") were probably Luo-speakers from the North. After arriving in Great Lakes Africa, they coalesced into a stratum of cattle-herding warriors with, it seems, a distinctive ethnic profile. Before long, some of these newcomers had conquered local farming peoples, who thus became "Hutus" for the first time.

In the next phase, the terms *Tutsi* and *Hutu* acquired a primary class connotation. Whereas nobles were still called Tutsis, this designation was no longer ethnic. Wealthy Hutus could acquire Tutsi status by an act of ritual, and poor Tutsis could sink to the level of ordinary Hutus. At this stage, however, colonialism intervened, and a third phase began. Convinced that the Tutsis were racial aristocrats, the colonialists granted them many privileges on expressly racist grounds. This action not only hardened the Rwandan class division but also gave this polarization a quasi-ethnic

---

2. Note, by the way, that this figure omits South Africa—which has been the site of much additional conflict.

flavor. Accordingly, the Tutsis became the objects of a passionate hatred among the Hutu peasantry. A class division thus became a quasi-ethnic division as well.

"Racial" hostilities burst into flame during the anti-Tutsi pogroms that marked the birth of Rwandan independence in the years from 1959 to 1964. In the next generation, animosities continued to smolder, even though most of the remaining Tutsis in Rwanda were now ordinary peasants. The actual "ethnic" and even class significance of the Tutsi-Hutu gulf was declining rapidly, but it remained very real, ideologically, to many Rwandans. Ethnicity, once invented, often leads to lasting ethnocentrism, which is clearly what happened in Rwanda. And this ethnocentrism, in turn, gave the predatory Rwandan state an opportunity. Pressured, in the early 1990s, by a guerrilla army (the RPF), by global banking agencies (for example, the International Monetary Fund and World Bank), and, perhaps most menacingly, by peasant dissent, the Rwandan rulers hoped to divide their enemies by exploiting residual ethnic hostility. The genocide proved that ethnocentrism is, indeed, a force to be reckoned with in latter-day Rwanda.

Besides local factors, there are, as well, powerful international forces that have undermined Rwandan stability. Historically, the most destructive of these forces have all been linked to the global market. It is worth noting, for example, that even Belgian colonialism was, for Rwanda, essentially market driven. Until 1929, Belgium treated Rwanda as an appendage to the world copper market, and thereafter, Belgium placed Rwandan peasants in thrall to the coffee market. This action was the crux of the colonial experience, and it has remained the basic postcolonial reality as well. Coffee, and again coffee, has spurred polarization in Rwanda. At every stage, Rwandans have been *forced* to labor for "the free market"—first by Belgians and their Tutsi adjutants, and then by a pair of anti-Tutsi regimes. The consequence has been mass death in several forms, from famine to genocide.

Never was this link between mass death and the market clearer, I would argue, than in the experience of the second postcolonial regime. Originating in a 1973 military coup led by Juvénal Habyarimana, and overthrown after the 1994 genocide, Habyarimana's "Second Republic" was a paragon of coercive violence and, at the same time, an icon of the market-driven "development" strategies so dear to free-trade ideologues. This blend of qualities is not strange or unusual, as fans of globalization might think. On the contrary, the vaunted "progress" of the Rwandan economy, which made Rwanda so appealing to the IMF and the World Bank, rested securely on a foundation of forced labor and top-down bureaucracy. Rwanda was an apparent success story for globalization precisely because it used force to guarantee "development." Here, as elsewhere in sub-Saharan Africa, forced labor was the guilty secret of "free trade."

When trade faltered—when the coffee market collapsed in 1987, yielding famine and dissent—the IMF and World Bank seized the opportunity to impose an even more stringent free-trade policy on the Habyarimana regime. This new policy, however, only worsened the underlying social and economic problems, and gave a fresh impetus to the forces leading to genocide. Unable to count on the global market for salvation, the Habyarimana clique turned to force.

Fans of globalization say that it benefits rich and poor alike—the postcolonial "new nations" as well as the ex-colonial powers that fund the IMF and World Bank. Rwanda, once cited to support this claim, now seems to tell a very different story.

◆   ◆   ◆

Chroniclers of the genocide have shown definitively that the genocide itself was not the "elemental outburst" depicted by the media, but was, rather, a quasi-military campaign meticulously planned by the predatory Rwandan ruling party, which sought to exploit residual Hutu racism in a vain effort to remain in power. Here, I emphasize two further points, namely, (1) that the Habyarimana regime turned to coercion because it could no longer count on consent to stay in power, and (2) that the global banking community played a shadowy but central role in driving Rwanda to the edge of the abyss—and over.

These two claims are intertwined, in the following sense: On the one hand, the legitimacy of the Rwandan state, which was gravely compromised by colonialism, declined still further as a result of the cupidity of the postcolonial rulers. This cupidity, in turn, was fired and fed by the IMF and World Bank, which thereby helped set the stage for the genocide itself.

In precolonial days, the Rwandan state had basked in the glory of its sacred kings. But kingship gave way to a venal colonial bureaucracy, which relied less on consent than on coercion. In the first flush of independence, the new rulers made minor concessions to the peasants. But in the 1970s and 1980s, when an influx of international loans reduced the state's dependence on the coffee market (and thus, on the peasantry), the rulers became even more predatory than before. Inequality rose to new levels, and the peasants grew even poorer. When, in 1987, coffee prices fell sharply, the rulers were forced to rely even more heavily on the global banks. Forced by the banks to embrace rigorous austerity as "shock therapy" for their ailing economy, the Rwandan rulers tried to recoup their losses by turning the screws on the peasantry. The peasants resisted, and when the RPF stepped up the pressure as well, the rulers felt trapped. Rather than accepting defeat, they opted for the most violent path open to them—total war against much of their own public.

Thinly veiled as an eruption of ethnic violence, the genocide was actually a desperate gamble. The aim was to retain power at all costs by murdering actual and potential enemies. Tutsi peasants bore the brunt of this genocide for several reasons: (1) the regime's wish to exploit lingering ethnic hatred, in a final bid for "Hutu" legitimacy; (2) the conviction that all Tutsis were born dissidents; and (3) a measure of real ethnocentrism on the part of the regime and its accomplices. But thousands of Hutus were also killed, for political reasons. They opposed the regime. They exposed—and could exploit—the rulers' fatal lack of legitimacy.

Ultimately, it was the rulers' loss of legitimacy that proved most decisive. Although aggravated by recent IMF–World Bank policy—as we will see below—this legitimacy crisis also has deep historic roots.

◆　◆　◆

When the Tutsis first arrived in Great Lakes Africa roughly five hundred years ago, they found sacred kingship well established among the Zigaaba, Sindi, and other peoples of the region. Until then, the Tutsis had been egalitarian, but they adapted to local norms. Under various names, including "Tutsi" and "Hima," they built sacred kingdoms of their own. Rwanda, which means "empire," was one such kingdom, in which power was entrusted to a sacred king, the *Mwami,* who was thought to preeminently personify *imana,* the mystic power of life and fertility.

Among the Barundi, whose outlook is similar, the verb *to rule* also means *to give.* In Rwanda the same word unites the ideas of *man, husband, virility, courage,* and *generosity.* The king, in this worldview, is the fount of wealth and well-being, the embodiment of the empire, the living, giving divinity who ensures the fertility of the land, cattle, and people by royal ritual.

In reality, of course, the *Mwami* was enriched and exalted by peasant labor. His court, granary, and herds were sustained by services and surpluses from his subjects—the now famous "Hutus." Supposedly above class divisions, the king was actually the emblem of Rwandan class relations. As the greatest Tutsi lord and bearer of the royal drum (akin to the European crown), the *Mwami* was the most voracious consumer of surplus Hutu labor. Yet, his reign was not simply exploitative. In reciprocal relations of the Rwandan type, the king seeks legitimacy, not merely domination. And for this authenticity, he must give as well as take.

Still, even in precolonial days, the ties between the state and public had begun to weaken as the kings claimed ever grander powers. This change was reflected in a late imperial saying, "The drum is greater than the shout," which meant, in effect, that the crown eclipses the vox populi. This sense of distance from power deepened when the final precolonial king, Rwabugiri, centralized many state functions in a period of growing disparity between rich and poor. Finally, with the advent of colonialism, the gulf between the state and people widened still further.

Germany, which annexed Rwanda in 1899, found the small empire in turmoil. Rwabugiri's death in 1895 had sparked a succession conflict, which resulted in coup d'état by the "matridynastic" Kagara lineage of the Tutsi nobility, the source of many Rwandan queens. In 1896, Kagara plotters (led by the queen mother, Kanjogera) overthrew the heir to the royal drum, declaring Kanjogera's son Musinga the new *Mwami*. This usurpation of power spurred a pair of rebellions, which were crushed in campaigns so rapacious that famine ensued. Soon the new regime was cynically known as *Cyiimyamaboko*, "It is force that rules." Even Kanjogera sensed that the sacredness of the kingship had been violated. She and her kinsmen had seized power, but could they claim to embody *imana*? It seemed dubious to many.

Equally fateful was Musinga's wish to conquer the Kigan peoples to the north. The Kigans, made up of many ethnic groups, were almost the only Great Lakes population without a history of sacred kingship, and they had long resisted conquest. Musinga realized, however, that the Europeans could help him overrun Kiga. The consequence, by the end of the 1920s, was that "Rwanda" had grown to encompass not only Tutsis and

Hutus in the South, but also Kigans, who were new to Tutsi-Hutu society—and who remained implacably hostile to the haughty Tutsi conquerors. The full menace of this hostility became apparent in 1994.

A new phase began when Belgium seized Rwanda in 1916. Significantly, the Belgians chose to rule the country through the nobility, thus marginalizing the king. By 1931, Musinga's anger over his reduced status had grown so disruptive that the Belgians decided to oust him in favor of his more pliant son, Rudahigwa. This move had a profoundly desacralizing effect, which was augmented in 1935 when a sacred royal dwelling became the site of a Catholic church.

In 1926, the Belgians reinvented the nobility as well. The precolonial system, which had balanced the claims of several different kinds of aristocrats, was abolished in favor of a centralized system of "chiefs." By 1935, there were fewer than seventy chiefs in all Rwanda, aided by nine hundred "subchiefs." These Tutsi chiefs, moreover, were treated as a "racially pure" ruling caste, with exclusive access to office, education, and luxury. Though there were a few holes in the Belgians' racist logic—for lack of a clear racial criterion, they defined Tutsis as anyone who owned at least ten cows—they were unbending in their effort to divide Rwanda into racial camps. The result, as many critics have observed, was a kind of apartheid. The subtleties of identity were flattened into a binary Tutsi-Hutu polarity. Instead of generosity and reciprocity, the Belgians imposed inequity. The result was that the class division between nobles and peasants turned into a yawning chasm—and assumed a "racial" profile as well.

The Belgians profited from this polarization. "We harass the chiefs without respite," an administrator wrote in 1932, and the chiefs bullied the peasants in turn. That same year—a decade after forced labor was introduced and a year after forced coffee cultivation began—a priest protested that the peasants were being driven so hard that they were in danger of famine. Forced road clearing, tree planting, farm labor, and construction consumed the labor of fully two-thirds of the 2,024 grown men in his parish every day. Indeed, so extreme were the Belgian exactions in this period that the very word for work, *akazi,* became synonymous with forced labor. Meanwhile, along with *akazi,* each taxpayer was forced to grow one hundred coffee trees, for sale on the export market (at prices set by the Belgians). By 1937, 20 million coffee trees had been planted in "Ruanda-Urundi," and many more were planted later.

By 1944, forced labor consumed 120 workdays per adult. Ultimately, even one of the governor-generals was appalled, writing, in 1955, that the chiefs extorted everything from the peasants save "the strict minimum needed to survive."

Suffice it to say that, under Belgian rule, the Rwandan state became a virtual suction pump for the extraction of peasant labor. This state of affairs remained true after independence was achieved, as well (a process that occurred in stages from 1959 to 1962. At this juncture, the king and thousands of Tutsis were forced into exile, the victims of a "Hutu revolution" led by a new party, PARMEHUTU, that drew its strength from Gitarama, in south-central Rwanda, and from the northern, largely Kigan provinces of Gisenyi, Ruhengeri, and Byumba. Though posing as an iconic bearer of republican virtue, PARMEHUTU soon proved to be a worthy heir to the Tutsi bureaucracy. By 1965, PARMEHUTU had established a one-party state, and soon afterward *"Gitaramistes"* controlled the party, elbowing northerners aside. Politicians from Gitarama (led by Gregoire Kayibanda) soon emerged as a "state nobility," bent on self-enrichment through control of the coffee trade. Their main instrument was the state-run marketing system, which monopolized export profits.

Northerners were incensed, not only because they were left out in the cold, but also because they saw Kayibanda as an enemy of traditional Kigan social relations. Unlike the *Gitaramistes,* for whom the state itself was the source of enrichment, the northerners wanted the state to serve the traditional Kigan landlord class. In 1973, Kayibanda crossed a fatal line when he vested a new bureau, ONACO, with exalted power over the private sector. In July 1973, a Kigan general, Habyarimana, seized power and "suspended" ONACO, which he vilified as "communist."

No populist, Habyarimana soon revived forced labor, requiring all adults to join labor teams every Saturday under state direction. The penalty for refusal was imprisonment.[3] In other respects, too, Habyarimana imposed an ever more elitist and predatory state. Standing at the very heart of the regime was an inner circle known as the *Akazu,* or "little hut," which consisted of Habyarimana's intimates, most of whom were from Gisenyi. Many other Kigans (politicians, traders, and the like) or-

---

3. The reactionary daring of this step can be gauged by the fact that forced labor had been expressly singled out in the revolutionary 1957 "Manifesto of the Bahutu" as a practice "no longer adapted to the situation and psychology of today." No other feature of Belgo-Tutsi rule had been more hated.

bited the *Akazu*. So wealthy did this group grow that Claudine Vidal spoke ironically of a "fourth ethnicity" in Rwanda—the ruling rich.

Although Habyarimana claimed to speak for all Rwandans, it was plain, a former ambassador reports, that "in reality he was only interested in the Bakiga people, . . .especially those from Gisenyi."[4] Gitarama and Kibuye, with 20 percent of the population, received just 1 percent of rural investments (excluding donor funds), whereas Gisenyi, Ruhengeri, Kigali (the capital), and Cyangugu shared almost 90 percent of the total. Analogous disparities were plain elsewhere.

Writing just months before the genocide, a Belgian specialist reported that the Tutsi-Hutu division had given way to a regional conflict. The North, prospering at the expense of the South, had made a mockery of the old rhetoric of "Hutu" unity. Yet even the North was not conflict free. When an anthropologist visited the North in 1977, he found that the old landlord-peasant relationship had grown even more unequal. For the Kigan poor, he reported, the "devil word is *amataranga*"—money. Kigan landowners had capitalized on the new money economy to seize land from indebted peasants, thereby opening an abyss between rich and poor.

Elsewhere conditions were equally desperate. Average landholdings shrank dramatically, landlessness became common, and peasant incomes fell sharply. This savage inequality inspired profound dissatisfaction. By the early 1990s, an open revolt was brewing. The genocide was a last-ditch effort to quash this revolt.

◆　◆　◆

The Rwandan state lost popular support, briefly, as it became the engine of an ever widening gulf between rich and poor. Class inequality, no less than ethnic hostility, played a leading role in unhinging Rwandan society—and the Rwandan state fanned both class and ethnic tensions. The state, in turn, was deeply affected by emergent globalism. Old-fashioned imperialism, represented mainly by France (which had displaced Belgium as Rwanda's principal ally), was still a powerful force, but the global lending community was, if anything, even more directly influential. This influence was, for the most part, destructive.

---

4. "Bakiga" is the Bantu way of saying "Kigan people," just as "Bahutu" means "Hutus."

The IMF and World Bank seldom deign to notice the political tumult they cause or aggravate. In 1988, for example, when the government of Burundi killed tens of thousands of its citizens, the World Bank was praised for showing interest! And they had good reason to show interest, because, not long before, they had made Burundi the world's largest per capita recipient of low-interest loans. These loans, accompanied by austerity policies demanded by the bank, contributed directly to Burundian destabilization and polarization. Yet, the bank soon concluded that the massacres were not "deliberate policy" and resumed their prior lending policy.

Elsewhere, the IMF and the World Bank have been equally inattentive to the social and political effects of their lending policies. But so much violence has accompanied bank and IMF programs that even IMF economists have begun to take note. The key figure in this respect is Jean-Dominique Lafay, who, with his associates Dessus and Morrisson, analyzed data on twenty-three African nations (including Rwanda) to learn whether IMF policies spur conflict and violence. Their conclusions are sobering.

Focusing on a trio of "decision-making forces"—the IMF and World Bank, the state, and civil society—Lafay tracks an arrow of causality that begins with the IMF–World Bank and runs, through the state, to the public. The public, injured by IMF–World Back austerity policies, resists until repressed.[5] State repression is thus a direct outgrowth of the familiar IMF–World Bank objectives: cuts in public spending, increased consumer prices, tax increases, cuts in public employment, and currency devaluations.

Empirically, IMF–World Bank interventions of this type have been almost universally unpopular.[6] Spending cuts, price hikes, tax increases, and job cuts normally prompt strikes and demonstrations, which almost always provoke state violence—arrests, measures to ban unions and parties, and efforts to censor the media and close the schools. This outcome, Lafay says, is because just about every African conflict quickly "turns into a dispute over the legitimacy of the regime." Yet, the IMF and World Bank continue to fuel these conflicts, seemingly heedless of the consequences.

Rwanda and Burundi are living proof of this point. When, in 1993,

---

5. From this point on, for ease of reading, I will refer to Lafay as the author of the study cited below. It should be kept in mind, though, that Morrisson and Dessus are his coauthors.

6. Fifteen of sixteen carefully coded cases.

the Burundian state massacred another hundred thousand people, two World Bank economists voiced belated regret about the effects of bank policies. The "lesson," they wrote, "is that in attempting to restructure an economy—which implies a redistribution of income and, along with it, power—a government must recognize not only the economic but also the social and political bonds that hold a society together" (Engelbert and Hoffmann 1994, 18).

In Rwanda, plainly, the very opposite occurred. The state, backed into a corner by forces both local and global, preferred genocide to solidarity. Forced to tailor the economy to World Bank specifications, Rwanda's rulers drew the line at the "redistribution of income and, along with it, power."

◆   ◆   ◆

Rwanda became a favorite of global donors in the wake of the 1973 coup, largely because the new regime—which declared 1974 the "year of agriculture and manual labor" and revived forced labor in 1975—was a model of exploitative efficiency. "In the eyes of the U.S. government and other donors," Lindsay Hilsum wrote, "Rwanda . . . was a model of development efficiency. Every Rwandan citizen had to participate in collective labor on Saturdays. The system was harsh but effective—roads were built, trees planted . . ." (1994, 14). And, even more profitably, coffee was grown. From 1965 to 1989, the GDP grew steadily in Rwanda—4.9 percent per annum—and coffee accounted for more than 80 percent of total export revenues. Coffee production was the sector of the economy "where force and pressure were most [widely] used," Peter Uvin reports, and it consumed the "overwhelming" majority of peasant energy even in the donor-supported agricultural extension system. In 1988, for example, peasant families were forced to devote nearly fifty-four thousand hectares to coffee cultivation, tending an average of 157 trees (more than in colonial times). In 1986, this increase resulted in export earnings of $150 million—of which, unsurprisingly, little trickled down to the cultivators (indeed, retail prices were twenty times what the peasants received). "The Rwandan peasant, silent and hardworking," Uvin concludes, "often resembled more an unpaid employee of a public enterprise than an independent farmer" (1998, 130).

Western banks and governments, impressed by the exploitative efficiency of the regime, made Rwanda one of the leading recipients of foreign aid. From 1980 to 1986, Rwanda received at least $200 million in new aid every year except one. In 1987, total aid soared to $340 million. From 1982 to 1987, foreign aid financed more than two-thirds of all public investment. Overall, more than 200 donors were active in Rwanda, and several gave Rwanda privileged treatment. Canada, for example, contributed $150 million to more than 150 development projects in Rwanda. Rwanda was also the largest beneficiary of Swiss and Belgian assistance. And the World Bank, in particular, was smitten by Rwanda's charms. In reports written as late as 1989–1991—when the coffee market and the economy were in crisis, war and famine had broken out, and ethnic tension and repression had worsened—the World Bank praised the Habyarimana regime for its humane spirit and prudence. As Peter Uvin writes, "the World Bank seemed to be the one with the strongest love affair with Rwanda. The reason for the intensity of this relation was in all likelihood that Rwanda's economic policies overall were quite liberal [in other words, market oriented] and thus very much in line with the Bank's ideology, which was a rarity in Africa before the second half of the 1980s" (46).[7]

The result, as Catharine Newbury once observed, is that "Rwanda depends, to an extraordinary degree, on foreign assistance" (1992, 199). In 1989–1990, Rwanda relied on foreign aid for 11.4 percent of its total GNP. This reliance made the regime all the more vulnerable when the coffee market collapsed in 1987 and exports fell sharply.

Two sad ironies call for attention at this point. First, Rwanda's long honeymoon with Western lending agencies was also a period of soaring poverty and inequality, despite rising productivity. And the coffee crisis that abruptly ended this honeymoon—a crisis that was, plainly, entirely the result of market vicissitudes—was exploited by the IMF to "marketize" Rwanda still further. And this exploitation, predictably, deepened poverty and conflict even further.

Thus did the market work its magic in Rwanda.

◆ ◆ ◆

If lending and "market reforms" actually reduced poverty and repression—as officially advertised—then Rwanda should be comparatively af-

---

7. As Andy Storey writes, "Rwanda's economy had already been extensively liberalised—for good or ill—before the formal adoption of a structural adjustment programme" (1991, 54).

fluent and untroubled by now. But, in fact, market-oriented lending often makes the poor even poorer, the rich even richer, and the privileged even harsher in defense of their privilege. This consequence plainly is what happened in Rwanda. In northern Rwanda, wealth had long been concentrated in the hands of the old Kigan landlord class, the so-called *abakonde*. In the 1960s, PARMEHUTU had enriched a parallel elite of southern businessmen and politicians. But after 1973, during the Habyarimana years, the concentration of wealth grew even more extreme, in both the North and the South. This fact was perhaps most visible, and most consequential, in the crucial realm of landownership.

Recall, first, that in 1949, after decades of colonial rule, the average peasant family still owned three hectares of land. By the 1960s, however, this average had fallen to two hectares, and by the early 1980s, it had plummeted to just 1.2 hectares. In 1984, in fact, more than half of all peasant families (57 percent) worked a single hectare or less, whereas just over a quarter (27 percent) owned more than 1.5 hectares. Overall, nearly half of all farms were rented by otherwise landless tenants, the poorest quartile of the population owned less than 7 percent of all cultivated land, and a wealthy minority (16 percent) owned nearly half the land (42.9 percent). The state, moreover, was legally entitled to expropriate peasants at will—and regularly did so. Asked, in 1982, whether they wanted their children to become farmers, nearly four out of five Rwandan peasants said no.

The wage sphere, however, was no more equitable. In 1986, the upper 1.1 percent of salary recipients received more than a quarter of total salaries (27.8 percent), whereas the bottom half (49 percent) earned just 7.6 percent. And so fast was Rwanda stratifying that just two years later, in 1988, the share of total salaries received by the top 1 percent had soared to nearly half (45.8 percent), whereas the bottom two-thirds (65 percent) now earned less than 4 percent of the total. All this, it should be noted, was true *before* Rwanda agreed to the IMF-dictated Structural Adjustment Program (SAP) in 1990. Afterward, matters grew even worse.

The root problem, once again, was market related—namely, the free fall of coffee prices that began in 1987 when the system of production quotas established under the International Coffee Agreement (ICA) came unglued. Two years later, at a "historic" meeting in Florida, the ICA reached a final impasse, Michel Chossudovsky reports, "as a result of political pressures from Washington on behalf of the large U.S. coffee traders" (1997, 111). In the next few months, coffee prices fell another 50 percent.

In Rwanda, the net effect was catastrophic. Overall, from 1985 to 1992, the world price of coffee fell by 72 percent, whereas the prices of Rwanda's other major exports (tea and tin) fell 66 percent and 35 percent, respectively. On balance, the real purchasing power of Rwandan exports fell by 59 percent in this period. In response, the government forced the peasants to increase the volume of coffee production by 40 percent in 1989 and 1990—though peasant coffee earnings *fell* 20 percent. At the same time, the production of each of the five major food crops fell at least 20 percent.[8]

The World Bank, sensing an opportunity, sent a mission to Rwanda in November 1988 to review government options. The outcome was a document, "With Strategy Change," proposing a deepening of Rwanda's "transition to the free market." Arguing, on the basis of computer simulations, that further marketization of the economy would yield a bevy of benefits by 1993—rising levels of investment and consumption, improved trade balances, and declining debt—the World Bank successfully pressured the Habyarimana regime to accept economic shock therapy in the form of a Structural Adjustment Program negotiated with the IMF, the World Bank, and the U.S. Agency for International Development (USAID).[9] The agreement to proceed with the SAP was reached at a meeting in Washington on September 17, 1990—just two weeks before the RPF, also seeking to exploit Habyarimana's vulnerability, invaded from Uganda.[10]

8. Maize production, for example, fell from 110,000 tons in 1983 to 90,000 tons in 1996, whereas sorghum, another staple, fell from 213,000 tons in 1982 to roughly 140,000 tons in 1988. The production of beans, the single most important source of peasant nutrients, fell 50 percent.

9. As the Organization of African Unity concluded in a recent report, "the Habyarimana government reluctantly concluded that it had little choice but to accept a Structural Adjustment Programme . . . in return for a loan conditional on the rigid and harsh policies that characterized western economic orthodoxy of the time. The premise was that Rwanda needed economic shock therapy" (Caplan and Sangare 2000, 5.5).

10. This period was an inauspicious time to begin an SAP, since the IMF had just decided to demand more rigorous compliance with stricter requirements. And the collapse of the USSR gave the IMF a freer hand to push for the decentralization of states that were blocking the free action of the market.

◆ ◆ ◆

The new SAP was inaugurated in November 1990 with a 40 percent devaluation of the Rwandan franc, followed, a few days later, by steep price hikes for fuel and other consumer necessities. Ultimately, the World Bank reminisced in 1997, the Rwandan "authorities implemented, in 1991–92, most of the agreed reform measures" (quoted in Storey 1999, 49). Interest rates, taxes, and school fees were raised, whereas producer prices for coffee, paid to farmers, were frozen at 1989 levels and then, in 1990, slashed 20 percent. Other notable features of the SAP included the privatization or liquidation of state enterprises; policies designed to commercialize and intensify peasant production, especially in the export sector; the abolition of import barriers; strict hiring and wage controls in the state sector; the removal of price and profit controls; the elimination of more than half of Rwanda's public investment projects; the abandonment of a program to reclaim swampland for farming, which the World Bank deemed "unprofitable"; and the introduction of user fees for state services, including health and education.

In June 1992, the government implemented a further 15 percent devaluation of the Rwandan franc, resulting in "a further escalation of the prices of fuel and consumer essentials." In 1993, prodded by the World Bank, the government announced plans to privatize the Electrogaz energy monopoly; shortly afterward, two thousand Electrogaz employees were fired. In September 1993, the government privatized the state telecommunications company, Rwandatel. These changes were, indeed, shock therapy with a vengeance.

The global lending community was appreciative. At a time when overall aid to Africa was declining, assistance to Rwanda greatly increased in 1991. By June, the IMF and World Bank had approved more than $100 million in unrestricted new Structural Adjustment loans.[11] That same year, the European Community gave Rwanda $15–$40 million, the United States gave $10–$25 million, France gave $12–$14 million, Austria gave $6–$10 million, Belgium BF 200 million, and Switzerland dedicated SwF

---

11. In April 1991, the IMF granted the regime an $11.91 million "Extended Structural Adjustment" loan, and two months later the World Bank approved a $90 million "Structural Adjustment Credit."

10.9 million—all to what the Swiss called "a friendly country in need." In 1992, Germany chipped in $16 million, Japan $6 million, and Belgium BF 720 million. France, from the start of the war, provided military support as well. And as late as January 1994, just months before the genocide, Japan contributed yet another $7 million.

For ordinary Rwandans, the effects of these policies were acutely painful. Inflation, in the capital city of Kigali, elevated the prices of basic consumer goods an average of 50 percent during the first seven months of the program. Overall, from 1989 to 1991, inflation rose from 1 percent to more than 19 percent. In 1992 and again in 1993, inflation rose 10 percent. As the Catholic relief agency Caritas reported, prices rose so high that people went hungry, homelessness soared, and (in a period of ongoing famine) children and the sick were in grave jeopardy. State enterprises went bankrupt, school enrollments declined, public services (including health and education) were sharply reduced, cases of severe childhood malnutrition rose steeply, and (in the first year of the program) the incidence of malaria rose 21 percent—mainly due to shortages of antimalarial medicines at public-health facilities.

As starry-eyed as ever, the World Bank reported in 1994 that, in Rwanda, "land is less unequally divided than elsewhere" (quoted in Uvin 1998, 111). This startling claim is belied by a host of facts. By the early 1990s, the average family landholding had fallen to a new low to 0.7 hectares—which, in fact, is precisely what the United Nations defines as the bare minimum for a family of five. Applying that criterion to Rwanda in 1991, the UN concluded that 43 percent of all Rwandan farm households had fallen below the absolute survival threshold and suffered chronic malnutrition as a result. Even the World Bank reported, in 1991, that the average daily intake of the poorer half of Rwandan society had fallen below 2,000 calories per person. Peasants who, in 1984, had produced an average of 2,055 kilocalories per day were reduced to just 1,509 per day by 1991—a decline of nearly 27 percent.[12] About half of all children were stunted.

In 1991, 26 percent of the rural populace was entirely landless. In 1993, a USAID report revealed that Rwanda now had the highest poverty rate in the entire world.

---

12. Calorie intake, in turn, was "perfectly correlated" with income and "almost perfectly correlated" with farm size (Uvin 1998, 112).

◆ ◆ ◆

On many levels, the Habyarimana regime now found itself in great difficulty. The economy, plainly, had been severely compromised. By 1992, external debt had increased 34 percent. By 1993, coffee revenues had fallen to just 20 percent of the precrisis 1986 figure ($150 million). By 1994, the state-run coffee marketing system had effectively ground to a halt. In all, from 1990 to 1993, the ratio of imports to exports doubled, with imports exceeding $300 million, whereas exports tumbled to about $50 million.

Meanwhile, domestically, after bowing to Western pressure to allow rival parties, Habyarimana witnessed a flowering of dissent. Old PARME-HUTU forces sprang to life, now joined by a plethora of new parties across the political spectrum. The peasantry, meanwhile, was growing dangerously restive. Many joined peasant associations, which were centers of dissent. In 1992, suffering the aftershocks of the coffee crisis doubly as the state intensified its exactions, peasants uprooted at least three hundred thousand coffee trees.[13] They refused to perform Saturday labor, stopped attending state rallies, occupied Western-sponsored demonstration and reforestation projects, and destroyed antierosion structures on their farms. These moves were all acts of defiance and desperation, and strictly illegal. They also terrified the embattled rulers, who saw both their political prospects and their coffee profits plunge still further.

All this occurred, meanwhile, as the state quadrupled military spending and (with French help) expanded its army eightfold. The object of this military buildup was to repel the RPF—but this plan, too, was a failure, since it soon became clear that the RPF had fought the army to a standstill. Even worse, from the IMF–World Bank standpoint, was the fear that military spending would undercut Rwanda's SAP-mandated fiscal austerity. In 1993, the World Bank president wrote Habyarimana a scolding letter that was widely circulated in the diplomatic corps, insisting that Habyarimana cut military spending and negotiate a peace pact with the RPF. Grudgingly bowing to pressure, the government joined the RPF in peace talks held in Arusha, Tanzania. Before long, though, it became clear that Habyarimana was dragging his feet. By July 1993, Alison Des Forges reports that "the donor nations—including France—had lost patience [with Habyarimana's

---

13. Chossudovsky calls this appraisal "a conservative estimate."

stalling tactics] and used the ultimate threat. In combination with the World Bank, they informed Habyarimana that international funds for his government would be halted if he did not sign the treaty by August 9. With no other source of funds available, Habyarimana was obliged to sign along with the other parties on August 4, 1993" (1999, 124).

This move was evidently the last straw for ruling-party extremists, who decided to continue fighting without Habyarimana's support. Upon leaving the Arusha talks, Col. Theoneste Bagosora, who was later a central figure in the genocide, told colleagues that he was returning to Rwanda "to prepare the Apocalypse" (Omaar and de Waal 1994, 79).

Death squads, thousands strong, had been in training since the early 1990s. Open threats of genocide became common, and it was well known that Tutsis and dissidents were in danger. Many were assassinated. The signal for the start of the genocide came on April 6, 1994, when the jet returning Habyarimana from abroad crashed upon arriving in Rwanda. In the ensuing days, death squads, aided by the military, fanned across Rwanda, killing as many actual and potential dissidents as possible. Peasants in many communities were bribed, coerced, and cajoled to participate in the slaughter; many did, and many did not.

In barely fourteen weeks, roughly 850,000 were killed. The genocide was halted, without foreign help, in mid-July, when the RPF captured Kigali and forced the remnants of Habyarimana's army and death squads into exile.

◆ ◆ ◆

From the start, the IMF and the World Bank showed remarkably little interest in the possible negative effects of structural adjustment in Rwanda. The danger of crisis as a result of shock therapy in a country on the edge of war might seem acute, but the World Bank was, in fact, so blasé about this risk that it blithely excluded all "noneconomic variables" when computing likely SAP outcomes. And, indeed, the World Bank was so adept at seeing no evil that, in a 1991 report, Rwanda was praised for its ethnic and socioeconomic homogeneity! That same year, outside monitors found "major donors . . . unwilling to admit that ethnic conflict posed serious risks," Alison Des Forges of Human Rights Watch reports. "When they advised donors to insist on the removal of ethnic classification on identity cards as a condition for continued aid, none of them took the advice" (1999, 92).[14]

This incident was not an isolated episode. In April 1993, the UN special rapporteur on summary, arbitrary, and extrajudicial executions went to Rwanda to investigate charges of widespread human-rights violations, including the violent repression of dissidents and the massacre of fifteen hundred Tutsi nomads, the so-called Bagogwe, in 1992. In August, the rapporteur released a report indicting the Habyarimana regime for a host of crimes, including acts of genocide as defined by the 1948 UN Convention for the Suppression and Punishment of Genocide. Once again, donors showed scant interest. As Uvin writes, "The fact that the development business continued as usual while government-sponsored human rights violations were on the rise sent a clear signal that the international community did not care too much about the racially motivated and publicly organized slaughter of citizens" (1998, 229).

Since the genocide, most critics have blamed the state and its death squads; France, for sending Habyarimana money, weapons, and military advisers; the UN, for pulling its troops out of Rwanda at the start of the genocide, and thus failing to prevent what Gen. Romeo Dallaire, the leader of the UN military mission, called a preventable genocide; the RPF, for putting domestic Tutsis and dissidents at risk; and, above all, the Rwandan people, who are accused of racism and authoritarian compliance with evil. Except for the latter charge—which understates the role of popular resistance to authority and exaggerates the level of public participation in the genocide—these criticisms are amply deserved. But it would be a mistake to minimize the role played by the avatars of globalization as well. As important as internal factors may have been, it seems highly unlikely that these factors, alone, would have generated a genocide.[15] And

14. Des Forges (1999) adds that the same consultants approached ambassadors and others from the U.S., French, Canadian, German, and Belgian embassies, with equally little effect.

15. The internal factor most often assigned a causal role vis-à-vis the genocide is overpopulation. This statement, in my opinion, is only modestly credible. Although population pressure is certainly a problem in Rwanda, it is wrong to think that violence is a simple reflex of crowding. As Peter Uvin (1998) notes, both earlier periods of civil violence in Rwanda (1959–1964 and 1973) took place during extended phases of high growth in per capita food production. And despite the well-advertised fact that Rwanda has the highest fertility

among the global forces implicated in the genocide, none (save perhaps French foreign policy) played a more consequential role than the IMF and World Bank.

David Woodward, otherwise a cautious critic of globalism in Rwanda, calls shock therapy "irresponsible in the extreme. Even if the adjustment programme did not contribute directly to the tragic events of 1994, such a reckless disregard for social and political sensitivities in such a conspicuously sensitive situation would unquestionably have increased the risk of creating or compounding a potentially explosive situation" (1996, 25). Gerald Caplan and Anatole Sangare, writing for the Organization of African Unity (OAU), have vigorously endorsed this criticism: "The World Bank, we should acknowledge, disagrees that it was responsible for exacerbating Rwanda's economic woes, though not," the OAU ironizes, "with its usual confidence" (2000, 5.7). Indeed, on May 16, 1994, at the height of the genocide, the World Bank argued, in halfhearted self-defense, that "it is difficult to analyze the effects of the adjustment program on the incomes of the poor *because overall economic conditions worsened and everybody was worse off*" (italics mine; quoted in ibid.). Fair enough.

More recently, in a classic case of twenty-twenty hindsight, the World Bank has suggested "social assessments, including explicit recognition of sources of social conflict and social tension, as a core aspect of development" (quoted in Storey 1999, 58). Yet, IMF and World Bank enthusiasm for structural adjustment remains undiminished. Even Lafay and Lecaillon, who understand well that ill-considered interventions may prompt "the triggering or acceleration of a revolutionary process or civil war, [or] the emergence or proliferation of acts of terrorism or . . . repressive action by the state," nevertheless continue to feel that the risk is worth taking (1993, 91).

Ways Out

"The old is dying and the new cannot be born," Antonio Gramsci once wrote, musing over the miscarriage of capitalism in southern Italy. "In this interregnum a great variety of morbid symptoms appear." For Rwanda

---

rate in sub-Saharan Africa (8.3 children per woman), Rwanda is actually only the sixth-ranked African country in terms of population density per square kilometer.

and much of Africa, the twentieth century was an epoch of arrested transition. Old ways died, yet the market millennium never arrived. Forced labor and coffee exports broke empires, but did not offer emancipation. Is there a solution? Is there a way forward?

Pundits say that Rwanda has been sabotaged by its own irrepressible past. Primitive hatreds, pulsing beneath the veneer of civilization, have been reawakened. The solution, hence, can lie only outside Rwanda. This thinking is the apparent rationale for William Pfaff's proposal, in *Foreign Affairs,* to revive colonialism: "If anybody is competent to deal sympathetically with these countries, the Europeans are" (1995, 4).

By now, the bald, comic effrontery of this claim should be plain. As long as Rwanda remains a pawn of the West and the market, it seems to have little chance of ceasing to be a forced-labor state. It is thus highly revealing, culturally, that the genocidal death squads were called *interahamwe*—a name once reserved for forced-labor teams. And the colloquial term for murder during the genocide was *work*. Evidently, the path from forced labor to forced murder is not as long as it might seem. To the extent, hence, that global forces continue to favor a forced-labor, coffee-based regime in Rwanda, there is likely to be continued strife.

Hope for Rwanda lies, in my opinion, in two realms: regionally, in the potential unity of the oppressed peoples of Great Lakes Africa, and in Rwanda, in the same forces of public dissent that sprang to life in the early 1990s.

In late 1994, the human-rights activist Monique Mujawamariya was asked, "What happened in your country?" Her reply is instructive:

> The people revolted against a well-armed dictatorial regime, and they are paying a high price for their attempt to install democracy. The dictator's clan knew that, as a result of international pressure and the mobilization of the people, it would have to share power. People had massively joined opposition parties; this threw the regime into a fever. So it decided to crush the moderate opposition, to eliminate the intellectuals, to kill everybody who could have laid claim to power. It is a revolution, within which a genocide has taken place. (Saint-Jean 1994, 13)

Only the Rwandan people, strengthened by unity with neighboring peoples, can take the steps needed to avert mass death in the future. The shining example of mass resistance in the early 1990s gives us reason to hope.

Suggested Reading

Caplan, Gerald, and Anatole Sangare. 2000. "The Preventable Genocide." On-line at <http://www.oau-oua.org/Document/ipep/ipep.htm>: Organization of African Unity.

Chossudovsky, Michel. *The Globalisation of Poverty: Impacts of IMF and World Bank Reforms.* London and Atlantic Highlands, N.J.: Zed Books; Penang, Malaysia: Third World Network.

Des Forges, Alison. 1999. *Leave None to Tell the Story: Genocide in Rwanda.* New York and Paris: Human Rights Watch.

Omaar, Rakiya, and Alex de Waal. 1995. *Rwanda: Death, Despair, and Defiance.* 2d ed. London: African Rights.

Smith, David Norman. 1998a. "Postcolonial Genocide." In *The Coming Age of Scarcity: Preventing Mass Death and Genocide in the Twenty-first Century,* edited by Michael Dobkowski and Isidor Wallimann, 220–44. Syracuse: Syracuse Univ. Press.

———. 1998b. "The Psychocultural Roots of Genocide: Legitimacy and Crisis in Rwanda." *American Psychologist* 53, no. 7 (July): 743–53.

Storey, Andy. 1999. "Economics and Ethnic Conflict: Structural Adjustment in Rwanda." *Development Policy Review* 17: 43–63.

Uvin, Peter. 1998. *Aiding Violence: The Development Enterprise in Rwanda.* West Hartford, Conn.: Kumarian Press.

12

The Feminization of Global Scarcity and Violence

Waltraud Queiser Morales

Structural violence especially affects the lives of women and other subordinated groups. When we ignore this fact we ignore the security of the majority of the planet's occupants.
—V. Spike Peterson and Anne Sisson Runyan, *Global Gender Issues*

GLOBAL SCARCITY and violence are part of a seamless web of relative deprivation and inequality that impacts the weakest members of human society disproportionately. Among the millions of the world's poor who suffer injustice and desperation today, women and children are systematically victimized. Their struggle to survive ever worsening resource scarcity and their social, political, and economic marginalization has had disproportionately negative consequences for global sustainability. If the dangers of global scarcity are to be avoided, the plight of the weakest members of human society must be addressed because the coming age of scarcity will not be gender free. As in the past, the underlying causes of economic and social disintegration in the twenty-first century include gendered scarcity and structural violence against women.

Feminization of Scarcity

For some, the emphasis on gender concerns within underdevelopment detracts from the important work at hand. However, the feminization of poverty, scarcity, and violence is a reality that cannot be ignored. The fact

173

that poor women in the Third World represent a new global underclass that the current economic order and traditional development models perpetuate is central to the crisis of scarcity in the twenty-first century. Peterson and Runyan (1993) have defined structural violence as the reduced life expectancy of women and children as a result of oppressive political and economic structures. The statistics are revealing. More than two-thirds of women's work is unpaid labor in the home, invisible to a country's official gross domestic product and the gross global output. However, women earn only one-tenth of the global income, and own less than 1 percent of the world's property. Women work one-third more hours daily than do men yet earn only 70 percent of a man's nonagricultural wage in the Third World. Nearly 50 percent of women in the developing world are below the poverty line compared to only 30 percent of men, and in many Third World countries women constitute some 60 percent of the rural poor. And despite their systematic exclusion from the economic systems of the Third World and their depressed earning abilities, women who head households spend more on food for the family than male-headed households.

Moreover, the deprivation of women also has a much greater negative multiplier effect on overall conditions of global scarcity. Conversely, employment opportunities, economic independence, and guaranteed education for women have proved to have positive multiplier effects on sustainable development. For this reason, Mieka Nishimizu, vice president of the World Bank, argued: "If you educate a boy you educate a human being. If you educate a girl, you educate generations" (quoted in Buvinic 1997, 234). Therefore, the problems of underdevelopment and scarcity are NOT gender neutral. The mistaken assumptions of traditional, unsustainable, and gender-biased development models have resulted in unintended consequences that have imposed greater hardships and obstacles for women in the developing world. Probably in no other area have unintended consequences of unsustainable development had more negative multiplier effects than in global population policy.

Women and the Population Crisis

Overpopulation is an integral component of the feminization of poverty, that vicious cycle of deprivation inherited by generations of women in the Third World. Approaches to population reduction have generally relied on birth-control policies almost exclusively. However, in the Third World, the relative disempowerment of women politically and economically has meant that birth-control programs have often been ineffective. Population programs have often ignored the fact that women's rights are also human rights and that cultural and traditional restrictions cannot deprive women of the same rights that men have under international, as well as national, laws. Typically, population policies have tended to focus on controlling women's choices without recognizing that women must have a voice in reproductive decisions. The tensions between an individual woman's right to reproductive choice and voluntary limitations in family size are resolvable. Recently, international conferences and movements—for example, the Beijing Fourth World Conference on Women in 1996—affirmed the rights of women over their own sexuality and their reproductive rights, and urged that national abortion laws achieve the goal of decriminalization.

Empowerment of women and the improvement in their social and economic positions in the Third World are critical components of population policy. Given a choice, experts argue, women will have only the number of children for whom they can adequately provide life opportunities. Studies have shown that educated women tend to have fewer children, that women with greater economic security tend to have fewer children, and that women whose social status is not based solely or primarily on their reproductive role tend to have fewer children. The conclusion seems to be that a global decrease in the birthrate becomes more possible with conscious gender analysis in development policies and with the improvement of the economic, political, and social status of women in the Third World (indeed, among the deprived women of the First World as well). A key caveat is that economic growth alone may not automatically translate into population reduction. The type of economic growth and its impact on gender roles and women will be critical.

Modernization and some free-market economic programs may actually leave women worse off, especially since joblessness, abuse, and deteriorating social services disproportionately impact women and children around the world. On October 12, 1999, the "Day of Six Billion," the United Nations issued the chill reminder that despite the greatest wealth the world has ever seen, 1 billion people lacked the fundamental elements of human dignity—clean water, food, secure housing, basic education, and basic health care. In the developing world, the majority were women denied access to decent health and whose reproduction constituted the single greatest threat to their lives. Indeed, one conclusion must be that if we take care of the world's women, then we will significantly reduce the global population crisis.

Women and Development

In the process of national development and economic growth, the women of the Third World have generally been ignored and victimized. Among the most powerless members of developing societies in Africa, Asia, the Middle East, and Latin America, women, especially women who belong to oppressed minority groups distinguished by color, class, or religion, have been impacted negatively and disproportionately. Nevertheless, in the past decades, these disadvantaged women have thrown off their oppression and have come to play decisive roles in the creation of independent grassroots political organizations and social movements. Through these new social movements and the revolutionary new development models of Women in Development (WID) and Women and Development (WAD), women have chartered new avenues for social change. Their collective success has proved decisive in the struggle to overcome global inequality, overpopulation, and resource scarcity.

Several decades of failed development led to the recognition that women are critical to the development process. In Africa, agricultural improvements floundered because traditional development programs excluded women and erroneously trained only men when women were the primary farmers and bore responsibility for food production. Although Third World women were also the key economic actors in the marketing of food, they had no access to new agricultural technology, training, and credits. UN statistics indicated that more rural women lived below the poverty line than men, but that agricultural assistance was almost exclusively directed to rural men despite the fact that these resources generally never found their way into family coffers or into agricultural improvements. As a result, these inefficient and wrongheaded development programs failed to alleviate the chronic problems of overpopulation, poverty, and starvation in the developing world. Failure led to critical reexamination of the most basic assumptions concerning women, underdevelopment, and global scarcity.

One revolutionary conclusion was the realization that women are key to development and reproduction. Nevertheless, development experts (most of whom were men) had routinely focused on men in dealing with population and family-planning programs. However, successful family planning has never been as simple as providing birth-control methods to women, because modernization unequally and unfairly impacted the women of the Third World. Unsustainable economic growth and technical advances actually eroded the precarious status and reduced the life opportunities of poor women. For example, mechanization improved agricultural productivity, but it also eliminated critical jobs for both men and women. And because women found themselves on the bottom of the economic ladder to begin with, they were impacted more extensively.

Globalization and industrialization have radically restructured the roles that women played in many developing economies. Routinely, women have been displaced into low-tech and low-wage assembly jobs, which involve the least labor costs. The significant wage differentials between men and women in the modernized sectors of the economy have also disadvantaged women most. In general, not only are women relegated to the less-valuable work, but also women's work tends to be ignored or undervalued in many developing (as well as developed) societies. Economic austerity measures, such as the economic Structural Adjustment Programs imposed by the International Monetary Fund and World Bank have also impacted Third World women disproportionately. Unemployment has increased in the short term as a result of structural adjustments, because governments and private employers are forced to reduce labor costs—that is, hire less workers, reduce the numbers currently on the rolls, as well as reduce salaries. Women lose jobs not only in the formal sector but also in the mainstay informal economy, where women are forced to compete with men for scarce resources and employment opportunities. And when women suffer, entire families, especially children, suffer. The informal economy represents the unregulated and rapacious markets of the streets and underground and illegal economies of the Third World, peopled with the desperately poor street peddlers and street children who are forced to make work and struggle with long hours in order barely to survive.

New development movements, such as Women in Development and Women and Development, recognized not only the central role of women in the development process, but also the critical relationship among economics, empowerment, and developmental change. Women represented more than 50 percent of the global population, yet they were being not only ignored, but victimized and oppressed as well. Only if women were empowered could they become independent actors able to control their lives, their bodies, their families, and their economic situations, and therefore, be able to effect the personal and social changes essential to sustainable development. Thus, the new development approaches not only encouraged the direct involvement of women in the problems of overpopulation and scarcity, but also emphasized the importance of fair access. If women were provided better access to education, the job market, and material resources, then many problems could be resolved. As long as the majority of Third World women remained systematically excluded from traditional avenues of advancement, individual efforts to improve their situations were certain to failure. Indeed, a more radical solution provided women development opportunities exclusive of men. The goal was for women to shake off the bonds of male domination and to assume roles of economic independence. The results were innovative women-only projects and small-scale economic programs such as the Grameen Bank that allowed women greater opportunities to devise their own development plans rather than compete in the "male-dominated development process."

Begun as an experiment in 1976 by Muhammad Yunus, by 1983 the Grameen Bank was firmly established as an independent bank in Bangladesh. The bank grew to serve more than thirty-six thousand poor villages and 2.1 million borrowers of whom 94 percent were poor women. Over the years, the bank not only had lent more than $1 billion dollars to the neediest in Bangladesh, but also had become part of a progressive international development movement. The bank's founder believed that his strategy of lending almost exclusively to women would reverse the gender discrimination of financial institutions in Bangladesh and the Third World where women were unable to be independent economic actors and hold title to property or contract loans. The microlending experiment was tried in 1992 in Bolivia by Banco Solidario, which became the first private commercial bank dedicated to microlending. The Bolivian bank came to serve some seventy-six thousand borrowers of whom 70 percent were women.

The success of microlending programs shook up the global development bureaucracy, challenging gender bias in development and the bigger-is-better approach of institutions such as the World Bank. Instead of financing primarily large-scale infrastructure development projects as in the past, the major international development institutions began to support grassroots microenterprises. In 1994, the UN International Conference on Population and Development gave special recognition to innovative development models such as microlending and microenterprises that helped to empower women economically. At the same time, the proliferation of grassroots women's organizations around the world has also increased both the social and the political power of women and has had an impact not only on how women conceptualize themselves and their personal and public roles, but also on how society views them. Many grassroots development organizations by women are also becoming feminist organizations, which are primarily focused on women's issues and the status of women in society. Overall, the politicization of both types of groups has resulted in an increase in women as visible social actors and in the greater acceptance of women as political leaders.

Gendered Violence

What the gendered division of violence constructs is a world shaped by hostile forces.
    —V. Spike Peterson and Anne Sisson Runyan, *Global Gender Issues*

Poverty, injustice, environmental degradation, and conflict interact in complex and potent ways. The discrimination against women is undeniably a critical part of the complex of causes of conflict and violence. Thus, population growth and environmental decline lead to social and political unrest and conflict; in turn, these conditions increase the potential for environmental and internal war-induced population displacement and international refugees, 80 percent of whom are women and children. However, refugees not only flee environmental destruction and internal conflict but also cause these conditions. Thus, the world's poorest of the poor (the majority of whom are women) cause as much natural-resource depletion as all the other 3 billion developing-world people put together. The principal agents of deforestation and water depletion in the Third World are the desperate refugees from civil war and rural poverty. For instance, in Rwanda's brutal civil war, more than 2 million refugees fled abysmal conditions of resource scarcity and genocide only to re-create these horrors in overcrowded and insecure refugee camps where violence against women and children became endemic.

In the same manner that scarcity and environmental depletion in-

crease the potential for violence generally, these factors also promote insti-
tutionalized violence against women. In the international and internal
wars of Rwanda and the former Yugoslavia, gender-related violations became recognized and ultimately prosecutable as war crimes for the first
time. Although systematic sexual assaults and rapes have served as gendered instruments of violence and warfare against women throughout
world history, only recently have these offenses been accepted as war
crimes and egregious violations of human rights. Most governments and
international institutions had permitted official and social tolerance of violence against women during conflicts, in great measure because of the extensive state-supported violence against women by Third World military
and police forces. However, in 1993, media reports of the systematic rape,
torture, sexual enslavement, and murder of Bosnian Muslim women and
children by Serbian military and paramilitary forces provoked the world's
condemnation of rape as a weapon of war and ethnic cleansing.

Gendered violence served as an integral and insidious component of
interethnic conflict and genocide. A survivor of the multiethnic strife in
the former Yugoslavia observed that "nationalism and sexism are deeply
interwoven, one nourishing the other and relying on the other" (Morokvasic 1998, 68). In the wars of Bosnia and Kosovo, women experienced multiple victimizations by enemies and friends alike as subjects and
objects of the strife. Not only were women absent from the halls of national and regional power where war policies had been made, but also they
became captive to the gendered ideologies and patriarchal symbolism of
the region's interethnic violence. Women were stereotyped as the
guardians of ethnic purity, and were "either excessively protected or violated," depending on whether they were "perceived as 'Ours' or 'Theirs' "
(ibid.).

Women are, therefore, the direct and indirect victims of everyday violence and the social disintegration, economic hardship, and political chaos
of international and internal war. Indeed, wars, especially multiethnic
wars, are primarily wars against women and children. Through gendered
violence, genocide takes on another pernicious meaning—the death of the
ethnic group and race. The intended goal is genocide or ethnic cleansing
by other means. In this way, the destruction of the ethnic Enemy and
Other is accomplished via the rape of women in the former Yugoslavia, as
well as in Rwanda, Somalia, Algeria, Haiti, East Timor, India, and the
many other countries in internal and multiethnic conflict. Precisely be-

cause this gendered violence is intended to threaten the entire out-group, torture and rape are perceived not as crimes against individual women but as collective sectarian violence against the ethnic and nationalist groups to which the women belong. It is in this way that sexual violence against women becomes politicized, ideologized, and gendered, in the process, further depersonalizing and dehumanizing its victims, and feeding that cycle of scarcity and violence.

Ending the Cycle

However, there are constructive ways to break the vicious cycle of scarcity and violence against women. The first step is to recognize the violence against women as part of a seamless web of humankind's inhumanity to man, and to encourage a normative examination and debate of the entrenched power relations that have caused gender discrimination and marginalization. A second important way to interrupt the cycle is to find and to adopt a new and more humanistic social paradigm based on gender equality and respect for all groups that are different because of race, ethnicity, class, religion, and gender. Third, planning for humanity's future must be taken away from those people who cannot challenge entrenched assumptions or accept a broader vision. Fourth, we must all realize and act upon the fact that women's security is vital for environmental security and human survival. The endangered status of the world's women serves as a challenge to prevailing power relations, including patriarchal forms of power, and is an accurate measure of the disenfranchisement of the powerless among us.

To effect these broader solutions, specific policies can also be implemented. The structural scarcity that confronts humankind is the result of an imbalance in distribution that is deeply rooted in institutions and class, gender, and ethnic relations. Moreover, the intimate relationship of the state of the world's women with global overpopulation, the crisis of unsustainable development, and catastrophic environmental decline makes it imperative that both short-term and long-term solutions to these problems include the world's women. Governments and international institutions must provide support for female education, for medical and health care, for family planning, for economic independence, and for political and social empowerment. Women's rights must be respected and protected as human rights, and systematic violence against women must be fully prosecuted as crimes under domestic and international laws. Only by relieving inequalities in gender relations and providing equal opportunities and life chances to women will women be able to fulfill and to formulate their needs. And as we begin this search for ways out of the coming global scarcity, the most important lesson to remember is that if we take care of the world's women, we will surely take care of the entire family of humanity.

Suggested Reading

Buvinic, Mayra. 1997. "Women in Poverty: A New Global Underclass." *Foreign Policy* 108 (fall): 38–53.

Elliott, Lorraine. 1998. *The Global Politics of the Environment.* New York: New York Univ. Press.

Haynes, Jeff. 1996. *Third World Politics: A Concise Introduction.* Oxford: Blackwell.

Jacobson, Jodi. 1992. *Gender Bias: Roadblock to Sustainable Development.* Worldwatch Paper 110. Washington, D.C.: Worldwatch Institute.

Morales, Waltraud Queiser, and Megan A. Duncanson. 2000. "Gender Theory and Women in Latin America: A Status Report." *South Eastern Latin Americanist* 43 (winter): 37–57.

Morokvasic, Mirjana. 1998. "The Logics of Exclusion: Nationalism, Sexism, and the Yugoslav War." In *Gender, Ethnicity, and Political Ideologies,* edited by Nickie Charles and Helen Hintjens, 65–90. New York: Routledge.

Peterson, V. Spike, and Anne Sisson Runyan. 1993. *Global Gender Issues.* Boulder, Colo.: Westview Press.

Scott, Catherine V. 1995. *Gender and Development: Rethinking Modernization and Dependency Theory.* Boulder, Colo.: Lynne Rienner.

Waylen, Georgina. 1996. *Gender in Third World Politics.* Buckingham, Eng.: Open Univ. Press.

Yuval-Davis, Nira. 1997. *Gender and Nation.* Thousand Oaks, Calif.: Sage.

13

Scarcity, Genocides, and the Postmodern Individual

Leon Rappoport

HOW ARE PEOPLE likely to react if future scarcities lead to increasing conflicts and genocidal events in much of the world? More specifically, what sort of social and psychological responses may be anticipated from "postmoderns"—people who have grown up in the high-tech and media-saturated environments of North America and Western Europe? This question is explored by first outlining the sorts of genocidal conflicts that seem probable in future conditions of scarcity, and then reviewing the personality attributes that many social scientists and culture critics already perceive to be characteristic of youth in postmodern environments. Finally, the various ways that such postmodern individuals may react to genocidal events are discussed.

Genocidal Conflicts

It takes no great leap of the imagination to understand the connection between scarcity and the deadly conflicts that can ultimately, and just as quickly, kill as many people as perished in the European or Cambodian Holocausts. The most obvious case in point is Africa, where scarcities appear endemic either because of crop failures, warfare, or government mismanagement and corruption, and often all three at the same time. Over the past decade, these conditions have created massive famines and genocidal conflicts with tens of millions of victims. Even where governments operate with integrity and goodwill, however, scarcities brought on by

183

overpopulation, soil erosion, water shortages, and epidemic diseases such as AIDS undermine the ability of authorities to implement humane policies. And as a result, their societies tend to deteriorate into a state of armed tribal rivalries.

If scarcities of one sort or another clearly stand as the cause of conflicts and mass death in much of Africa, then the reverse appears to be true in Eastern Europe. Here, sociopolitical conflicts have emerged as the apparent cause of scarcities, but the end result has been the same for the victims of ethnic cleansing in the former Yugoslavia, or of the Russo-Chechin war. The destructive effects of such "low"—or "moderate"-intensity conflicts are similar throughout the world. In the Middle East, there is the perennial Arab-Israeli conflict, whereas in Iraq, people continue to die from the indirect effects of U.S. bombings that have destroyed much of the country's physical infrastructure. In the Far East, the civil war in Afghanistan and the wars of rebellion in Sri Lanka and Indonesia claim their victims more directly, whereas, in Latin America, victims accrue from the effects of guerrilla warfare, narco-terrorism, death squads, and counterinsurgency campaigns.

There is also a "breeder effect" in all these cases whereby the male children who survive but are left destitute and traumatized by their exposure to violence become teenagers who are easily recruited into the factions that perpetuate ongoing campaigns of warfare and terrorist violence. It deserves emphasis, furthermore, that powerful, prosperous countries such as the United States are not immune to the dynamics of violence associated with scarcity. The social dislocations produced as the United States has become a postindustrial state geared to global corporate economics appear closely linked to the rise of private militias, armed religious cults, and gang violence. Although the death toll thus far from cults, gangs, suicidal paranoids, terrorist bombers, and alienated schoolboys who turn their guns on students and teachers is still relatively small, it may well show a dramatic increase under the impact of serious scarcity. And according to recent news reports, our government is already preparing contingency plans against the threat of chemical—or biological-weapon attacks by domestic or foreign terrorists.

No discussion of potential genocidal events associated with scarcity would be complete without mention of the rogue-nation nuclear-weapon scenario. The theme here is that the sociopolitical pressures created by scarcity would increase the likelihood that either nations or the terrorists they support will acquire and eventually use nuclear weapons against the United States or Western Europe. Scarcity in the former Soviet Union is also presumed to be the reason that material and technology from the Soviet nuclear arsenal have apparently been offered for sale to any high bidder.

Postmodern Culture and Personality

Detailed discussion concerning the end of the modern and beginning of the postmodern era is beyond the scope of this chapter, but some brief perspectives on the issue may be noted. One view I presented elsewhere is that the modernity ideal died at Auschwitz and Hiroshima. That is, the fundamental assumption of modernity, that human progress toward a better world could be achieved through increased rationality, technological efficiency, and social control, has been, on the evidence of the Nazi death camps and nuclear bombing of Japan, shown to be false. Nothing in modern science, law, or religion served to forestall or seriously mitigate the mass genocides of the twentieth century. Indeed, more than one historian has argued that the mass killings of the twentieth century were facilitated by various mechanisms associated with rationality, technology, and social control.

Another perspective was offered by the architecture critic Charles Jencks, who proclaimed the end of modernity when the Pruitt-Igoe housing project in St. Louis was demolished in 1972. Designed according to the rationalized, functional criteria of modernity, this low-income, high-rise housing complex was finally seen to be unfit for human habitation. Yet another way that some writers have distinguished the postmodern from the modern is through a series of simple material comparisons. Accordingly, electronic clocks are postmodern, whereas mechanical clocks are modern; nuclear weapons, computers, and television are all postmodern, whereas gunpowder, adding machines, typewriters, and radio are all modern. In broader cultural terms, the postmodern versus modern distinction may be seen in comparisons such as feminism versus sexism, the Internet versus the telephone, MTV versus the hit parade, and almost all of the films of the 1980s and '90s versus those films of the '30s, '40s, and '50s.

Films and television have a particularly important role in postmodern culture because they allow individuals to evade domination by established, normative realities and encourage awareness of alternative possible worlds. Commentators on postmodernity further suggest that in some respects the electronic media technologies have advanced to such an extent that the images and simulations they produce have become more significant than the objects or conditions they claim to represent. As Marshall McLuhan famously observed, the medium becomes the message. What this statement implies is that our perception of persons, issues, and events tends to be ruled by media imagery.

Taken together, all of the aspects of postmodernity discussed above, and many more that could be cited, cannot fail to influence the culture base that social scientists recognize as the foundation for human development and personality. Indeed, it is a truism in the social sciences that in any society, personality is grounded upon culture, and culture reflects the "collective personality" of the society. Consequently, over the past decade, an increasing number of personality theorists have begun to discuss and investigate the effects of postmodern culture on the personality development of the youths growing up in it. Most of this work has been based on the premise that an individual's core sense of self or identity is based on the systems of meaning (language, roles, norms, and values) provided by his or her culture. It therefore appears axiomatic that major changes in a culture will inevitably bring about major changes in the self-concepts or personalities of its inhabitants.

But how do such changes occur? In premodern and early modern societies, the mechanisms of identity formation or change or both were not considered problematic. One's self-concept or identity was seen to be largely determined by the cultural meanings attached to one's gender, status in the family (first or later born), and the status of the family (particularly the father) in society, as often indicated by the family name: Baker, Hunter, Smith, and so on. With the rise of industrial societies, and even more so in postindustrial, postmodern societies, however, identity and the self have become profoundly problematic because the traditional meanings of gender and family-background factors have become increasingly irrelevant. This state of affairs was already beginning to be understood in the 1940s and '50s, and was described in popular works by theorists such as David Reisman (*The Lonely Crowd,*) Erich Fromm (*Escape from Freedom,*) and Erik Erikson (*Childhood and Society*). But it was Erikson who had the greatest impact. During the 1960s and '70s, his concept of the adolescent "identity crisis" became something of a household phrase.

The conditions these writers originally saw as emerging threats to healthy social adjustment and stable personality development have now, in postmodern societies, become the rule rather than the exception. Thus, it is unusual today to find strong, intact families able to model a clear sense of independent selfhood to their children, as in the classic TV series *Father Knows Best*. And even where such families exist, they can hardly succeed in this task because the meanings and values they represent often do not connect with the situations challenging young people in the postmodern environment. In the larger social context, moreover, identity has become increasingly problematic because structural and process changes now occur so rapidly as to offer only an amorphous basis for identity formation. The former certainties provided by predictable gender roles and career paths have disappeared along with the industrial economy that once supported them. Instead, young people now encounter an "information economy" emphasizing consumption rather than production and fluid, rapid adaptations to changing technologies and markets.

In general, therefore, for many young people, the former ideal of an integrated, unitary self-concept has gone beyond the problematic and, like the manual typewriter and rotary telephone, taken on the quality of a historical artifact. What has emerged instead is a sense of self characterized by diversity, flexibility, and multidimensionality—an adaptable self that has the potential to project more than one possible identity. In other words, what is valued is an ability to reinvent the self to suit changing demands and situations.

Popular-culture examples of this type of "postmodern self" abound in the form of celebrity performers such as Madonna, who seems able to easily reinvent her persona to fit the demands of changing trends in music and films. At another level, in the now-defunct TV series *Highway to Heaven*, the lead characters were angels who took on a variety of novel identities as they went about aiding people in distress. And surely at the head of any list of famous people who represent the qualities of postmodernity in themselves would be Bill and Hillary Clinton. Indeed, much of the controversy surrounding the Clintons follows from what many critics see as their excessive "flexibility" concerning personal and political issues.

The underlying attraction of both the fictional and the real models of a pluralistic self and diversified personal identity lies in the exciting transformational possibilities they present. On the one hand, they dramatize the rich potentials that may become available when the social construction of reality principle is applied to personality development, and on the other, they represent a glamorous alternative to the prosaic qualities associated with a single, unitary identity. Particularly for young people reared in the postmodern environment of rapid socioeconomic changes and a 50 percent divorce rate, therefore, the older ideal of an identity based on consistent, one-dimensional loyalties to a specific career and specific mate can appear only arbitrary.

Human-potential psychologists and therapists who often appear on TV talk shows also contribute to the culture trend toward pluralism by warning against becoming trapped in a fixed sense of self that can inhibit personal growth. Therapies designed to encourage self-transformation are readily available, and by recourse to body-work facilities and cosmetic surgery, the body itself may be harnessed to the task of self-transformation.

Some psychiatric theorists consider that this trend encouraging pluralism and change signals a dangerous public vulnerability to mental disorders. The American Psychiatric Association's diagnostic manual defines an identity disorder as the "inability to integrate aspects of the self," and a recent survey reported a significant rise in the number of persons diagnosed with such disorders. But other theorists do not agree. At least one has argued that a "schizoid consciousness" is adaptive to contemporary social life, and another suggests that it is normal for people to have several "subpersonalities."

There is mounting research support for the more positive viewpoint. One study has shown that normal college students think about their future development as consisting of a range of different "possible selves." Another reports that persons with more complex, pluralistic self-concepts are better able to cope with stress, the premise being that if a loss of self-esteem occurs in one self-domain, it can be offset by success in a different one. And there is a third study indicating that persons with high scores on a measure of personality multiplicity show higher levels of creativity than those persons with low scores.

Although most theorists agree that the self is changing under the impacts of postmodern culture and technology, there is no consensus about the long-term effects. Kenneth Gergen (1991) has suggested that the postmodern self is "saturated"—overstimulated and fragmented from the impacts of exposure to nonstop communications media. But the same environmental conditions are seen by another theorist as producing an "empty self" in postmodern individuals who then try to smother their interior emptiness with consumer goods. And a third perspective has been developed by Edward Sampson, who theorizes that the problems of contemporary selfhood are due to the irrelevancy of the traditional American ideal of "self-contained individualism." He suggests that in the global world system today, the individual can no longer find meaning in assertive independence, but must find it through relationships and integration with a larger community. Accordingly, Sampson sees the postmodern individual adapting by maintaining a pluralistic manifold of self-concepts.

Taken together, the burden of evidence accumulating from analyses of popular culture, empirical research studies, and theoretical discussions clearly points to multiplicity or pluralism as the defining quality of the postmodern personality. This definition poses a major challenge to the unitary, hierarchical personality system that has dominated modern psychological theory in the past. Based on the view that personality is a centrally organized, vertically integrated system in which lower-order impulses and emotions are controlled by higher-order cognitive (ego) processes, the hierarchical model now appears obsolete. It seems destined to be replaced by a more decentralized, horizontally organized system. In the latter, cognitive and emotional processes are understood to be interpenetrating rather than opposed, and the model for consciousness is a "conversation of equals" rather than a struggle for power.

When viewed in this perspective, the modern idea that personal morality involves a conscience or superego that struggles against basic instincts in order to enforce obedience to internalized moral values seems obsolete, and reminiscent of a Victorian steam engine. By contrast, the postmodern perspective would conceptualize personal morality as based on context-dependent evaluative possibilities. As one theorist has already suggested, the postmodern individual rejects the idea of universal moral principles in favor of diverse, locally grounded moral alternatives, and seeks to define morality in terms of relationships and communal values. This type of morality can be summarized as agnostic, highly relativistic, and independent of any single system of rationality. It follows that moral decisions or choices are thus no longer a matter of obedience to "natural laws" or religious values, but have instead become reduced to the status of an act of will dependent upon how individuals interpret their situation.

Postmoderns' Reactions to Genocidal Events

Before examining the issue of how postmoderns may respond to genocidal events, it will be helpful to first clarify the basis of the discussion. Although focused on the postmodern individual, the question is not addressed in a genuinely postmodern voice. If this were to be done, then it would immediately require a critical, contextualist analysis of the question itself: who is asking it, and for what purpose, and what particular sorts of genocidal events are involved? To do this would be to adopt the methodology of discursive textual analysis known as deconstruction, and the likely final answer would be simply that "it all depends."

It should also be acknowledged that like modern and premodern individuals, postmoderns are not all the same. If traditional social class distinctions have become more complex and difficult to interpret today than in the past, they are, nevertheless, still relevant. At least metaphorically, there are the postmodern proletarians who in one way or another maintain the information highways versus the plutocrats who cruise on them. And there also are those "lumpen" and outlaw inhabitants of cyberspace, forever seeking new thrills via pornography, fraudulent Web sites, or the creation of viruses, as well as the avant-garde technocrats always pushing the limits of global linkage. But piecemeal analyses based on the foregoing distinctions would be impractical here. Instead, for the sake of convenience, the following discussion assumes an "average" postmodern individual. And when considering how such individuals may respond to genocidal events, the primary psychological factor involves empathy.

A large body of research indicates that empathy, a reflexive emotional feeling of identification with the suffering of victims, is the main motivation for observers to respond sympathetically. Drawing on this research evidence for his analysis of how people responded to the major genocides of the twentieth century, Ervin Staub concluded that two general conditions inhibit empathy. One is material scarcity, which drives people toward preoccupation with their own personal needs and reduces their sense of connection with others. This circumstance was the case in Weimar Germany, the former Soviet Union, and many other places. The other condition is an inner psychological state that Staub describes as being associated with a weak ego or poorly articulated self-concept. This condition is characteristic of people who have been traumatized during childhood by severe abuse, the chaotic deprivation occurring in war zones, or by family breakups in bitter divorce conflicts. Such people tend to deal with anxiety and stress by using paranoid defense mechanisms, blaming others for their difficulties.

There is no substantial evidence showing that the multiplicity characterizing postmoderns leads to paranoid defense mechanisms, or equates to a weak ego, but there is enough similarity between these states and multiplicity to suggest parallel reactions to scarcity-induced stress. Moreover, something like a "blaming the victim" reaction would certainly fit the free-market orientation of postmodern culture. Illustrative examples might include the defensive reactions of Bill Clinton to the Lewinsky scandal, or the way Bill Gates has blamed weak competitors for the government lawsuit against Microsoft.

Another explanation for why reflexive feelings of empathy may be repressed or ignored has been suggested by the social psychiatrist Robert Lifton (1986). Based on his studies of the German physicians who performed atrocious acts in the Nazi death camps, he concluded that they were able to remain indifferent to their victims through a process of "doubling." This process is defined as a form of dissociation whereby the individual adopts two or more alternative self-concepts. Thus, Lifton found that the German doctors saw themselves, on the one hand, as sensitive humanitarians, and, on the other, as respectable objective scientists while performing horrific experiments on helpless women and children. In a subsequent study, Lifton and Erik Markusen found a similar but less intense form of doubling among American nuclear-warfare planners.

Insofar as doubling is a valid mechanism allowing people to accommodate themselves to genocidal activities, and since doubling appears to be a variant of the general multiplicity, if not "schizoid consciousness," of postmoderns, it is plausible to assume that postmoderns would probably not find it very difficult to tolerate genocidal events. In short, it may well be that the same adaptive qualities of a pluralistic self-concept that can make for creativity, flexibility, and effective stress coping can also insulate against empathy.

Prevalent culture trends expressed through language and imagery have also been identified as a source of indifference to atrocious events. Studies of the Nazi SS personnel and other organized perpetrators of extreme violence indicate that an abstract, "nonfeeling" language of euphemisms, acronyms, and metaphors allows people to distance themselves or dissociate from the realities of human destruction intrinsic to their work. There is a fairly direct parallel here to the semiotics typical of postmodern culture, in that much of contemporary language and imagery is manifestly "nonfeeling." One need consider only the rapid collage imagery, metaphors, and language of music videos, video games, computer icons, passwords, PINs, and the trivialization of violence in films and TV.

Immersion in such a semiotic environment may not produce full-blown dissociation but is likely to facilitate a significant degree of indifference or desensitization toward genocidal events. And this condition would be particularly relevant to situations in which victims lack the sign qualities that can evoke empathy among observers. In a rudimentary way, such desensitization may already be apparent from the way postmoderns deal with the homeless people cluttering urban centers, either treating them as invisible or dropping a handout without breaking stride.

A final issue concerns the difference between modern and postmodern morality noted earlier. Recall that in contrast to the modern ideal of universal moral values, postmodern values were described as context-dependent possibilities. Postmoderns, therefore, are not likely to show knee-jerk moral responses to genocidal events, but to reflect on them in a more complex, exploratory fashion. The contrast can be seen clearly in the ways that moral issues are treated in modern as compared with postmodern media dramas. Such postmodern productions as *Pulp Fiction* and *The Sopranos* deliberately confound modern moral values by having attractive characters placed in ambiguous, amoral situations such that no simplistic moral principles can be applied to their behavior. The modern films made by John Ford and John Wayne impose a straightforward, "predigested" morality on viewers, whereas the moral issues in films made by Quentin Tarentino are confabulated. The former succeeded as popular entertainment because they gave assurances of moral certainties; the latter succeed today because they emphasize moral ambiguities. A relevant citation—life imitating art?—might be seen in the way the O. J. Simpson murder trial became a major media entertainment.

Other aspects of postmodern culture also promote complex, ambiguous moral perspectives. During the Gulf War, television often presented near-simultaneous reports from both sides of the conflict, and viewers could be led to cheer for the bombers while almost at the same time experiencing sympathy for the bombees. Postmodernism even acknowledges the logic of terrorism: when anyone can become a victim, governments are shown to be impotent; when terror attacks generate wide media coverage, they become a public relations tactic; and when everyone can be defined as a direct or indirect participant in the world system, there are no innocent bystanders. This statement is not to suggest that the logic of terrorism is accepted as legitimate. What *is* accepted, however, is that as soon as yesterday's terrorists (for example, the PLO or the IRA) agree to renounce violence, they become legitimate participants in the world system.

In general, therefore, given the qualities of multiplicity associated with postmodern personality development, and the increasing climate of moral ambiguity characterizing postmodern culture, the only plausible estimate that can be made of how postmodern individuals would respond to genocidal events is that it will be tentative, complex, and multifaceted. That is, in situations where the events are not persistently presented in the media, and where victims do not evoke a significant level of empathy in observers, the response will tend toward indifference or apathy. This outcome appears to be the case with current genocidal conflicts in sub-Saharan Africa. The contrary is indicated by reactions to the conflict in Kosovo, where conditions finally provoked an affirmative public response, but one that was carefully programmed to minimize involvement. The operative principle of postmodern public and government responses to the forces responsible for genocidal events may sum up to something like this: "If you can't wait them out, talk them out, or buy them out, then blow them up, but only if the cost-benefit ratio is very favorable."

Conclusion

Although most predictions of the future notoriously turn out to be wrong, given the conclusions presented here, that might be a good thing. However, all of the relevant cultural factors—the language, imagery, and climate of moral ambiguity—suggest that a growing process of desensitization is at work. And all of the relevant personality theory and research suggest that the multiplicity characterizing postmoderns facilitates the adoption of desensitizing stress-coping or defense mechanisms.

What this may mean for the future remains problematic. The pessimistic view is that in the short run, it portends a dark era in which a privileged postmodern minority will become smugly indifferent to an increasing number of genocidal conflicts. But there is also a more optimistic long view, whereby in due time, the postmodern minority will find the means, however slowly and tentatively, to save what can be saved while encouraging the spread of a liberating, humanitarian multiplicity.

Ways Out

There are no simple ways out from the likelihood that postmodern individuals will be relatively insensitive to genocidal events. However, this tendency might be substantially reduced through a combination of efforts in the popular media, churches, and education systems to counteract indifference. An illustrative example would be the film *Schindler's List* that was not only a popular success but also used in schools to convey knowledge of the Holocaust and foster empathy toward its victims. Sympathetic attention to the plight of other genocide victims has also been stimulated by celebrity musicians who have organized special concerts for this purpose. Finally, the effects of government policies should not be underestimated. If governments in Western Europe and North America committed themselves to respond quickly to genocidal conflicts by deploying effective relief and military forces, then postmodern individuals might be encouraged to participate or offer significant support.

Suggested Reading

Baumgardner, S. R., and Rappoport, L. 1996. "Culture and Self in Postmodern Perspective." *Humanistic Psychologist* 24: 116–40.

DeBerry, S. T. 1993. *Quantum Psychology: Steps to a Postmodern Ecology of Being.* Westport, Conn.: Praeger.

Gergen, K. J. 1991. *The Saturated Self.* New York: Basic Books.

Kaplan, Robert D. 1994. "The Coming Anarchy." *Atlantic Monthly* (Feb.): 44–76.

Kvale, S. 1992. "Postmodern Psychology: A Contradiction in Terms?" In *Psychology and Postmodernism,* edited by S. Kvale, 31–57. Newbury Park, Calif.: Sage.

Lifton, R. J. 1986. *The Nazi Doctors: Medical Killing and the Psychology of Genocide.* New York: Basic Books.

Rowan, J., and M. Cooper. 1999. *The Plural Self.* London: Sage.

Works Cited

Abernethy, Virginia. 1979. *Population Pressure and Cultural Adjustment*. New York: Human Sciences Press.

———. 1993. "The Demographic Transition Revisited: Lessons for Foreign Aid and U.S. Immigration Policy." *Ecological Economics* 8: 235–52.

———. 1994. "Optimism and Overpopulation." *Atlantic Monthly* (Dec.): 84–91.

———. 1999. *Population Politics*. 1993. Reprint. Piscataway, N.J.: Transactions Press.

Arens, Richard, ed. 1976. *Genocide in Paraguay*. Philadelphia: Temple Univ. Press.

Athanasiou, Tom. 1996. *Divided Planet*. Boston: Little, Brown.

Barnet, Richard, and John Cavanagh. 1994. *Global Dreams: Imperial Corporations and the New World Order*. New York: Simon and Schuster.

Bartlett, Albert, and Edward P. Lytwak. 1995. "Zero Growth of the Population of the United States." *Population and Environment* 16, no. 5: 415–28.

Baumgardner, S. R., and L. Rappoport. 1996. "Culture and Self in Postmodern Perspective." *Humanistic Psychologist* 24: 116–40.

Bello, Walden, with Shea Cunningham and Bill Rau. 1994. *Dark Victory: The United States, Structural Adjustment, and Global Poverty*. London: Pluto Press, for the Institute for Food and Development Policy, or Food First.

Blumberg, Paul. 1980. *Inequality in an Age of Decline*. New York: Oxford Univ. Press.

Bookman, Milica Z. 1997. *The Demographic Struggle for Power: The Political Economy of Demographic Engineering in the Modern World*. London and Portland, Oreg.: Frank Cass.

Borjas, George. 1995. "Know the Flow." *National Review* (Apr. 17): 44–49.

Borjas, George, and Richard B. Freeman. 1992. *The Economic Effects of Immigration in Source and Receiving Countries*. Chicago: Univ. of Chicago Press.

Briggs, Vernon M., Jr. 1990. "Testimony Before the U.S. House of Representatives Judiciary Committee Subcommittee on Immigration, Refugees, and International Law." *Congressional Record* (Mar. 13).

Brittain, Victoria. 1995. "The Continent That Lost Its Way." In *Global Issues,* edited by Robert M. Jackson, 150–52. Guilford, Conn.: Dushkin.

Brown, Lester, Christopher Flavin, and Sandra Postel. 1991. *Saving the Planet: How to Shape an Environmentally Sustainable Global Economy.* New York: W. W. Norton.

———. 2000. *Vital Signs, 2000.* New York: W. W. Norton.

———, eds. 1995. *Nature's Limits.* In *State of the World, 1995,* 3–20. New York: W. W. Norton.

Brown, Lester, and Hal Kane. 1980. *Building a Sustainable Society.* New York: W. W. Norton.

———. 1994. *Full House: Reassessing the Earth's Population Carrying Capacity.* New York: W. W. Norton.

Buchanan, Patrick J. 1998. *The Great Betrayal.* Boston: Little, Brown.

Buvinic, Mayra. 1997. "Women in Poverty: A New Global Underclass." *Foreign Policy* 108 (fall): 38–53.

Campbell, Colin. 1998. *The Future of Oil and Hydrocarbon Man.* Houston and London: Petroconsultants.

Caplan, Gerald, and Anatole Sangare. 2000. "The Preventable Genocide." On-line at <http://www.oau-oua.org/Document/ipep/ipep.htm>: Organization of African Unity.

Chatterjee, Pratap, and Matthias Finger. 1994. *The Earth Brokers: Power, Politics, and World Development.* New York: Routledge.

Chomsky, Noam. 1994. *World Orders Old and New.* New York: Columbia Univ. Press.

———. 1997. *Profit over People.* New York: Seven Stories.

Chossudovsky, Michel. 1997. *The Globalisation of Poverty: Impacts of IMF and World Bank Reforms.* London and Atlantic Highlands, N.J.: Zed Books; Penang, Malaysia: Third World Network.

Cobb, John B., Jr. 1994. *Sustaining the Common Good: A Christian Perspective on the Global Economy.* Cleveland: Pilgrim Press.

———. 1998. "The Threat to the Underclass." In *The Coming Age of Scarcity: Preventing Mass Death and Genocide in the Twenty-first Century,* edited by Michael Dobkowski and Isidor Wallimann, 25–42. Syracuse: Syracuse Univ. Press.

———. 1999. *The Earthist Challenge to Economism: A Theological Critique of the World Bank.* New York: St. Martin's Press.

Cohen, M. N. 1977. *The Food Crisis in Prehistory.* New Haven: Yale Univ. Press.

Connelly, Matthew, and Paul Kennedy. 1994. "Must It Be the Rest Against the West?" *Atlantic Monthly* 274 (Dec.): 61–83.

Conquest, Robert. 1986. *The Harvest of Sorrow: Soviet Collectivization and the Terror-Famine*. New York: Oxford Univ. Press.

Crossette, Barbara. 1995. "UN Parley Ponders Ways to Stretch Scarce Aid Funds." *New York Times,* Mar. 7, A6.

Daly, Herman E. 1977. *Steady-State Economics: The Economics of Biophysical Equilibrium and Moral Growth*. San Francisco: Freeman.

———. 1992. *Steady-State Economics*. 2d ed. London: Earthscan.

Daly, Herman E., and John B. Cobb Jr. 1994. *For the Common Good: Redirecting the Economy Toward Community, the Environment, and a Sustainable Future*. 2d ed. Boston: Beacon Press.

Danaher, Kevin, and Roger Burbach, eds. 2000. *Globalize This!* Monroe, Maine: Common Courage Press.

DeBerry, S. T. 1993. *Quantum Psychology: Steps to a Postmodern Ecology of Being*. Westport, Conn.: Praeger.

Des Forges, Alison. 1999. *Leave None to Tell the Story: Genocide in Rwanda*. New York and Paris: Human Rights Watch.

Dilworth, Craig. 1997. *Sustainable Development and Decision Making*. Uppsala: Department of Philosophy, Uppsala Univ.

———. 1998. *The Vicious Circle Principle*. In *The Coming Age of Scarcity: Preventing Mass Death and Genocide in the Twenty-first Century*, edited by Michael Dobkowski and Isidor Wallimann, 117–43. Syracuse: Syracuse Univ. Press.

Dobkowski, Michael, and Isidor Wallimann, eds. 1998. *The Coming Age of Scarcity: Preventing Mass Death and Genocide in the Twenty-first Century*. Syracuse: Syracuse Univ. Press.

Douthwaite, R. 1996. *Short Circuit*. Dublin: Lilliput.

Ehrenfeld, David. 1978. *The Arrogance of Humanism*. New York: Oxford Univ. Press.

Ehrlich, Paul R., and Ann H. Ehrlich. 1981. *Extinction: The Causes and Consequences of the Disappearance of Species*. New York: Random House.

———. 1990. *The Population Explosion*. New York: Touchstone.

Elliott, Lorraine. 1998. *The Global Politics of the Environment*. New York: New York Univ. Press.

Ellul, J. 1964. *The Technological Society*. New York: Vintage Books.

Engelbert, Pierre, and Richard Hoffmann. 1994. "Burundi: Learning the Lessons." In *Adjustment in Africa: Lessons from Country Case Studies,* edited by Ishrat Husain and Rashid Faruqee, 11–71. Washington, D.C.: World Bank.

Enzensberger, Hans Magnus. 1993. *Civil Wars: From Los Angeles to Bosnia*. New York: New Press.

Escobar, Arturo. 1995. *Encountering Development: The Making and Unmaking of the Third World*. Princeton: Princeton Univ. Press.

Esman, Milton J. 1994. *Ethnic Politics*. Ithaca: Cornell Univ. Press.

Estrada, Richard. 1991. "The Impact of Immigration on Hispanic Americans." *Chronicles* (July): 24–28.

Etzold, Thomas H., and John Lewis Gaddis, eds. 1978. *Containment: Documents on American Policy and Strategy*. Vol. 2, *1945–1950*. New York: Columbia Univ. Press.

Fein, Helen. 1993. "Accounting for Genocide after 1945: Theories and Some Findings." *International Journal on Group Rights* 1: 79–106.

Ferguson, R. Brian. 1995. *Yanomami Warfare: A Political History*. Santa Fe: School of American Research Press.

Ferguson, R. Brian, and Neil L. Whitehead, eds. 1992. *War in the Tribal Zone: Expanding States and Indigenous Warfare*. Santa Fe: School of American Research Press.

Finsterbusch, Kurt. 1973. "The Sociology of Nation States: Dimensions, Indicators, and Theory." In *Comparative Social Research: Methodological Problems and Strategies,* edited by Michael Armer and Allen Grimshaw, 417–66. New York: John Wiley and Son.

———. 1983. "Consequences of Increasing Scarcity on Affluent Countries." *Technological Forecasting and Social Change* 23: 59–73.

French, Hillary. 1995. "Forging a New Global Partnership." In *State of the World, 1995,* edited by Lester Brown et al., 170–90. New York: W. W. Norton.

———. 2000. *Vanishing Borders*. 1995. Reprint. New York: W. W. Norton.

Frey, William. 1995. "Immigration and Internal Migration 'Flight': A California Case Study." *Population and Environment* 16, no. 4: 353–75.

Friedman, Thomas L. 2000. *The Lexus and the Olive Tree*. Rev. ed. New York: Anchor Books.

Fukuyama, Francis. 1989. "The End of History." *National Interest* (summer): 3–20.

Gardels, Nathan. 1995. "Tide of Globalization." *New Perspectives Quarterly* 12 (winter): 2–3.

Georgescu-Roegen, Nicholas. 1971. *The Entropy Law and the Economic Process*. Cambridge: Harvard Univ. Press.

———. 1976. *Energy and Economic Myths*. San Francisco: Pergamon Press.

Gergen, K. J. 1991. *The Saturated Self*. New York: Basic Books.

Goldin, Claudia. 1993. "The Political Economy of Immigration Restriction in the United States, 1890 to 1921." NBER Working Paper 4345. Cambridge: Harvard Univ.

Gore, Al. 1992. *The Earth in Balance: Ecology and the Human Spirit.* Boston: Houghton Mifflin.

Gowdy, John M. 1998. *Limited Wants, Unlimited Means: A Reader on Hunter-Gatherer Economics and the Environment.* Washington, D.C.: Island Press.

Gruhn, Isebill. 1995. "Collapsed States in Africa." Paper given at the 1995 American Society for Environmental History, Las Vegas.

Gurr, Ted Robert. 1970. *Why Men Rebel.* Princeton: Princeton Univ. Press.

———. 1985. "On the Political Consequences of Scarcity and Economic Decline." *International Studies Quarterly* 29: 51–75.

———. 1993. *Minorities at Risk: A Global View of Ethnopolitical Conflict.* Washington, D.C.: U.S. Institute of Peace.

Hauchler, Ingomar, and Paul Kennedy, eds. 1994. *Global Trends: The World Almanac of Development and Peace.* New York: Continuum.

Hawken, Paul. 1993. *The Ecology of Commerce.* New York: HarperCollins.

Haynes, Jeff. 1996. *Third World Politics: A Concise Introduction.* Oxford: Blackwell.

Heilbroner, Robert. 1992. *An Inquiry into the Human Prospect: Looked at Again for the 1990s.* New York: W. W. Norton.

Hertsgaard, Mark. 1999. *Earth Odyssey.* New York: Broadway Books.

Hilsum, Lindsay. 1994. "Settling Scores." *Africa Report* 39, no. 3: 13–17.

Hirsch, Herbert. 1995. *Genocide and the Politics of Memory: Studying Death to Preserve Life.* Chapel Hill: Univ. of North Carolina Press.

Hobbes, Thomas. 1960. *Leviathan; or, The Matter, Forme, and Power of a Commonwealth Ecclesiasticall and Civil.* 1651. Reprint. Oxford: Blackwell.

Homer-Dixon, Thomas F. 1991. "On the Threshold: Environmental Changes as Causes of Acute Conflict." *International Security* 16: 76–116.

Homer-Dixon, Thomas F., Jeffery Boutwell, and George Rathjens. 1993. "Environmental Change and Violent Conflict." *Scientific American* (Feb.): 33–45.

Huddle, Donald L. 1993. "Dirty Work: Are Immigrants Taking Jobs That the Native Underclass Does Not Want?" *Population and Environment* 14, no. 6: 515–38.

Human Rights Watch. 1995. *Slaughter among Neighbors: The Political Origins of Communal Violence.* New Haven: Yale Univ. Press.

Ihonvbere, Julius O. 1992. "The Third World and the New World Order." In *Developing World,* edited by Robert J. Griffiths, 6–16. Guilford, Conn.: Dushkin.

Jacobson, Jodi. 1992. *Gender Bias: Roadblock to Sustainable Development.* Worldwatch Paper 110. Washington, D.C.: Worldwatch Institute.

Jakubowska, Longina. 1992. "Resisting 'Ethnicity': The Israeli State and Bedouin Identity." In *The Paths to Domination, Resistance, and Terror,* edited by Carolyn Nordstrom and JoAnn Martin, 85–105. Berkeley and Los Angeles: Univ. of California Press.

Kane, Hal. 1995. "The Hour of Departure: Forces That Create Refugees and Migrants." *World Watch Paper* 125 (June): 5–56.

Kaplan, Robert D. 1994. "The Coming Anarchy." *Atlantic Monthly* (Feb.): 44–76.

———. 1996. *The Ends of the Earth.* New York: Vintage Books.

———. 2000. *The Coming Anarchy.* New York: Random House.

Kates, Robert, Billie L. Turner II, and William Clark. 1990. "The Great Transformation." In *The Earth as Transformed by Human Action,* edited by Billie Turner et al., 1–18. New York: Cambridge Univ. Press.

Kellas, James G. 1991. *The Politics of Nationalism and Ethnicity.* New York: St. Martin's Press.

Kennan, George. 1995. "On American Principles." *Foreign Affairs* 74, no. 2: 116–25.

Kennedy, Margrit. 1988. *Interest and Inflation Free Money.* Steyerberg: Permaculture.

Kennedy, Paul. 1987. *The Rise and Fall of the Great Powers: Economic Change and Military Conflict from 1500 to 2000.* New York: Random House.

Korten, David C. 1995. *When Corporations Rule the World.* West Hartford, Conn.: Kumarian Press.

———. 1999. *The Post-Corporate World.* San Francisco: Berrett-Koehler.

Kuper, Leo. 1981. *Genocide: Its Political Use in the Twentieth Century.* New Haven: Yale Univ. Press.

Kuznets, Simon. 1955. "Economic Growth and Income Inequality." *American Economic Review* 45: 1–28.

Kvale, S. 1992. "Postmodern Psychology: A Contradiction in Terms?" In *Psychology and Postmodernism,* edited by S. Kvale, 31–57. Newbury Park, Calif.: Sage.

Lafay, Jean-Dominique, and Jacques Lecaillon. 1993. *The Political Dimension of Economic Adjustment.* Paris: Development Center of the Organisation for Economic Co-operation and Development.

Lee, Ronald D. 1980. "A Historical Perspective on Economic Aspects of the Population Explosion: The Case of Preindustrial England." In *Population and Economic Change in Developing Countries,* edited by R. E. Easterlin, 517–57. Chicago: Univ. of Chicago Press.

———. 1987. "Population Dynamics of Humans and Other Animals." *Demography* 24, no. 4 (Nov.): 443–65.

Lenski, Gerhard. 1966. *Power and Privilege: A Theory of Social Stratification.* Chapel Hill: Univ. of North Carolina Press.

Lifton, R. J. 1986. *The Nazi Doctors: Medical Killing and the Psychology of Genocide.* New York: Basic Books.

Linden, Eugene. 1998. *The Future in Plain Sight.* New York: Simon and Schuster.

Malcolm, Noel. 1995. "The Case Against 'Europe.' " *Foreign Affairs* 74, no. 2: 52–61.

Malthus, T. R. 1970. *An Essay on the Principle of Population.* 1798. Reprint. Harmondsworth, Eng.: Penguin Books.

Mander, Jerry, and Debi Barker. 2000. *Beyond the World Trade Organization.* Sausalito, Calif.: International Forum on Globalization.

Mander, Jerry, and E. Goldsmith, eds. 1997. *The Case Against the Global Economy.* San Francisco: Sierra Club.

Marshall, Jonathan. 1995. "How Immigrants Affect the Economy." *San Francisco Chronicle,* Jan. 9, B3.

McDaniel, Carl N., and John M. Gowdy. 2000. *Paradise for Sale: A Parable of Nature.* Berkeley and Los Angeles: Univ. of California Press.

Meadows, D. H., et al. 1992. *Beyond the Limits: Global Collapse or a Sustainable Future?* London: Earthscan.

Milbrath, Lester W. 1989. *Envisioning a Sustainable Society: Learning Our Way Out.* Albany: State Univ. of New York Press.

Morales, Waltraud Queiser. 1998. "Intrastate Conflict and Sustainable Development." In *The Coming Age of Scarcity: Preventing Mass Death and Genocide in the Twenty-first Century,* edited by Michael Dobkowski and Isidor Wallimann, 245–68. Syracuse: Syracuse Univ. Press.

Morales, Waltraud Queiser, and Megan A. Duncanson. 2000. "Gender Theory and Women in Latin America: A Status Report." *South Eastern Latin Americanist* 43 (winter): 37–57.

Morokvasic, Mirjana. 1998. "The Logics of Exclusion: Nationalism, Sexism, and the Yugoslav War." In *Gender, Ethnicity, and Political Ideologies,* edited by Nickie Charles and Helen Hintjens, 65–90. New York: Routledge.

Morris, Frank L., Jr. 1990. "Illegal Immigration and African American Opportunities Testimony Before the U.S. House of Representatives Judiciary Committee Subcommittee on Immigration, Refugees, and International Law." *Congressional Record* (Apr. 5).

Mumford, L. 1967. *The Myth of the Machine.* Vol. 1, *Technics and Human Development.* San Diego: Harcourt Brace Jovanovich.

Newbury, Catharine. 1992. "Rwanda: Recent Debates over Governance and Rural Development." In *Governance and Politics in Africa,* edited by Goran Hyden and Michael Bratton, 193–220. Boulder: Lynne Rienner Publishers.

Norgaard, Richard B. 1994. *Development Betrayed.* New York: Routledge.

O'Connor, James. 1994. "Is Sustainable Capitalism Possible?" In *Is Capitalism Sustainable?* edited by Martin O'Connor, 152–75. New York: Guilford Press.

Omaar, Rakiya, and Alex de Waal. 1994. *Rwanda: Death, Despair, and Defiance.* 2d ed. London: African Rights.

Ophuls, William, and A. Stephen Boyen Jr. 1992. *Ecology and the Politics of Scarcity Revisited: The Unraveling of the American Dream.* New York: W. H. Freeman.

Parker, Geoffrey. 1988. *The Military Revolution: Military Innovation and the Rise of the West, 1500–1800.* Cambridge: Cambridge Univ. Press.

Peterson, V. Spike, and Anne Sisson Runyan. 1993. *Global Gender Issues.* Boulder, Colo.: Westview Press.

Petrella, Ricardo. 1995. "A Global Agora vs. Gated City-Regions." *New Perspectives Quarterly* 12 (winter): 21–22.

Pfaff, William. 1995. "A New Colonialism?" *Foreign Affairs* 74, no. 1 (Jan.-Feb.): 2–6.

Pimentel, David C. Harvey, et al. 1995. "Environmental and Economic Costs of Soil Erosion and Conservation Benefits." *Science* 267 (Feb. 24): 1117–23.

Ponting, Clive. 1991. *A Green History of the World: The Environment and the Collapse of Great Civilizations.* New York: St. Martin's Press.

Raghavan, Chakravarthi. 1990. *Recolonization: GATT, the Uruguay Round, and the Third World.* Penang, Malaysia: Third World Network.

Rasler, Karen, and William R. Thompson. 1989. *War and State Making: The Shaping of the Global Powers.* Boston: Unwin Hyman.

Redclift, Michael. 1987. *Sustainable Development: Exploring the Contradictions.* New York: Routledge.

Renner, Michael. 1996. *Fighting for Survival.* New York: W. W. Norton.

Rist, G. 1997. *The History of Development.* London: Zed Books.

Rowan, J., and M. Cooper. 1999. *The Plural Self.* London: Sage.

Sahlins, Marshall. 1972. *Stone Age Economics.* Chicago: Aldine.

Saint-Jean, Armande. 1994. "Rwanda: An Activist Reflects on Her Nation's Trauma and History." *MS* 5, no. 3 (Nov.-Dec.): 10–14.

Schnaiberg, Allan, and Kenneth Alan Gould. 1994. *Environment and Society: The Enduring Conflict.* New York: St. Martin's Press.

Schwarz, Benjamin. 1995. "The Diversity Myth: America's Leading Export." *Atlantic Monthly* 275 (May): 57–67.

Schwarz, W., and D. Schwarz. 1998. *Living Lightly.* London: Jon Carpenter.

Scott, Catherine V. 1995. *Gender and Development: Rethinking Modernization and Dependency Theory.* Boulder, Colo.: Lynne Rienner.

Shaw, R. Paul, and Yuwa Wong. 1987. "Ethnic Mobilization and the Seeds of Warfare: An Evolutionary Perspective." *International Studies Quarterly* 31, no. 1 (Mar.): 5–31.

Sitarz, Daniel, ed. 1994. *Agenda 21: The Earth Summit Strategy to Save Our Planet.* Boulder, Colo.: Earthpress.

Smith, David Norman. 1998a. "Postcolonial Genocide." In *The Coming Age of Scarcity: Preventing Mass Death and Genocide in the Twenty-first Century,* edited by Michael Dobkowski and Isidor Wallimann, 220–44. Syracuse: Syracuse Univ. Press.

———. 1998b. "The Psychocultural Roots of Genocide: Legitimacy and Crisis in Rwanda." *American Psychologist* 53, no. 7 (July): 743–53.

Smith, Roger W. 1987. "Human Destructiveness and Politics: The Twentieth Century as an Age of Genocide." In *Genocide and the Modern Age: Etiology and Case Studies of Mass Death,* edited by Isidor Wallimann and Michael N. Dobkowski, 21–39. Westport, Conn.: Greenwood Press.

———. 1998. "Scarcity and Genocide." In *The Coming Age of Scarcity: Preventing Mass Death and Genocide in the Twenty-first Century,* edited by Michael Dobkowski and Isidor Wallimann, 199–219. Syracuse: Syracuse Univ. Press.

Speth, James Gustave. 1992. "A Post-Rio Compact." *Foreign Policy* (fall): 145–61.

Steiner, Stan. 1976. *The Vanishing White Man.* Norman: Univ. of Oklahoma Press.

Storey, Andy. 1999. "Economics and Ethnic Conflict: Structural Adjustment in Rwanda." *Development Policy Review* 17: 43–63.

Sundberg, Ulf, et al. 1994. "Forest EMERGY Basis for Swedish Power in the Seventeenth Century." *Scandinavian Journal of Forest Research* 1 (supp.).

Tainter, Joseph A. 1988. *The Collapse of Complex Societies.* New York: Cambridge Univ. Press.

———. 1992. "Evolutionary Consequences of War." In *Effects of War on Society,* edited by G. Ausenda, 103–30. San Marino, Calif.: Center for Interdisciplinary Research on Social Stress.

———. 1998. "Competition, Expansion, and Reaction: The Foundations of Contemporary Conflict." In *The Coming Age of Scarcity: Preventing Mass Death and Genocide in the Twenty-first Century,* edited by Michael N. Dobkowski and Isidor Wallimann, 174–93. Syracuse: Syracuse Univ. Press.

Tilly, Charles. 1978. *From Mobilization to Revolution.* Reading, Mass.: Addison-Wesley.

Trainer, F. E. 1989. *Developed to Death.* London: Green Print.

———. 1995a. "Can Renewable Energy Save Industrial Society?" *Energy Policy* 23, no. 12: 1009–26.

———. 1995b. *The Conserver Society: Alternatives for Sustainability.* London: Zed Books.

———. 1998. *Saving the Environment: What It Will Take.* Sydney: Univ. of New South Wales Press.

———. 1999. "The Limits to Growth Case in the 1990s." *Environmentalist* 19: 329–39.

Turner, Billie L., II, et al., eds. 1990. *The Earth as Transformed by Human Action: Global and Regional Changes in the Biosphere over the Past 300 Years.* New York: Cambridge Univ. Press.

Union of Concerned Scientists, eds. 1993. *World Scientists Warning Briefing Book.* Cambridge, Mass.: Union of Concerned Scientists.

United Nations Development Program. 1995. "Redefining Security: The Human Dimension." *Current History* 94, no. 592 (May): 229–36.

Uvin, Peter. 1998. *Aiding Violence: The Development Enterprise in Rwanda.* West Hartford, Conn.: Kumarian Press.

Van Crevold, Martin L. 1991. *The Transformation of War.* New York: Free Press.

Wackernagel, N., and W. Rees. 1995. *Our Ecological Footprint.* Philadelphia: New Society.

Wall, Alex de. 1994. "The Genocidal State: Hutu Extremism and the Origins of the 'Final Solution' in Rwanda." *Times Literary Supplement* 4761 (July 1): 3–4.

Wallach, Lori, et al. 1999. *Whose Trade Organization?* Washington, D.C.: Public Citizen.

Wallimann, Isidor. 1994. "Can the World Industrialization Project Be Sustained?" *Monthly Review* (Mar.): 41–51.

Waylen, Georgina. 1996. *Gender in Third World Politics.* Buckingham, Eng.: Open Univ. Press.

Weatherford, Jack. 1994. *Savages and Civilization: Who Will Survive?* New York: Crown.

Wilkinson, R. G. 1973. *Poverty and Progress: An Ecological Perspective on Economic Development.* New York: Praeger.

Wilson, Edward O. 1992. *The Diversity of Life.* Cambridge: Harvard Univ. Press.

Woodburn, James. 1982. "Egalitarian Societies." *Man* 17: 431–51.

Woodward, David. 1996. *The IMF, the World Bank, and Economic Policy in Rwanda: Economic and Social Implications.* Oxford: Oxford Univ. Press.

Young, John. 1990. *Sustaining the Earth.* Cambridge: Harvard Univ. Press.

Yuval-Davis, Nira. 1997. *Gender and Nation.* Thousand Oaks, Calif.: Sage.